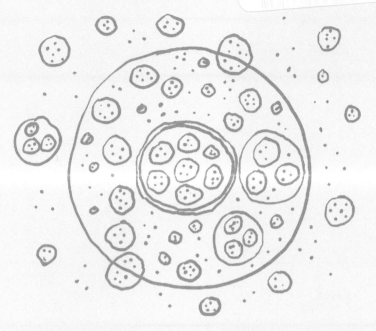

THE CONNECTED COMPANY

Holarchy
Fractal work units

Autonomy

Flexible

Adaptive in uncertain environments

THE
CONNECTED
COMPANY

BY DAVE GRAY

WITH THOMAS VANDER WAL

TO MARTY!

DAVE

O'REILLY®

BEIJING | CAMBRIDGE | FARNHAM | KÖLN | SEBASTOPOL | TOKYO

The Connected Company
By Dave Gray with Thomas Vander Wal

Published by O'Reilly Media, Inc., 1005 Gravenstein Highway North, Sebastopol, California 95472.

O'Reilly books may be purchased for educational, business, or sales promotional use. Online editions are also available for most titles at *http://safari.oreilly.com*. For more information, contact our corporate/ institutional sales department: (800) 998-9938 or *corporate@oreilly.com*.

EDITOR: Julie Steele

COVER & INTERIOR DESIGN: Bill Keaggy

ILLUSTRATIONS: Dave Gray

PRODUCTION EDITOR: Holly Bauer

PROOFREADER: Holly Bauer

INDEXER: Lucie Haskins

PRINTING HISTORY

September 2012: First edition

REVISION HISTORY FOR THE FIRST EDITION

2012-08-20: First release

See *http://oreilly.com/catalog/errata.csp?isbn=0636920023333* for release details.

Set in Trade Gothic and Scala.

ISBN: 978-1-449-31905-2
[CW]

TO MICHELLE

TABLE OF CONTENTS

PART ONE

Customers are adopting disruptive technologies
faster than companies can adapt.

Customers are connecting, forming networked communities that allow them
to rapidly share information and self-organize into powerful interest groups.
Companies will have to be more responsive to customer needs and demands if they
want to survive.

Industrialization is a phase, and in developed nations that phase is ending. Growth
in developed economies will increasingly come from services.

Services cannot be designed and manufactured in isolation, like products. They
are cocreated with customers and are interdependent with wider service networks
and clusters.

Services introduce customers into operations, which creates a lot of complexity
and variability that is hard to plan for in advance. Companies must find ways to
accommodate variety at the edge of the organization, where people and systems
interact directly with customers, partners, and suppliers.

Companies tend to lose touch with customers as they grow, for a variety of reasons.
They must find ways to create, maintain, and develop deep connections as they grow.

PART TWO

How does a connected company work?

A connected company learns and adapts by distributing control to the points of interaction with customers, where semi-autonomous pods pursue a common purpose supported by platforms that help them organize and coordinate their activities.

12. Wrangling complexity

The good news is that many of the problems of addressing complexity and change have already been solved by the very people who started the complexity problems in the first place: technologists. They solved these problems because they had to.

13. The future is podular

Connected companies are not hierarchies, fractured into unthinking, functional parts, but holarchies: complex systems in which each part is also a fully functional whole in its own right. A holarchy is a different kind of template than the modern, multidivisional organization. It's podular.

14. Pods have control of their own fate

The core building block of a podular organization is the pod: a small, autonomous unit that is authorized to represent the company and deliver results to customers. Pods are flexible, fast, scalable, and resilient.

15. Pods need platforms

A podular organization requires support structures that network the pods together so they can coordinate their activities, share learning, and increase the company's overall effectiveness. Platforms are support structures that increase the effectiveness of a community.

16. How connected companies learn

Connected companies grow and learn over time. Like all life forms and complex systems, their growth is governed by natural rhythms and patterns. As individuals and teams learn, they must find ways to share their knowledge with the larger community. As communities learn, platforms must learn how to support them.

PART FOUR

How do you lead a connected company?
Connected companies are living, learning networks that live within larger networks. Power in networks comes from awareness and influence, not control. Leaders must create an environ-  ment of clarity, trust, and shared purpose, while management focuses on designing and tuning the system that supports learning and performance.

PART FIVE

How do you get there from here?...........239

Any enterprise involves risk, and connected companies are no exception. Connected companies can fail. But in times of change and uncertainty, their ability to learn and adapt faster than their competitors gives them an edge. If you want to become a connected company, there's no reason you can't start today.

INTRODUCTION

More business books are published today than ever before in the history of mankind. Who has time to read them all? We designed this book with today's busy reader in mind. In the front of the book you will find a Table of Contents that also serves as an executive summary and detailed outline of the book. This summary is designed to allow you to quickly and easily understand the book's main argument.

If you decide to read the book from beginning to end, you will have the most complete and thorough experience. Reading the book in sequence will give you a guided tour of the connected company, starting with the challenges of today's connected world and walking you through the core concepts of the connected company, step by step, concluding with some first steps you can take today to start moving your company into the connected age.

But you don't have to read it that way. You can start by reading the summary and then dip in wherever you want. We have designed the book with the goal of making it as skimmable as possible: each chapter begins with a summary of its core ideas, and is broken into sections, marked with bold headlines. Diagrams and illustrations are peppered throughout the book to make the concepts easier to understand. We have also put some discussion questions in the back, in case you want to start a conversation at work about how your company can become a more connected company.

Our overarching goal was to make the book easy to read and navigate, a book that makes it easy for busy people to quickly find what they want and take away what they need. Enjoy!

– Dave Gray
@davegray
July 2012

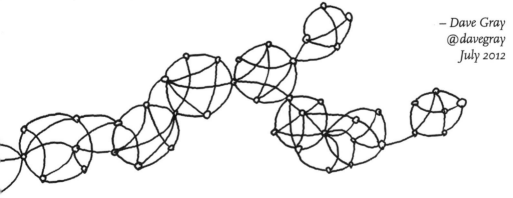

Safari.

Safari Books Online is an on-demand digital library that delivers expert content in both book and video form from the world's leading authors in technology and business. Technology professionals, software developers, web designers, and business and creative professionals use Safari Books Online as their primary resource for research, problem solving, learning, and certification training.

Safari Books Online offers a range of product mixes and pricing programs for organizations, government agencies, and individuals. Subscribers have access to thousands of books, training videos, and prepublication manuscripts in one fully searchable database from publishers like O'Reilly Media, Prentice Hall Professional, Addison-Wesley Professional, Microsoft Press, Sams, Que, Peachpit Press, Focal Press, Cisco Press, John Wiley & Sons, Syngress, Morgan Kaufmann, IBM Redbooks, Packt, Adobe Press, FT Press, Apress, Manning, New Riders, McGraw-Hill, Jones & Bartlett, Course Technology, and dozens more. For more information about Safari Books Online, please visit us online at *http://my.safaribooksonline.com*.

WE'D LIKE TO HEAR FROM YOU

Please address comments and questions concerning this book to the publisher:

O'Reilly Media, Inc.
1005 Gravenstein Highway North
Sebastopol, California 95472 U.S.A.

+1 (707) 829-0515 for international or local
(800) 998-9938 in the United States or Canada
(707) 829-0104 to send a fax

We have a web page for this book, where we list errata, examples, and any additional information. You can access this page at: *http://oreil.ly/connected_company*. To comment or ask technical questions about *The Connected Company*, send email to *bookquestions@oreilly.com*.

Find us on Facebook: *http://facebook.com/oreilly*
Follow us on Twitter: *http://twitter.com/oreillymedia*
Watch us on YouTube: *http://youtube.com/oreillymedia*

ACKNOWLEDGMENTS

A book like *The Connected Company* is not an individual effort. Its ideas build on those of generations of thinkers and innovators. A book like this one evolves slowly, through countless conversations that lead to countless suggestions of people who must be spoken to, companies that must be understood, books and articles that must be read.

And though the task was impossible, I did try to speak to everyone, understand every company, and read every book and article that was suggested. My desk piled high with books, papers, and transcribed interviews, which were soon were marked, folded, plastered with sticky notes, and supplemented with boxes and boxes of cross-referenced index cards, diagrams, and sketches.

So many people contributed to this effort that it would be impossible to recognize them all in such a small space. But I must single out a few people whose contributions loom large.

The book would not have happened without a series of conversations with Thomas Vander Wal, which led to my initial blog post, "The Connected Company." It also could not have happened without Tim O'Reilly, who read the blog post and saw that it could become a book.

I soon collected a small posse of people who were tremendously helpful as a sounding board for the ideas as they developed. That group included, in no particular order, Thomas Vander Wal, Michael Dila, James Macanufo, Aaron Silvers, Elliot Felix, Gary Thompson, Bo and Kristi McFarland, Rawn Shah, Gordon Ross, Matt Ridings, Amber Naslund, Ben Reason, Scott Mitchell, Chris Messina and Brynn Evans, Larry Irons, Kevin Hoffman, Andrew Hinton, Chris Heuer, Ian Fenn, Bill DeRouchey, Marcel Botha, Mike Bonifer, Richard Black, Jim Benson, Tom Graves, Alex Baumgartner, Jerry Michalski, Alison Austin, Andy Budd, Christopher Allen, Chris Carfi, Joe Sokohl, Johanna Kollman, Joachim Stroh, Megan Bowe, Kevin Clark, Peter Merholz, Christian Crumlish, Sheila Kim, Monique Elwell, Rachel Happe, Kevin Jones, Todd Sattersten, and Dr. Richard Gray.

I also had tremendous help and support from my colleagues at Dachis Group, specifically: Jeff Dachis, Dion Hinchcliffe, Peter Kim, Ethan Farber, Brian Kotlyar, Susan Scrupski, Amanda Johnson, Lara Hendrickson, Lee Bryant, John De Oliveira, Erik Huddleston, Jen van der Meer, David Mastronardi, W. Scott Matthews, and Aric Wood.

I have also had the privilege to receive help and advice from true luminaries, such as Richard Saul Wurman, Saul Kaplan, Kevin Kelly, Jared Spool, Peter Vander Auwera, Dan Roam, Thor Muller, Paul Pangaro, Lane Becker, Peter Morville, Lou Rosenfeld, Nilofer Merchant, John Hagel III, JP Rangaswami, Doc Searls, Stowe Boyd, Jay Cross, Marcia Conner, Ben Cerveny, Chris Brogan, Bob Logan, David Armano, Alex Osterwalder, and Don Norman.

Although I don't know them personally, for the ideas in this book, I owe a deep debt of gratitude to the works of Gary Hamel, Clayton Christensen, Arie de Geus, Ricardo Semler, Eric Beinhocker, Daniel Pink, Richard Florida, Stewart Brand, Bill McKelvey, Stafford Beer, Herbert Simon, John Boyd, and perhaps most of all, Dr. W. Edwards Deming, many of whose groundbreaking ideas are only now being realized.

For the access they provided to connected companies and their inner workings, I must thank Ray LaDriere, Kevin Kernan, Michael Bonamassa, Jerry Rudisin, Sunny Gupta, Adrian Cockcroft, Harry Max, Mary Walker, Mark Interrante, Ben Hart, Livia Labate, Sherri Maxson, and Sharif Renno.

I must single out for special recognition my friend, Bo McFarland, who took the whole project under his wing and spent many hours providing detailed feedback and serving as a high-level advisor to the project. Special mention is also due to Jay Cross, Sheila Kim, Larry Irons, Shara Karasic, Dan Miller, Richard Black, and Monique Elwell, who provided detailed and much-appreciated feedback on the manuscript.

I cannot neglect the stellar team who worked ceaselessly on the design, production, and promotion of the book: Bill Keaggy, Julie Steele, Edie Freedman, Jenny Murphy, Betsy Waliszewski, Steve Weiss, and Sara Peyton.

And most of all, I need to thank my family, for their help and forbearance: Michelle, Isaac and Aly, Rick, Dan, Mom, and Dad.

To all of you: *thank you!*

FOREWORD

L ong gone are the days of a predictable world in which you could take your time to make decisions, manage an organization from the top, or get away with mediocre products and services.

Pointing to today's mind-boggling speed of commerce, exploding computing power, ever-sinking communication costs, and fierce global competition is stating the obvious. We all know that the competitive environment has changed forever.

Yet, surprisingly, while surpassing themselves at innovating with products and services, most companies are terribly slow at reinventing their management style, organizational structure, or institutional culture. They remain inapt to a fast-paced and connected world in which customers instantaneously and globally voice their dissatisfaction over anything less than outstanding products and services. These expired ways of organizing often result in unhappy clients, demotivated employees, and missed opportunities for new value creation.

In my work on business model innovation with large, global companies, I am constantly confronted with this. In the face of a changing competitive environment, companies are forced to take action. Smart and energetic executives generate amazingly innovative business models that have the potential to produce future growth, but then the organization is incapable of making things happen. More senior or more established executives get the company to fall back on their historic business model and old ways of working, which made them successful originally. In the short term, this might offer the comfort of a known model, less risk, and maybe even short-term gains. In the longer term, this often represents the roots of a decline into irrelevance or an increased risk of disruption by more nimble and often totally new competitors with innovative business models.

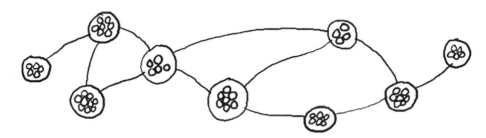

What I have come to realize is that without organizational and management innovation, business model innovation and adaptation to today's fast-changing world rarely happens. To make it happen, we need to build new spaces for experimentation and learning. We need new organizational principles and platforms for autonomous teams to succeed. We need new incentive systems and institutional cultures to get employees motivated again. In short, companies need management innovation.

In his book, *The Connected Company*, Dave Gray offers answers for organizing in this new world. Refreshingly, Dave, who I've come to know as a deep thinker, practical "doer," and good friend over the years, is not satisfied with quick fixes. In an approachable style, with explanatory visualizations and fascinating examples, he weaves together the core elements you need to take into account when designing the connected company: transparent interaction and communication platforms, organizational structures favoring autonomy and adaptation, a culture of experimentation and learning, and a new governance and reward system encouraging new behavior and holding it all together.

— Alexander Osterwalder
Echandens, Switzerland
June 2012

PART ONE

Why change?

Customers are adopting disruptive technologies faster than companies can adapt.

THE DIVIDED COMPANY

If you make customers unhappy
in the physical world, they might
each tell six friends. If you make
customers unhappy on the Internet,
they can each tell 6,000 friends.

—*Jeff Bezos, Founder & CEO, Amazon.com*

CHAPTER ONE

The connected customer

Customers are connecting, forming networked communities that allow them to rapidly share information and self-organize into powerful interest groups. Companies will have to be more responsive to customer needs and demands if they want to survive.

THE BALANCE OF POWER IS SHIFTING

The balance of power is shifting from companies to the networks that surround them. Connected, communicating customers and employees have more choices, and more amplified voices, than ever before. They have more knowledge than ever before. These trends are only increasing with time. This means the network—customers, partners, and employees—will increasingly set the agenda, determine the parameters, and make the decisions about how they interact with companies.

A WAKE-UP CALL AT STARBUCKS

In February 2007, Starbucks chairman Howard Schultz sat down to write a difficult memo.

Schultz, always in the habit of visiting stores around the world, had noticed that the Starbucks experience was deteriorating. And in 2006, Starbucks' legendary growth had started to slow. The amount of money customers were spending was starting to dip.

In his 2007 memo, "The Commoditization of the Starbucks Experience," Schultz laid out his concerns. Espresso machines, which increased efficiency, were too tall; they created a wall that blocked the line of sight between customers and baristas, a barrier to conversation and connection. Flavor-locked packaging, which guaranteed fresh roasted coffee in every cup, also made the stores more antiseptic, depriving them of their rich, flavorful, coffee aromas. Streamlining store designs increased efficiency, but many customers perceived them as sterile, cookie-cutter designs.

"We have all been part of these decisions," wrote Schultz. "I take full responsibility myself, but we desperately need to look into the mirror and realize it's time to get back to the core and make the changes necessary to evoke the heritage, the tradition, and the passion that we all have for the true Starbucks experience."

The memo was meant to be a wake-up call to the senior executive team as they embarked on their yearly strategic planning process. But it soon became much more than that. A little over a week later, a colleague stepped into Schultz's office. "Someone leaked the memo," he said. "It's on the internet."

Schultz was shocked.

Reporters were already calling, but Schultz was too shaken up to grant any interviews. This had been a confidential memo to the CEO and a small group of senior executives in the company. He couldn't believe any of them would have done such a thing.

The memo had first appeared on a blog called Starbucks Gossip and was quickly picked up by the mainstream media. The speed at which word spread, and the breadth and depth of the online conversations that ensued, astonished Schultz:

> The day after the memo was posted, the mainstream media picked it up like a whirlwind. *The Wall Street Journal. The New York Times.* The Associated Press. Bloomberg, Reuters, the *Financial Times.* Online financial news sites and independent blogs. Articles quoted the memo and parsed my words, usually under dour headlines that implied, or stated outright, that trouble was brewing at Starbucks. Online, readers posted comments one after the other. Many of them stung. Stunned as I was that the memo had been leaked, I was also astonished by the depth of conversation it unleashed, as well as the speed. It seemed that everyone—customers, partners, analysts, reporters, industry insiders, and business "experts"—had an opinion about the memo, its motive, what it meant for the future of the company as well as what it said about me as a leader.

HOWARD SCHULTZ

Schultz says he took two very important lessons from his experience. First, nothing can be presumed confidential. Second, Starbucks did not have a voice in the global conversation:

> The heated online conversations about the memo were beyond Starbucks' influence, more so than any other controversy we had experienced...the good things about us, our values and the acts that distinguished us, these were getting lost in the public conversation. The millions of dollars we invested in local communities. The health-care coverage and stock we extended to part-timers, at a considerable cost to the company. While we never put forth press releases about many of these initiatives—believing they were just the right things to do—we also were not getting credit for them...

> Our website, with its beautifully designed pages...was primarily a one-way dialogue, inadequate in the digital age. Starbucks had no interactive presence online. No way to speak up quickly on our own behalf, to talk directly to customers, investors, as well as partners, or let them talk directly to us...we were losing control of our story, in the stores as well as the real world.

The leaked memo and its aftermath were a wake-up call for Schultz. "I was not sure where to begin," he writes today, "but we had to do something."

SOMETHING'S HAPPENING HERE

If Starbucks didn't have a voice in the global conversation, who did? The Starbucks Gossip blog, the mainstream media, readers, customers, analysts, and so on—in other words, anyone and everyone who was interested: the network. And because the memo was interesting, it cascaded through the network, gaining momentum as it went, like a tidal wave.

These kinds of cascading effects are common in networks. An initial event strikes a chord: it's interesting, funny, sad, disgusting, or enraging. As a result, it is shared, commented on, analyzed, and argued about. And as it moves through the network, it is amplified, sometimes to an exponential degree.

CASCADING EFFECTS CAN BE INITIATED BY CUSTOMERS

In 2005, Dell learned a tough lesson when they shut down peer-to-peer customer forums, and Dell customer (and blogger) Jeff Jarvis, who had recently bought a machine that almost immediately malfunctioned, expressed his dissatisfaction on the Web in a post titled, "Dell lies. Dell sucks." Jarvis coined the term "Dell Hell," saying Dell didn't "respect [customers] enough to listen to them."

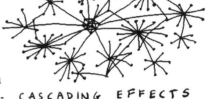

CASCADING EFFECTS

Within a week, Dell Hell was a story in *The New York Times* and *Business Week*. Hundreds of other bloggers chimed in to tell their "Dell Hell" stories. At the time, Dell had an internal policy not to reply publicly to blogs. So the company remained silent, and the PR nightmare snowballed. Sales plummeted, along with Dell's reputation.

Dell has learned from its mistake, and in 2010 launched a "customer listening command center" to monitor and proactively respond to online conversations. Founder and CEO Michael Dell is active on social media, engaging with customers directly.

In another incident, Canadian musician Dave Carroll was traveling on United Airlines in 2008 and had checked his guitar into baggage, when his plane landed at Chicago's O'Hare airport en route to Omaha. He became concerned as he watched baggage handlers on the runway throwing guitars. When he arrived in Omaha, he found that indeed the neck of his $3,500 Taylor guitar had been broken. He filed a claim with the airline, but they refused to honor it because he had failed to make the claim within 24 hours. For nine months, he tried to negotiate with the airline. Finally, in frustration, he wrote a song titled "United Breaks Guitars" and released a music video on YouTube. The song's refrain: "I should have flown with someone else, or gone by car, 'cause United breaks guitars."

The video was an Internet hit. Within one day of its release, it had amassed 150,000 views. In a few weeks, that number had risen to 5 million, and in December, Time magazine listed it as number 7 on a list of top viral videos of 2009.

Once the video was released, United contacted Carroll to try to right the wrong, but it seems that their efforts were too little, too late. Bob Taylor, owner of Taylor Guitars, gave Carroll two free guitars, and Carroll refused compensation from United, asking instead that they revise their customer service policies and give the money to charity. United donated $3,000 to the Thelonious Monk Institute of Jazz as a gesture of goodwill, but by that point, the damage had been done.

CASCADING EFFECTS CAN BE INITIATED BY EMPLOYEES

In 2009, two Dominos workers videotaped themselves doing disgusting things to food—one put cheese up his nose and mucus on sandwiches while the other narrated—and they posted the video on the internet. One of the employees, who identified herself as Kristy, said, "In about five minutes it'll be sent out on delivery where somebody will be eating these, yes, eating them, and little did they know that cheese was in his nose and that there was some lethal gas that ended up on their salami. Now that's how we roll at Domino's."

Within the week, the video had garnered over a million views. "We got blindsided by two idiots with a video camera and an awful idea," said Dominos spokesman Tim McIntyre to *The New York Times*.

Kristy Hammonds, 31, later said in a company email that it was just a joke and that she was sorry. But the damage had been done.

CASCADING EFFECTS CAN BE INITIATED BY ENEMIES OR COMPETITORS

In March 2011, conservative activist James O'Keefe, posing as a member of a Muslim education group, secretly videotaped NPR fundraising chief Ron Schiller saying republicans were "racist" and "xenophobic," and that NPR didn't need federal funding. Schiller resigned and the CEO was forced to step down shortly thereafter.

CASCADING EFFECTS CAN BE INITIATED BY SENIOR EXECUTIVES

On June 30, 2011, tech blog The Boy Genius Report published an anonymous memo from an executive at Blackberry maker Research in Motion (RIM), addressed to the RIM Senior Management team, starting with the words, "I have lost confidence. While I hide it at work, my passion has been sapped." The letter went on to plead for drastic changes.

The company issued an official reply, saying, "It is particularly difficult to believe that a high-level employee in good standing with the company would choose to anonymously publish a letter on the web rather than engage fellow executives in a constructive manner...RIM is nonetheless fully aware of and aggressively addressing both the company's challenges and its opportunities."

The Boy Genius Report published the response, but at the same time also published more anonymous letters from RIM employees supporting the original memo and accusing RIM of poor leadership, leading to low morale throughout the company.

THE ATM REVOLT

In September of 2011, Bank of America announced that it would start charging customers $5 per month to shop with their debit cards. In early October, a 27-year-old gallery owner in Los Angeles named Kristen Christian set up a Facebook event page, inviting 500 of her Facebook friends to move their accounts to local credit unions by November 5, which she called "Bank Transfer Day."

"Together we can ensure that these banking institutions will always remember the 5th of November," she wrote. "If we shift our funds from the for-profit banking institutions in favor of not-for-profit credit unions before this date, we will send a clear message that conscious consumers won't support companies with unethical business practices."

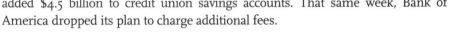

Christian's groundswell movement quickly snowballed. Within three days, 8,000 people had signed up to attend the event.

"I was tired," wrote Christian in another post. "Tired of the fee increases, tired of not being able to access my money when I need to, tired of them using what little money I have to oppress my brothers & sisters. So I stood up. I've been shocked at how many people have stood up alongside me. With each person who

KRISTEN CHRISTIAN

RSVPs to this event, my heart swells. Me closing my account all on my lonesome wouldn't have made a difference to these fat cats. But each of YOU standing up with me...they can't drown out the noise we'll make."

By November 4, the day before Bank transfer Day, at least 650,000 people had added $4.5 billion to credit union savings accounts. That same week, Bank of America dropped its plan to charge additional fees.

POWER IN THE NETWORK

By changing the way we create, access, and share information, social networks are changing the power structure in society.

Customers like Kristen Christian can pick up a megaphone at any time, and if they have a message that resonates with the network, it can gain momentum very fast.

Rogue individuals can target you in sting operations, as James O'Keefe did, or they can simply act stupidly, as the Domino's employees did.

Disgruntled employees can get their message out through leaks or anonymous memos like those from Starbucks and RIM.

However it happens, once something is released to a network, it can rapidly spin out of control.

Clearly, social networks such as Twitter and Facebook, which didn't exist in 1999, have gained momentum far more quickly among the general population than they have in corporations. Customers are connecting and sharing information at a far faster rate than the companies that serve them. There's no question that when it comes to social networking, companies lag behind their markets.

Networked customers can easily bypass formal channels to get information and support directly from each other.

Think about where you go when you want to make a buying decision today. In general, you go to peers first. If you want to go to a restaurant, you might go to Yelp! or Urbanspoon to read recommendations and reviews from customers. Booking a hotel? If you care about comfort and service, you might go to Hotels.com to read some reviews, or if price is a priority, you might go to Priceline, where you can set your own price. Want to watch a movie? You can find the best picks at Rotten Tomatoes, Netflix, or IMDB, where movie-watchers have a voice.

These peer-to-peer conversations subvert traditional marketing channels. Customers trust each other more than they trust companies, who have a vested interest in making themselves look good. A 2009 Nielsen study found that 90% of customers trusted recommendations from other customers more than any other form of advertising. And customers have begun to recognize, and exercise, their power.

This power, in and of itself, is not necessarily new. Customers have always had the power to choose what they wanted to buy. Customers and workers have always had the power to share their experiences with friends and peers. They have always had the power to promote—or demote—a company based on what it promised and what it delivered. Customers have always been able to vote with their wallets.

But they weren't connected to a global network with the potential to amplify their opinions and experiences to hurricane strength. And that little thing we call "linking" makes all the difference.

Any dictator will tell you that in order to control the state, you must control the media. So ask yourself: who controls the media today? And which way are the trends heading?

In February 2010, a nonprofit organization called WikiLeaks began releasing classified cables between the US State Department and its consulates, embassies, and diplomatic missions around the world. It was the largest leak of classified material in the history of the world, and there was nothing the US government could do about it. Once information is released to a network, it can't be pulled back. Wikileaks has demonstrated definitively that no secret, corporate or political, is safe for long.

We've been saying the customer is king so long that it has become a cliché. And in most cases, our actions don't match those words. But customers will be kings and queens, not only in name, but in fact. One by one, customers are recognizing the power that comes from a world in which their choices are infinite and their voices are amplified. They are connecting. They are organizing. They are gaining mass and momentum.

Customers don't need to revolt in an active way. All that is required is for a new company to come along and offer a better service. Connected customers will become aware of such services far more easily than they have in the past, and share the information more quickly, too. If the new service is interesting, it will quickly cascade through the network.

Some companies have figured out how to create these kinds of direct relationships. Amazon allowed customers to write negative reviews on the store's website since the day they launched. That was a controversial decision at the time. Why would a retailer allow anyone to post information that would help a customer decide to not to buy something? Jeff Bezos recalls a publisher calling him and saying, "I don't think you understand your business. You make money when you sell books." But Bezos knew better. He understood that what connected customers value is a company that will help them make better buying decisions. And today we all understand that.

To think that this customer revolution won't affect your business is naive. It will affect every business. It is already shifting the balance of power. It is changing the way power is controlled and exercised. It will change the way companies are organized and the way they do business.

Eventually, every customer will be a connected customer. And if you want to win over connected customers, you will need to become a connected company.

NOTES FOR CHAPTER ONE

Most of the stories here can easily be found by Google search. Influential sources include the sayings and writings of Doc Searls, David Weinberger, Clay Shirky, Peter Kim, and Dion Hinchcliffe. If you haven't read it yet, check out *The Cluetrain Manifesto* (see bibliography).

STARBUCKS
For that anecdote, I'm indebted to the candid thoughts Howard Schultz expressed in his book, *Onward: How Starbucks Fought for its Life without Losing its Soul*, (New York: Rodale Inc., 2011).

DOMINO'S
Stephanie Clifford, "Video Prank at Domino's Taints Brands," *The New York Times*, April 15, 2009.

BANK OF AMERICA
Bank withdrawal numbers from the Credit Union National Association newsletter, November 4, 2011.

CUSTOMER RECOMMENDATIONS
2009 Nielsen Global Online Consumer Survey.

AMAZON
"Jeff Bezos recalls a publisher calling him and saying 'I don't think you understand your business. You make money when you sell books.'" From "A Conversation with Jeff Bezos" by François Bourboulon, *Les Echos* (blog), June 23, 2011.

In today's world, where ideas are increasingly displacing the physical in the production of economic value, competition for reputation becomes a significant driving force, propelling our economy forward. Manufactured goods often can be evaluated before the completion of a transaction. Service providers, on the other hand, usually can offer only their reputations.

—*Alan Greenspan, former Federal Reserve Chairman*

CHAPTER TWO

The service economy

Industrialization is a phase, and in developed nations that phase is ending. Growth in developed economies will increasingly come from services.

THE GREAT RESET

In *The Great Reset: How New Ways of Living and Working Drive Post-Crash Prosperity*, Richard Florida points to a shift from an economy based on making things to one that is increasingly powered by knowledge, creativity, and ideas:

> Great Resets are broad and fundamental transformations of the economic and social order and involve much more than strictly economic or financial events. A true Reset transforms not simply the way we innovate and produce but also ushers in a whole new economic landscape.

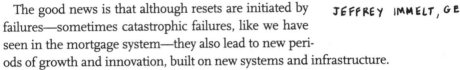

Jeffrey Immelt, CEO of General Electric, agrees:

> This economic crisis doesn't represent a cycle. It represents a reset. It's an emotional, raw social, economic reset. People who understand that will prosper. Those who don't will be left behind.

JEFFREY IMMELT, GE

The good news is that although resets are initiated by failures—sometimes catastrophic failures, like we have seen in the mortgage system—they also lead to new periods of growth and innovation, built on new systems and infrastructure.

There's little doubt that a fundamental economic restructuring is underway. There will be winners and there will be losers.

AN AGE OF ABUNDANCE

As we stand on the verge of a new era, it's easy to disparage the old-school industrial economy. But let's not forget that the industrial economy gave us an abundance of material wealth we now take for granted, including many things that were unavailable—and unimaginable—in previous centuries.

Economist J. Bradford DeLong points out that in 1836, the richest man in the world, Nathan Rothschild, died of a common infection that would have been easily curable with modern antibiotics.

In the 1890s, even the richest of the rich could not go to the movies or watch football on TV, and traveling from New York to Italy took at least a week.

The material abundance we all enjoy was made possible by an industrial economy that focused primarily on mass-producing material goods. The philosophy of mass production was based on Henry Ford's big idea: If you could produce great volumes of a product at a low cost, the market for that product would be virtually unlimited. In the early days, his idea held true, but eventually, every market gets saturated and it gets more and more difficult to sell more stuff. By 1960, 70% of families owned their own homes, 85% had a TV, and 75% had a car.

As markets became saturated with material goods, producers found a new way to apply the principle of mass production in mass marketing. With a TV in nearly every house, producers had a direct line to customers. Customers became known as consumers, because their role in the economy was to consume everything that producers could make. Increasingly, this producer-consumer economy developed into a marketing-industrial complex dependent on consumer dissatisfaction and the mass creation of desire for the next new thing.

New technologies of communication have splintered the channels of mass communication into tiny fragments. It's no longer possible for mass marketers to reach out and touch all of their customers at once. The megaphone is gone. And with the rise of blogs, social networks and other peer-to-peer communication channels, every customer can have his own megaphone.

To many mass marketers, this feels like a chaotic cacophony of voices, and it's hard to be heard in the crowd. But to most customers, it's an empowering feeling to have a voice, to be heard. Even if a company ignores your complaint, the world will hear, and if companies don't respond, they will eventually feel the pain, as customers find new places to go to get what they want.

The producer-driven economy is giving way to a new, customer-centered world in which companies will prosper by developing relationships with customers—by listening to them, adapting, and responding to their wants and needs.

The problem is that the organizations that generated all this wealth were not designed to listen, adapt, and respond. They were designed to create a ceaseless, one-way flow of material goods and information. Everything about them has been optimized for this one-directional arrow, and product-oriented habits are so deeply embedded in our organizational systems that it will be difficult to root them out.

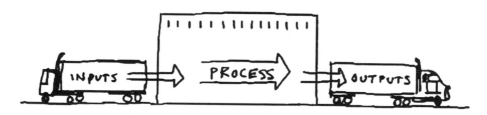

It's not only companies that need to change. Our entire society has been optimized for production and consumption on a massive scale. Our school systems are optimized to create good cogs for the corporate machine, not the creative thinkers and problem-solvers we will need in the 21st century. Our government is optimized for corporate customers, spending its money to bail out and protect the old infrastructure instead of investing in the new one. Our suburbs are optimized to increase consumption, with lots of space for products and plenty of nearby places where we can consume more stuff—including lots of fuel—along the way. Our entertainment and advertising industries are designed to drive demand and keep the whole engine running.

While workers are being laid off in many industries, technology companies like Facebook and Google are suffering from critical shortages, struggling to fill their ranks and depending heavily on talent imported from other countries that place a higher priority on technical education:

> The whole approach of throwing trillions of public dollars at the old economy is shortsighted, aimed at restoring our collective comfort level. Meaningful recovery will require a lot more than government bailouts, stimuli, and other patchwork measures designed to resuscitate the old system or to create illusory, short-term upticks in the stock market, housing market, or car sales. –*Richard Florida*

We no longer live in an industrial economy. We live in a service economy. And to succeed in a service economy, we will need to develop new habits and behaviors. And we will need new organizational structures.

AN EMERGING SERVICE ECONOMY

Since 1960, services have dominated US employment. Today's services sector makes up about 80% of the US economy. Services are integrated into everything we buy and use. Nine out of every ten companies with fewer than 20 employees are in services. Companies like GE and IBM, which started in manufacturing, have made the transition, and now make the majority of their money in services.

What's driving the move to services? Three things: product saturation, information technology, and urbanization.

US EMPLOYMENT GROWTH SINCE 1939

Source: US Bureau of Labor Statistics

PRODUCT SATURATION

When people already have most of the material goods they need, they will tend to spend more of their disposable income on services. Increasingly, the products that companies want to sell us are optional; they offer not functionality, but intangible things like status, pride of ownership, novelty, and so on.

And products, we have found, not only make life easier, but can also be a burden. When you own a house, you have to spend money to fix the roof or the plumbing. Where's the fun in that? And moving can be a big hassle when you have a truckload of stuff to lug along with you.

A recent study found that Great Britain, where the industrial revolution began, reached "peak stuff" levels between 2001 and 2003—long before the 2008 recession—and material consumption has been declining ever since (it's now down to the 1989 level).

INFORMATION TECHNOLOGY

A post-industrial revolution is delivering a new kind of abundance: an abundance of information, along with networks and mobile devices for moving that information around, and much faster processing, which allows us to do more interesting kinds of things with the information we have.

Think about how you use the Web. While at first this shift was driven by the kinds of things we traditionally think of as information containers, like pages and images, now it has exploded to include many things that were previously undocumented: your network of friends and acquaintances, the things you do, the places you go, the things you buy and what you think about them. Even your random, throwaway thoughts are being captured in Foursquare check-ins, tweets, status updates, photo and video uploads, and other kinds of "data exhaust" that you may not even know you're generating, simply by using your phone and other devices.

This digital revolution is ushering in new ways to deliver, combine, and mix up services, resulting in all kinds of enticing combinations: streaming music, following other people's book highlights, renting strangers' apartments or cars by the day, negotiating bargain prices from airlines and 4-star hotels, and much more.

URBANIZATION

In addition, there is an increasing trend toward urbanization. Throughout the world, city populations are growing much faster than rural populations. We are becoming an urban society and living more urban lifestyles.

Fifty percent of the world's population today lives on 2 percent of the earth's crust. In 1950, that number was 30%. By 2050, it is expected to be 70%.

Why are people moving to cities? Because cities are where the action is. There are more jobs—and more kinds of jobs—available in cities, and even when the same job is available in the country and the city, the job in the city pays more.

Urban workers make, on average, 23% more than rural workers. And the more highly skilled you are as a worker, the more you stand to gain financially by moving to a large city.

Also, if you happen to get laid off or your company goes out of business, it's much easier to find a new job in a city without having to pick up and move.

As work becomes more complex and more skills are required, cities become more attractive to companies, too, because that's where the skilled workers are. Cities pack a lot of people and businesses into a relatively small space, which is good for services companies in several ways.

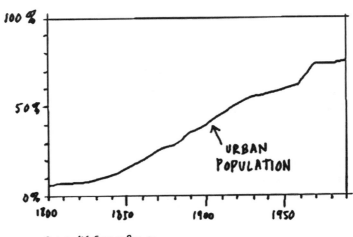

CHANGES IN US URBAN/RURAL POPULATION

Source: US Census Bureau

Space: People living in small city apartments just don't have a lot of room for products, and because they are making more money than their rural counterparts, they tend to spend more on services. Why take up space with a washer and dryer when there's a laundry service right down the street?

Density: Urban density makes it more attractive for companies to provide a wide variety of services. For example, a cable company can wire a city apartment building and serve hundreds of households for a fraction of the cost to do the same thing in a suburb or rural area. Taxis find customers quickly in densely packed urban centers. One city block can support several specialty stores and a variety of restaurants. And in a reciprocal loop, that wide variety of services makes cities even more attractive places to live.

Consider the quintessential industrial-age product, the automobile: for many, it is a symbol of individuality, status, personality, and freedom. In suburban and sparsely-populated rural areas, a car provides you with unlimited mobility and choice. But in a densely populated urban environment, a car quickly becomes more trouble than it's worth. A permanent parking space in New York costs more than a house in many other areas.

Density creates demand for more services, like taxis, limousine services, buses, and subways. It also creates opportunities for new services. For example, Zipcar is a car-sharing service that gives customers shared access to a pool of cars located throughout their city. RelayRide and Whipcar are peer-to-peer services that allow car owners to rent their cars to neighbors by the hour or by the day. Uber connects a network of professional limo drivers with city dwellers, who can order a car by SMS or mobile phone app; orders are routed to the nearest available driver, payments are automated, and driver tips are included, creating a simple, easy, seamless customer experience.

Cars themselves will increasingly become platforms for delivering services. In 1995, GM created OnStar, an in-car subscription service that offers turn-by-turn directions, hands-free calling, and remote diagnostics. If your car is stolen, GM can track the vehicle, slow it down, or shut off the ignition remotely. But that's just the beginning. Automakers will increasingly be integrating with digital services, and cars will become platforms for a broad array of apps and services that will help you lower your fuel costs, stream music, avoid collisions, find parking, notify you if friends are near, and a whole host of other things we can't yet imagine. Ford announced recently that they are creating an open platform that will allow tinkerers and developers to electronically "hot-rod" their cars. And Google is working on cars that will drive themselves. How's that for a service?

If a car can be a service, anything can.

WE ARE BECOMING AN URBAN SPECIES

The majority of business growth in the coming decades—new jobs and new businesses—will come from services.

Some people argue that the majority of services growth comes from low-wage jobs. But according to the US Bureau of Labor Statistics, job growth will be led by health care, followed by professional, scientific, and technical services, as well as education.

NOTES FOR CHAPTER TWO

JEFFREY IMMELT
GE CEO Jeffrey Immelt, quoted in *The Great Reset: How New Ways of Living and Working Drive Post-Crash Prosperity* by Richard Florida, (New York: HarperCollins, 2010).

NATHAN ROTHSCHILD
"In 1836, the richest man in the world, Nathan Rothschild, died of a common infection..." from "Cornucopia: The Pace of Economic Life in the Twentieth Century" by J. Bradford DeLong. Working Paper, National Bureau of Economic Research, (March 2000): *http://www.nber.org/papers/w7602*.

PEAK STUFF
"A recent study found that Great Britain, where the industrial revolution began, reached "peak stuff" levels between 2001 and 2003..." "From Peak Stuff: Did the UK reach a maximum use of material resources in the early part of the last decade?" By Chris Goodall, *http://carboncommentary.com*, (October 13, 2011).

CITY POPULATION
"City populations are growing much faster than rural populations" from US Census Bureau, *http://www.elderweb.com/node/2836*.

POPULATION PROJECTIONS
"Fifty percent of the world's population today lives on two percent of the Earth's crust. In 1950, that number was 30%, and by 2050 it is expected to be 70%." Projection by the United Nations, *http://en.wikipedia.org/wiki/File:Percentage_of_World_Population_Urban_Rural.PNG*.

URBAN WORKERS
Urban workers make, on average, 23% more than rural workers." "Explaining the Gap in Pay Between Rural and Urban Work," *The Daily Yonder*, March 3, 2008, *http://www.dailyyonder.com/explaining-gap-pay-between-rural-and-urban-work*.

WAGE GAP
"Wage Gap Widens, Especially in Cities," by Christopher H. Wheeler. *The Regional Economist*, January 2005.

PARKING SPACES
"A permanent parking space in New York costs more than a house in many other areas." From "For Parking Space, the Price is Right at $225,000" by Vivian S. Toy, *The New York Times*, July 12, 2007.

FORD
"Ford announced recently that they are creating an open platform that will allow tinkerers and developers to electronically 'hot-rod' their cars." From "Hack your car with OpenXC, a platform for modding Ford car computers," by Dean Takahashi, *VentureBeat*, September 12, 2011, *http://www.venturebeat. com/2011/09/12/hack-your-car-with-openxc-platform-for-modding-ford-car-computers/*.

SELF-DRIVING CARS
"Google is working on cars that will drive themselves." From "Google Cars Drive Themselves, in Traffic," by John Markoff, *The New York Times*, October 9, 2010.

JOB GROWTH
"Job growth will be led by health care..." From "Occupational Outlook Handbook: 2010-20 Projections," Bureau of Labor Statistics, March 29, 2012, *http://www.bls. gov/ooh/About/Projections-Overview.htm*.

Our mission statement about treating people with respect and dignity is not just words but a creed we live by every day. You can't expect your employees to exceed the expectations of your customers if you don't exceed the employees' expectations of management.

—*Howard Schultz, Founder & CEO, Starbucks Coffee*

CHAPTER THREE

Everything is a service

Services cannot be designed and
manufactured in isolation, like products.
They are co-created with customers and
are interdependent with wider service
networks and clusters.

THE INDUSTRIAL MODEL

Most companies today are designed to produce high volumes of consistent, standard outputs, with great efficiency and at low cost. Even many of today's services industries still operate in an industrial fashion. Schools efficiently produce standardized students. Hospitals efficiently move the sick and injured through a diagnostic and prescriptive production line. Drive-through restaurants efficiently move drivers through an order-fulfillment pipeline.

SERVICE-DOMINANT LOGIC

But most of these services are not really services at all. They are factory-style processes that treat people as if they were products moving through a production line. Just think of the last time you called a company's "customer service line" and ask yourself if you felt well served.

Sure, many services require some level of efficiency, but services are not production processes. They are experiences.

Unlike products, services are often designed or modified as they are delivered; they are co-created with customers. Services are contextual—where, when, and how they are delivered can make a big difference. They may require specialized knowledge or skills. The value of a service lies in the interactions: it's not the end product that matters, so much as the experience. Service providers often must respond in real time to customer desires and preferences.

To this end, a company with a service orientation cannot be designed and organized around efficiency processes. It must be designed and organized around customers and experiences. This is a complete inversion of the mass-production, mass-marketing paradigm, which will be difficult for many companies to adopt.

In "Evolving to a New Dominant Logic for Marketing," Stephen L. Vargo and Robert F. Lusch describe a new paradigm they call service-dominant logic, a fundamental shift in worldview and orientation toward marketing as a social process. In this view, products are not ends in themselves but means for provisioning services. The customer is seen as a co-producer, and knowledge is the source of competitive advantage.

In product-dominant logic, production is the core of the value-creation process, while customer service is a cost to be minimized. But in service-dominant logic, products are the cost centers, and services become the core value-creation processes.

Why such a fundamental shift?

Products are costly and require large investments of capital in R&D, factories, and manufacturing before money can be made. Furthermore, products are anchors. Investments in manufacturing take time to provide returns, and during this time period, customer needs are likely to change. Investing in physical products "hardens" the offering and reduces the company's ability to respond and adapt to changing customer preferences.

Investing in services "softens" the offering and increases the company's flexibility. Since costs aren't sunk into a single product, it's easier to shift the offering and keep pace with customer demands.

Like looking through a telescope the wrong way around, for many people who have become habituated to a product orientation, this inversion to service-dominant logic will at first feel unnatural and uncomfortable.

The good news is that there is huge room for improvement, and companies that dedicate themselves to improving services stand to make significant gains in profitability and competitive advantage.

According to an Accenture survey, customer satisfaction is declining in every area they measure, and 64% of customers have switched companies in the past year due to poor service. Three out of four people say they don't trust the companies with which they do business.

Another survey by American Express found that two-thirds of customers have not noticed improvements in customer service, and that fewer than 1 in 10 customers think companies are exceeding their expectations. An overwhelming majority of customers are willing to spend more to get excellent service, and more than half of them will switch companies to get it.

The same survey also found that while 40% of customers are willing to tell their friends about good service experiences, even more of them—60%—will tell their friends about poor service experiences.

It doesn't take a genius to figure out that poor service will result in lost sales, and good service will result in repeat business. And for most companies, the biggest growth opportunities in the coming years will come through services.

A PRODUCT IS A SERVICE AVATAR

The first step to a service orientation is to change the way we think about products. Instead of thinking about products as ends in themselves, we need to think of them as just one component in an overall service, the point of which is to deliver a stellar customer experience.

Today, many people think of an avatar as the face or icon that represents you in your Twitter stream, or on your Facebook page. But the original word *avatar* comes from ancient Sanskrit, based on the root words *ava* (descent, coming down) and *tatari* (crossing over). The original meaning is the divine made flesh: an incarnation or physical manifestation of an idea or god. In Hindu belief, Buddha was an avatar of the god Vishnu—a physical manifestation of the deity descended to earth. Energy transformed into matter.

AVATAR

In the same way, a product can be considered to be a physical manifestation of a service or set of services: a service avatar.

Products come with knowledge and services embedded within them. A car is the manifestation of years of learning, accumulated through research, crash testing, metallurgy, electrical engineering, design, and a score of other disciplines, including good old trial and error. And as we have seen, a car itself provides the service of getting you comfortably from one place to another.

The ratio of knowledge to matter in any product increasingly favors knowledge. A modern car contains more computing power than the system that guided Apollo astronauts to the moon. Consider the difference between a TV and a TiVo.

The knowledge and services embedded in a product are what give the product its value. Consider an iPhone. Its value comes from the services it provides you: you can talk to friends, send messages to them, and access a wide variety of applications, songs, books, and even movies if you care to. Having an iPhone allows you to carry around a whole city's worth of services in your pocket. The job of the iPhone is to provision you with services.

The words we use to describe products are a dead giveaway. Think about the number of product names that are essentially verbs or job descriptions.

SERVICE AVATARS

PRODUCTS AS VERBS

You use an iron to iron things, a brush to brush things, and a bottle to bottle things. You ladle with a ladle and hose things down with a hose. You step on a step, drum a drum, handle a handle, and grill with a grill. When you're driving, you brake with the brake, accelerate using the accelerator, and steer with the steering wheel. You mail the mail, drink a drink, lock a lock, and microwave things with the microwave. Cups cup things. You tape things together with tape.

PRODUCTS AS JOB DESCRIPTIONS

A blender's job is to blend things. A washer washes things and a dryer dries things. The lawn mower mows the lawn. The heater heats, the boiler boils, and the air conditioner conditions the air. In your kitchen, the refrigerator refrigerates and the freezer freezes. At work, the copier copies, the scanner scans, the printer prints, and the computer computes. The doorstop stops the door. Lipstick sticks to your lips and eye shadow shadows your eyes.

Products aren't just things. They are servants.

"The Kindle is not a device, it's a service," said Jeff Bezos in a recent interview. On the Kindle, you can go to the store, browse for stuff, read reviews, and start reading a book, listening to music, or watching a film in less than a minute. Kindle's service aspect becomes even more clear when you use it with more than one device. Open a Kindle book on your iPad, and the service syncs to the last page you were on. It doesn't matter what device you're using; Kindle follows you from device to device and always remembers your place. The Kindle is a physical manifestation and extension of the services Amazon provides to its customers: an avatar for its company's services.

SERVICES ARE CO-CREATED

A company can't create value on its own: value is only created through exchange. The customer must participate in defining and determining that value. That car, beautiful as it may be, has value in an economic sense only to the degree that a customer is willing to pay for it. The company can only create an offer, value proposition, or proposal. The customer must accept in order to create value. The bus can make an offer, but the customer still must step onto the bus for the value to be delivered.

Co-created value requires a relationship: products can play a role in relationships—even a key role—but products can't have relationships. The relationship between a company and its customers develops gradually, as customers build trust in the company and its ability to deliver on its promises over time.

The product is an intermediate step, not an end in itself: even after customers buy a product, they must learn how to use it, maintain it, repair it, and enjoy it. If the company is lucky, they will like it enough to tell friends about it, educate others, promote it, buy additional services around it, and so on.

SERVICES ARE CO-CREATED

A service-dominant world changes the game significantly. Service-orientation is a fundamental shift and creates opportunities for new business strategies, new sources of competitive advantage, new ways of interacting with customers, and new ways of organizing work.

A PROCESS IS NOT A SERVICE

We have developed a tendency to think of flows in terms of process, but services and processes are not the same. Processes are linked, linear chains of cause and effect that, when managed carefully, drive predictable, reliable results.

A service is different. While processes are designed to be consistent and uniform, services are co-created with customers each and every time a service is rendered. This difference is not superficial but fundamental.

A process has only one customer: the person who receives the final result. A process is rule-bound and tightly regulated. The quality of a process's output can be judged by the customer at the end of the line.

A service, on the other hand, is at its core a relationship between server and served. Service is work performed in support of another person. At every point of interaction, the measure of success is not a product but the satisfaction, delight, or disappointment of the customer.

SERVICE NETWORKS

Because services map to increasingly demanding customer preferences, companies must find ways to make them more granular, as well as easier to bundle with other complementary services—even services from other providers. Customers want services to be convenient for them, not for you.

Consider insurance. Even though insurance is a service, in many ways it is sold like a product. A product-dominant mindset says, "We sell life insurance, car insurance, and homeowner's insurance. Our customers come to us when they need insurance." But if a company can find a way to offer business partners' insurance as a configurable service, a lot more options open up.

For example, Whipcar allows car owners to rent their cars out when they are not using them. Part of the Whipcar service involves bundling car insurance along with the rental, which requires that the "insurance service" be available on demand in increments as small as one hour. The more networked and linkable an insurance service, the more easily it can be blended and bundled with Whipcar's other services.

SERVICES DO BETTER
WHEN THEY CLUSTER TOGETHER

PayPal is a super-granular payment service that is easy to plug in to any ordering system. Some of PayPal's customers are so happy with the service, and so loyal, that they will not buy from merchants who don't offer PayPal payment service. After all, buying from another vendor is usually just one click away.

Service networks thrive by making a set of complementary services more easily available to customers. A restaurant does better if it's within a short walk of a movie theater and shopping. Customers tend to like convenient clusters of services. For example, it's nice if you can go grocery shopping, drop off your laundry, and get a coffee in a single stop or within a short distance.

But to be effective in networks, companies need to learn how to navigate and interact successfully in environments that are fluid, ever-changing, and mostly outside of their control.

NOTES FOR CHAPTER THREE

ACCENTURE

Accenture 2010 Global Consumer Survey, February 18, 2011, *http://www.accenture. com/us-en/pages/insight-accenture-customer-satisfaction-survey-2010-summary.aspx.*

AMERICAN EXPRESS

2011 Global Customer Service Barometer, a research paper prepared for American Express by Echo, *http://about.americanexpress.com/news/docs/2011x/AXP_2011_ csbar_market.pdf.*

COMPUTING POWER

"Your Car Has More Computing Power than the System that Guided Apollo Astronauts to the Moon," Institute of Physics, *http://physics.org/facts/apollo.asp.*

KINDLE

"Bezos: Kindle Fire is an End-to-End Service," by Erick Schonfeld, *Seeking Alpha,* September 29, 2011, *http://seekingalpha.com/article/296777-bezos-kindle-fire-is-an-end-to-end-service.*

Most corporate systems were not built
with customer delight in mind.

—*Fred Reichheld, Fellow, Bain & Company*

CHAPTER FOUR

Services are complex

Services introduce customers into operations, which creates a lot of complexity and variability that is hard to plan for in advance. Companies must find ways to accommodate variety at the edge of the organization, where people and systems interact directly with customers, partners, and suppliers.

DEMANDS ON COMPANIES ARE INCREASING IN VOLUME, VELOCITY, VARIETY

I have a friend who works at the U.S. Food and Drug Administration (FDA). One of the challenges the FDA is facing is that more and more drugs and devices are coming up for approval all the time, and the FDA has limited resources for evaluating and approving them. The more drugs and devices that come in to the system for approval, the fewer the FDA can actually look at in detail. In a world of limited budgets, this presents a major challenge that will only increase over time.

The same thing is happening in microchips. At one time, the chip business was focused primarily on chips for servers and PCs. Based on Moore's Law, chipmakers could predict the price and performance that would be required in 18 months and work to achieve it. The production cycles were predictable. But today, the world of devices has fractured into devices that serve all kinds of purposes, with all kinds of production cycles. Chips are embedded in almost everything, from sneakers to smart phones.

Competitive intensity is rising all over the world. Global competition and the Web have given customers more choices than they have ever had before. This means that customers can choose from an ever-widening set of choices, and it seems that variety only breeds more variety. The more choices that become available, the more choices it seems people want.

Customers have lots of things they are trying to do, and lots of ways they are trying to do them. And you have lots of competitors who are trying to offer them better, cheaper, faster, easier ways to do those things. And while customers are always looking for these better, faster, cheaper ways to do things, technology isn't standing still. As the front edge of technological change gets bigger, its surface area also grows, like an ever-expanding balloon. Every new technology adds one more set of capabilities that the next generation of technology can expand on.

Technology has a lot of effects. It reduces the friction of distance, it increases the variety of options and possibilities, it increases the velocity of just about everything, and it tends to also increase complexity and interdependency as more and more technologies build on and interoperate with each other.

In the coming century, the world will create a lot of variety. This is great for people who want more choices, but it creates a real problem for companies.

From drugs to microchips, from food service to entertainment, your customers will be expecting a lot of variety from you. They will want better quality, and they will want it faster and cheaper. They will expect you to respond quickly to their demands for personal and customized services. This change is real and it's accelerating.

For most companies, business as usual just won't cut it. What the market requires is not incremental improvement, but order-of-magnitude increases in performance. Are you ready to respond to these rising expectations?

COMPETITIVE INTENSITY
Percent of US manufacturers classified as "hypercompetitive"

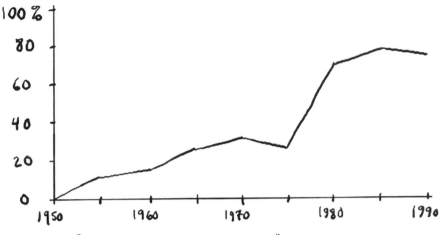

Source: "The Rise of Hypercompetition from 1950 to 2002" by L.G. Thomas and Richard D'Aveni, 2004

CUSTOMERS INTRODUCE COMPLEXITY AND VARIABILITY INTO OPERATIONS

You can't run service operations like a factory, because customers just walk onto the factory floor and mess everything up. They interfere. You can't schedule when they show up. They just come in massive waves at the most inconvenient times. Then they get angry when they have to wait. Why can't they make an appointment?

They don't understand how things work, so you have to train them to use the equipment. Sometimes they can be really slow to figure things out.

They ask for things that aren't on the menu. They want everything to be customized and personalized for them. They have no interest in efficient operations.

They don't follow the processes we lay out for them. As soon as you design a perfect voice menu system, they come up with some new problem that isn't on the menu and they have to talk to you. If you make a form, they need something that isn't on the form. They want to have a conversation.

And customers want to get on with their days. They don't want to wait in the waiting room or stay on hold for the next customer representative. They want services to be convenient for them. They want to get a coffee, get their hair done, and have lunch.

So customers introduce a massive amount of complexity into the Company Formerly Known as The Well-Oiled Machine. At the same time, competitors and even cooperating partners continually change the system as well. Instead of a stable landscape with peaks and valleys, you find yourself in a fluid landscape that looks more like waves in the ocean. As customers, competitors, and partners make adaptive moves and countermoves, they not only affect each other but they affect the landscape itself, so an organization that was fit for yesterday's world cannot be certain that they will be fit for tomorrow's world.

Our companies have all been optimized for a perfect one-way stream, the line of production, and these pesky customers are mucking about in our operations, and we have now a completely different problem to solve. We need to optimize not for the line of production but for the line of interaction, the front line—the edge of the organization—where our people and systems come into direct contact with customers. It's a whole different thing.

WHY IS IT SO HARD TO KEEP YOUR SERVICE PROMISES?

Since services are created as they are delivered, the only way to sell them is by making a promise to perform. But most service companies fail to keep their promises, leaving customers frustrated, confused, and abused. Why do so many service companies fail to keep their promises to customers?

A 2011 study by American Express found that fewer than 1 in 10 customers say companies are exceeding their service expectations. Customers are not getting the service they want. Many feel abused. When they call your customer service line and hear a recorded voice saying, "Your call is important to us," guess what? They don't believe you.

Customers have become accustomed to being abused by the companies they buy services from. Their expectations for most services are low, low, low. The most hated companies, and the most hated industries, are service providers.

CUSTOMERS RESIST STANDARDIZATION

Many service companies just aren't designed for service delivery. They are designed like factories, optimized for the mass production of inputs into outputs. This makes perfect sense in a rapidly-industrializing economy. But in an economy where manufacturing is shrinking and services are expanding, it doesn't work anymore.

Traditional management thinking looks at a customer service call as an input to the service factory. For a factory, it's not difficult to get standard inputs from suppliers. But inputs from customers come in all kinds of different shapes and sizes. Every problem, every job that customers need to do, has its own unique profile. Most companies try to standardize these inputs as much as possible so they can process them efficiently. The factory's job is to produce "resolutions." This is how we end up with complicated voice menu systems that attempt to route calls to the appropriate department while keeping costs as low as possible.

As companies try to fit customer demands into standard boxes, customers become frustrated and angry. They give up. Sometimes they leave to find another provider, but even then they often hold little hope that anything will change.

CUSTOMER SUPPORT: EFFICIENT FOR YOU, PAINFUL FOR THEM

Consider your last experience with your telephone, cable, or satellite provider; your utility provider; your airline; or your bank. Did you talk to a real person or an automated system? Did you have to ask to speak with a supervisor? Did you lose your temper? Did you swear? Did you hang up the phone in disgust? Did you not even call at all, because you knew it would not be worth the time and effort? You are not alone.

When customers are dissatisfied, there are only two possible outcomes. Either the issue is resolved to the customer's satisfaction or it isn't. When it isn't, it becomes costly to your company. Trying to reduce or outsource your customer support costs might actually cost you a lot more in the long run, as you lose customers and they badmouth you to all their friends.

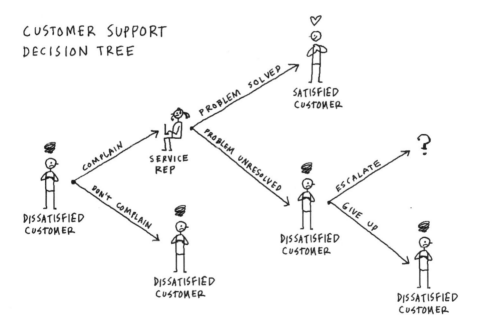

Consider what happens when you focus on costs in your customer service operations: the cheapest customer support call is the one that doesn't happen at all. Of course, you don't know why the customer didn't call you. Maybe they were happy with your service, or maybe they just didn't have the time or energy to fight their way upstream through your draconian support system. There's just no way to know.

If you're lucky and they do call you, there are still two possible outcomes. You satisfy the customer or you don't. Probably the cheaper outcome from a functional, departmental, cost-accounting perspective is the one where you quickly tell them it's not possible or it's not your department. You can mark that "resolved, not my department" and forget about it. Maybe the customer will give up at that point.

If you're still lucky, your customer will be patient as you bounce them around your system until they find the department that might be able to solve their problem. Once again, you have two possible outcomes: you satisfy the customer or you don't. Of course, while the customer bounces around they might get a little frustrated, but that's okay, because that's not your cost, it's the customer's cost. It's an "externality" and it doesn't show up in your cost-accounting system.

Now that the customer has finally reached the right department, you still have two possible outcomes: you can resolve their problem or not. It's probably going to be cheaper not to solve their problem, because most of the time solutions have some kind of cost. You might have to accept a return, or credit the customer's account. If the situation is not in the service representative's rule book, the service rep might not be able to help.

If you're lucky, the customer will ask to speak to a supervisor. At that point, there are still two possible outcomes. You can solve the customer's problem or say no. It's probably cheaper to say no, for the reasons outlined above. But maybe the supervisor will say yes, in which case there's a chance your customer will be satisfied.

Customers will put up with this kind of treatment only for so long. Eventually, they will find another company that treats them better. That would be great for you though, right? Because the cost of serving someone else's customer is zero! Yay for the cost savings team!

Then, when your customer tells all her friends about her experience, you will lose more customers. Your call center costs will continue to go down. At some point, when the last customer has left, you can eliminate your call center altogether. Total cost victory achieved.

COST AND QUALITY ARE NOT MUTUALLY EXCLUSIVE

Once you're making a profit at something, and you feel like you've got as many people buying it as are happy to buy it (market saturation), the next move is to try and to cut costs. Many companies assume that cutting costs will lead to lower quality. But that is not necessarily so.

Quality expert W. Edwards Deming once said that this is easy to understand. If you talk to a line worker in any factory, he said, just ask: "How does improving quality reduce costs?" The answer will be simple: "Less rework."

Cost-cutting can be a dangerous business. It's easy to cut costs in one area while unintentionally raising costs in another. Consider the costs that accrue when a customer calls in several times and talks to several people to get a single thing from the company. Consider the cost of a frustrated customer who gives up and finds another provider. Consider the costs involved in replacing customers that you lose through bad service. A company that truly serves customers well has vastly lower marketing and customer acquisition costs. Happy customers are the best marketing department any company could ever have.

All these costs are extremely important, but they are not easily counted. Many companies focus on those costs that are easily identified on the financial statements. But by cutting those costs, they are playing a shell game. In actuality, they are just moving those costs around. They are eating their own future: reducing today's costs at the expense of long-term customer relationships and customer loyalty. Pissed-off customers won't stay any longer than they have to.

CUSTOMER SERVICE DOESN'T HAVE TO BE PAINFUL

As a contrast, consider the Vanguard Group, an investment management company with $1.6 trillion in assets, offering mutual funds, financial products, and services to individual and institutional investors.

Calling a company for support is usually a headache. Usually, you start with a voicemail system and then you mess around for a while trying to find the right menu. Often, none of the menus exactly fit what you need, and it takes a while to get a real person on the phone. Then, when you finally get someone, you have to give them all your information even though you have already entered it into the system. They usually can't solve your problem, so they need to transfer you somewhere, where you need to give them your information all over again, and so on. We've all been there, right?

Vanguard customers have a vastly different experience. When you call Vanguard, you get a person on the phone, right off the bat. If the person can't help you, they will connect you to an expert, but they don't transfer you. They stay on the call.

"We have very high client loyalty," says Richard Dalton, Senior User Experience Manager at Vanguard. "Loyalty is pretty much everything to us...the client is really at the center of literally everything we do."

CONTROL AT THE EDGE

What does Vanguard do differently? They have inverted the traditional concept of control. The customer service representative has the control and authority to take ownership of the customer's issue, and the rest of the company operates as a support network, available to the front-line representative as needed to answer the customer or solve their problem in one go.

Contrast this with the typical approach to customer service, where each person is so specialized that no single person can own a customer issue or resolve it, where the only person with a single view of the customer's problem is the customer, who is then forced to deal with the company as if it were a fragmented, fractured personality.

CUSTOMER SERVICE IN THE DIVIDED COMPANY

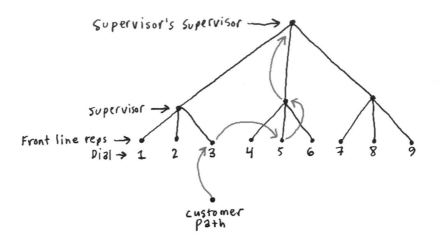

CUSTOMER SERVICE IN THE CONNECTED COMPANY

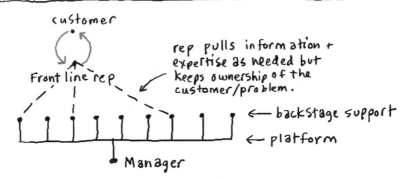

Source: John Seddon, Vanguard Group

The Vanguard rep can focus on the customer's needs, with easy access to the entire company's database of information and expertise, as if it were a service. This means the Vanguard rep can truly act as an agent, working on behalf of the customer until the customer's needs are met.

"We put our crew right at the center of our success. We've said that consistently that the crew are fundamental to the success of this company, and we invest quite heavily in them."

To truly accommodate customers, companies must invest real power and authority in the people and systems that interact directly with customers, at the edge of the organization.

NOTES FOR CHAPTER FOUR

AMERICAN EXPRESS
2011 Global Customer Service Barometer, a research paper prepared for American Express by Echo, *http://about.americanexpress.com/news/docs/2011x/AXP_2011_ csbar_market.pdf.*

HATED COMPANIES
"The most hated companies, and the most hated industries, are service providers." From "Banks, Utilities, Telecoms Top Most Hated Companies List," by Jason Chupick, *PRNewser*, October 14, 2011, *http://www.mediabistro.com/ prnewser/banks-utilities-telecoms-top-most-hated-companies-list_b28712.*

VANGUARD
Vanguard Mutual Funds information based on interviews conducted by the author, 2011.

Your most unhappy customers are your greatest source of learning.

—*Bill Gates, Cofounder & Chairman, Microsoft*

CHAPTER FIVE

How companies lose touch

Companies tend to lose touch with customers as they grow, for a variety of reasons. Companies must find ways to create, maintain, and develop deep connections as they grow.

WHY DO COMPANIES LOSE TOUCH?

Running through every business success story is a common theme: stay connected to customers, stay connected to your market, anticipate and expect change. This seems pretty obvious. It's simple and it's easy to understand. Customers, after all, are the one thing no business can do without. They are the key to every company's survival.

Paying attention to customers seems like such a fundamental thing. So why do so many companies do it so poorly? How do companies lose touch with their customers, and lose their grip on the realities of the marketplace?

As any athlete will tell you, just because something's fundamental, that doesn't mean it's easy.

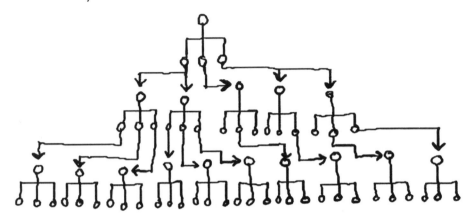

With growth, distractions and complications multiply.

Without question, customers are the single biggest factor in any company's long-term growth and profitability. And yet, as companies grow, distractions multiply. Success can create such a dazzling array of opportunities that companies try to capitalize on too many of them, over-expanding and diluting their offerings. Internal efficiency and organization become paramount as companies struggle to maintain their growth trajectories and keep the factories and supply chain moving. Political squabbles can erupt as people jockey for status, attempt to seize greater authority and control, or take credit for successes. Bureaucracies that emerge to handle increasing complexity and organizational challenges can also stifle creativity and innovation.

Focusing on the complexities and intricacies of growth, many companies take their eyes off of the customer, their most important asset.

Ironically, a history of success may be the biggest reason companies lose touch with customers. Success can fuel enormous growth and even lead to market dominance. But it can also lead to over-expansion, blind spots, and risk-avoidant cultures.

OVER-EXPANSION

Caught up in whirlwind growth, some companies become distracted by a landscape of opportunity and try to do everything just because they can.

HOW STARBUCKS LOST TOUCH

In the early 2000s, Starbucks focused on growth, expanding globally, opening new stores, and populating their stores with more and more products, like songs and books. New stores were opening every day, and a seemingly endless parade of new products entered stores, until every Starbucks seemed to double as a gift shop.

"Obsessed with growth, we took our eye off operations and became distracted from the core of our business," says Howard Schultz, Starbucks CEO, in *Onward: How Starbucks Fought for Its Life without Losing Its Soul* (Rodale Books, 2011).

"Every new store increased the company's profits, and every incremental product increased sales and profitability in each store. It wasn't any single new store or new product introduction that hurt the company, but as these incremental changes added up, Starbucks slowly lost touch with what its customers cared about— fast, great service, great coffee and a place to enjoy it."

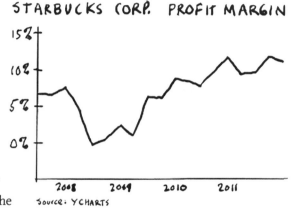

Schultz recalls a day when he realized the need for change.

"Once, I walked into a store and was appalled by a proliferation of stuffed animals for sale. 'What is this?' I asked the store manager in frustration, pointing to a pile of wide-eyed cuddly toys that had absolutely nothing to do with coffee. The manager didn't blink. 'They're great for incremental sales and have a big gross margin.' This was the type of mentality that had become pervasive. And dangerous."

Schultz called this "hubris born of a sense of invincibility."

In 2008, Starbucks closed 600 stores, narrowed its product line, and temporarily closed stores around the world to retrain employees on how to make a great espresso.

Since 2008, Starbucks has refocused on its core business; profits are up, and most investors are bullish.

HOW KRISPY KREME FLAMED OUT

It seemed as if Krispy Kreme had created the perfect business with all the right ingredients: a secret recipe, donuts that tasted so good they were addictive, and media that had a crush on the company. Krispy Kreme had grown organically since its founding in 1937, and after going public in 2000, the company entered into a phase of aggressive growth. It opened a flurry of new stores, selling its donuts in convenience stores, drug stores, gas stations, and big-box retailers like Walmart. The company's stock more than doubled in the two years following its IPO. New store openings were heralded on local news stations and customers lined up outside stores for a first taste of the fantastic donuts. Krispy Kreme's marketing plan boldly stated, "Our market is everyone, everywhere."

But the company grew too fast, and spread itself too thin. Donuts, it turned out, might not be so addictive after all. By opening so many franchises so quickly, Krispy Kreme forced franchisees to compete for a limited market. In addition, franchisees were required to buy equipment directly from Krispy Kreme at marked-up prices. But by maximizing its short-term profits from franchisees, Krispy Kreme shot itself in the foot. Many stores struggled to make a profit and some went out of business or had to declare bankruptcy.

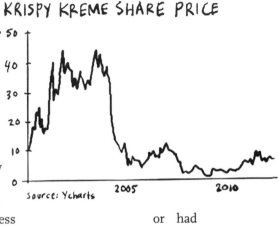

Sales dropped. One of its biggest franchisees defaulted on payments and later filed for bankruptcy. Other franchisees also declared bankruptcy, and Krispy Kreme found itself saddled with more stores than it could operate profitably. Krispy Kreme's troubles worsened when shareholders filed lawsuits, charging company executives with ignoring signs that the company was expanding too quickly. The SEC launched an investigation—never a good sign.

Krispy Kreme stock fell from a high of $50 in 2003 to $3 in 2007.

Krispy Kreme retrenched, sorted out its finances, and settled with the SEC in 2009. Today, the company is expanding again—more cautiously this time.

BLIND SPOTS

While trying to do too many things can be a problem, a focus that's too narrow can be equally problematic. As companies grow, they increase in expertise and efficiency as they attempt to increase profits and market share. But that expertise can narrow the company's focus so much that it develops gaping blind spots. When new technologies and business models inevitably come along to disrupt the status quo, the company has stuck all its eggs in one basket.

HOW XEROX MISSED THE PC REVOLUTION

In 1970, Xerox set up its PARC (Palo Alto Research Center) to envision and develop the office of the future. To that end, the group was wildly successful and has been credited with the invention of laser printers, bitmapped graphics, the mouse, the graphical user interface (GUI), what you see is what you get (WYSIWYG) text editors, and Ethernet. But when it came to introducing these innovations to the marketplace, Xerox faltered.

Xerox PARC was based in Silicon Valley, a far remove from Xerox headquarters in Rochester, NY. While this gave researchers great freedom to pursue new ideas, it also made it more difficult for them to convey the opportunities to senior executives. At the time, copiers were generating huge profits, and Xerox still saw itself as a copier company.

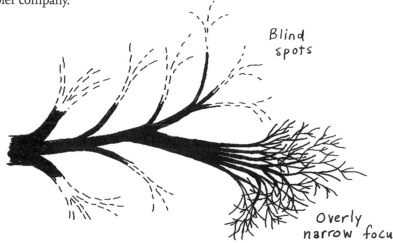

In a recent interview, Gary Starkweather, inventor of the laser printer and former Xerox PARC researcher, told Malcolm Gladwell: "They just could not seem to see that they were in the information business... Xerox had been infested by a bunch of spreadsheet experts who thought you could decide every product based on metrics. Unfortunately, creativity wasn't on a metric."

Apple founder Steve Jobs paid a visit to Xerox PARC in 1979. He was inspired. Xerox PARC engineer Larry Tesler reported to Gladwell: "Jobs was pacing around the room, acting up the whole time. He was very excited. Then, when he began seeing the things I could do onscreen, he watched for about a minute and started jumping around the room, shouting, 'Why aren't you doing anything with this? This is the greatest thing. This is revolutionary!'"

Jobs went back to Apple, and the rest is history.

Xerox may have learned its lesson. Today, the company is focused on moving from being a copier company to a services company. Since 2006, revenue from services—such as outsourcing its customers' document management and other business processes—has risen from 25% to almost 50%. The jury is still out, but Xerox may be turning itself around.

HOW KODAK FADED AWAY

Kodak introduced one of the first consumer cameras in history, in 1888, with the slogan, "You press the button, we do the rest." For 100 years, it sold cameras and film. Its highly profitable business was based on the classic "give away the razor and sell the blades" strategy: it sold cheap, easy-to-use cameras and reaped profits from the film business over time.

In 1975, Kodak engineer Steve Sasson invented the world's first digital camera, a prototype cobbled together using existing technologies, including a super-8 camera lens and cassette tape. After taking your photos with the camera, you could remove the tape and put it into a playback device to display the images on a standard TV. He and his colleagues demonstrated this "filmless technology" to Kodak executives throughout 1976.

EASTMAN KODAK SHARE PRICE

Source: Ycharts

But Kodak had a blind spot when it came to anything that might disrupt the company's profitable film business. Sasson reports the executive reaction: "Why would anyone ever want to view his or her pictures on a TV? How would you store these images? What does an electronic photo album look like? When would this type of approach be available to the consumer?"

Sasson and his team did not have the answers. But by applying Moore's law, the team came up with an estimate: In 15 to 20 years, the devices would be available to consumers.

Kodak sold low-cost cameras but made the lion's share of profits on film. The company's core product was threatened, and Kodak had a 15-year head start to figure out what to do about it. What did Kodak do? Nothing.

Over time, it became more and more evident that the predictions were coming true. In 1988, the JPEG and MPEG formats were introduced. Consumer digital cameras followed in the 1990s. While Kodak's film business faded, the giant slowly awoke, and the company struggled to find a strategy. One Kodak Senior VP and Director of Research said in 1985: "We're moving into an information-based company, [but] it's very hard to find anything [with profit margins] like color photography that is legal."

In the early 1990s, CEO Kay Whitmore vowed to "set the standard in film-based digital imaging." You may ask, as I did, "What's film-based digital imaging?" One example is the Photo CD. Customers could take film to a processor and get a CD back instead of prints. They could then view the CD on their TV with a special player. Kodak executives met with technology companies, trying to find a way to partner. (Bill Gates remembers Whitmore; he remembers Whitmore falling asleep in a meeting.)

More "strategies" followed. First digital cameras, but it turned out the margins in that competitive industry were way too thin. Next, online services to help people manage their photos. Today, it's cheap inkjet printers.

No doubt, times are tough in the film business. But consider rival Fuji. As early as the 1960s, it was producing videotape, computer tape, and audio cassettes. In the 1970s, it was selling VHS tapes and floppy disks. In the 1980s, Fuji started an Electronic Imaging Division and introduced the first digital, computerized X-ray system as well as the world's first consumer digital still camera.

Today, Fuji is building on its experience and expanding into other industries, such as medical systems, digital imaging, optical devices, and specialty materials like the thin films used in making flat-panel displays and solar cells.

Fuji stayed in touch with customers and the changing market. In January 2012, Kodak filed for bankruptcy.

RISK-AVOIDANT CULTURES

When a company is large and successful, its size can be its worst enemy, especially when it is so dominant that it lacks serious competition. A company culture that drove success in the early days can become overly codified, rigid, and ritualistic. Over time, bold new moves become much more risky; new business models may compete with existing businesses and cannibalize their sales. Even when it's obvious that change will someday be necessary, it's not hard to find excuses to put it off just a little bit longer. Slowly, great companies can lose touch with reality.

Cultural rigidity

HOW GE REVITALIZED ITS BUSINESS

GE was founded in 1890 by inventor Thomas Edison, and over time it grew to dominate many industries, including power generation, turbine engines, electrical appliances, and many others. When the Dow Jones Industrial Average was created, GE was one of the 12 companies listed (it's the only one of the original 12 that still exists).

Bureaucratic rigidity reigned supreme when young executive Jack Welch moved into GE headquarters in 1974. In his memoir *Jack: Straight from the Gut* (Warner Business Books), he remembers that, "a set number of ceiling tiles signified one's status in the corporation."

There were as many as a dozen layers between the CEO's office and front-line workers. All those layers insulated the company's executives from its customers, like a person who was wearing too many sweaters. Says Welch, "When you go outside and you wear four sweaters, it's difficult to know how cold it is."

In GE's power business, says Welch, "There was an attitude that customers were 'fortunate' to place orders for their 'wonderful' machines."

"The bigger the business, the less engaged people seemed to be. From the forklift drivers in a factory to the engineers packed in cubicles, too many people were just going through the motions. Passion was hard to find."

A mid-70s tour of Japanese manufacturing plants galvanized Welch into acting early and proactively, while the company was still healthy and profitable:

> The incredible efficiency of the Japanese was both awesome and frightening...And the Japanese, benefiting from a weak yen and good technology, were increasing their exports into many of our mainstream businesses from cars to consumer electronics. I wanted to face these realities.

"I came to the job without many of the external CEO skills," says Welch, "but I did know what I wanted the company to 'feel' like. I wasn't calling it 'culture' in those days, but that's what it was."

Change wasn't easy. In fact, it was war. Welch declared war on the bureaucracy and entitled culture at GE. "I was throwing hand grenades, trying to blow up traditions and rituals that I felt held us back."

He cut the levels of hierarchy in half and instituted a competitive, performance-oriented culture, insisting that top achievers were rewarded handsomely and low performers were fired. The

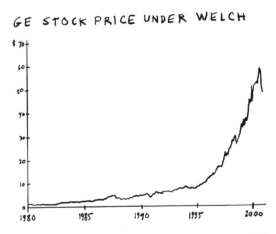

GE STOCK PRICE UNDER WELCH

strategy he laid out was to focus only on industries where GE could be number 1 or number 2. If they couldn't be number 1 or 2, they would fix, sell, or close the business.

In Welch's 20 years as CEO, GE refocused on customers and market realities and grew revenue from $27 billion to $130 billion while increasing profit margins. GE has been consistently profitable since 1991.

HOW IBM REDISCOVERED CUSTOMERS

IBM was also founded in the 1800s. Its early "business machines" included scales, electric tabulation machines, and company time clocks. As the company grew, it continued to focus on its business customers and helping them process and manage the data it took to run their businesses. IBM successfully managed to stay ahead of the technology curve for most of its history, combining investments in R&D and innovation with customer service and support for its complex, leading-edge technologies.

But by the early 1990s, the company's culture had atrophied into an internally-oriented, ritualistic web of territorial fiefdoms. IBM's sales and profits were falling at an alarming rate. They needed a change agent. In his book *Who Says Elephants Can't Dance? Leading a Great Enterprise through Dramatic Change* (HarperBusiness), Lou Gerstner remembers the culture he inherited in 1993:

> An institutional viewpoint that anything important started inside the company—was, I believe, the root cause of many of our problems...They included a general disinterest in customer needs, accompanied by a preoccupation with internal politics. There was general permission to stop projects dead in their tracks, a bureaucratic infrastructure that defended turf instead of promoting collaboration, and a management class that presided rather than acted.

Gerstner didn't come from inside the company. He was an outsider and former IBM customer as CEO of American Express. As a customer, he had been enormously frustrated by IBM's territorial geographic structure:

> The fact that American Express was one of IBM's largest customers in the United States bore no value to IBM management...It was enormously frustrating, but IBM seemed to be incapable of taking a global customer view or a technology view driven by customer requirements.

One of Gerstner's first moves was "Operation Bear Hug," in which every member of the senior management team, and every one of their direct reports, visited at least five of their biggest customers in a three-month period, to listen, show the customer they cared, and initiate action as necessary. For every visit, Gerstner wanted a one- to two-page report sent to him and anyone in the company who could solve that customer's problems.

The prevailing plan when Gerstner came on board was that the company should be broken apart into individual businesses—so-called "Baby Blues"—so they could compete more effectively. But Gerstner took a different tack.

Realizing that IBM's strength with customers came from its global reach and broad, deep expertise, he reorganized the company from geographic territories into global, customer-oriented segments that cut across geographic lines. Like Jack Welch's "hand-grenade" approach at GE, this was tantamount to a declaration of war. IBM regional managers were like powerful heads of state, and resisted him at every turn:

> During a visit to Europe I discovered, by accident, that European employees were not receiving all of my company-wide e-mails. After some investigation, we found that the head of Europe was intercepting messages at the central messaging node. When asked why, he replied simply, 'These messages were inappropriate for my employees.' And: 'They were hard to translate.'

> One particularly stubborn—and inventive—country general manager in Europe...simply refused to recognize that the vast majority of the people in his country had been reassigned to specialized units reporting to global leaders. Anytime one of these new worldwide leaders would pay a visit to meet with his or her new team, the country general manager, or GM, would round up a group loyal to the GM, herd them into a room, and tell them, 'Okay, today you're database specialists. Go talk about databases.' Or for the next visit: 'Today you're experts on the insurance industry.' We eventually caught on and ended the charade.

Changing the culture was the key to the transformation. Gerstner, like Welch, wanted a high-performance culture. "Culture isn't just one aspect of the game—it is the game," he says.

But culture isn't something any one person can control. It lives and breathes in the actions and behaviors of every person in the company, and it's acted out every day. Culture is deeply embedded in the ongoing habits and routines that permeate any company. Changing a culture is a Herculean task and it doesn't happen overnight.

"You can't mandate it, can't engineer it. What you can do is create the conditions for transformation. You can provide incentives. You can define the marketplace realities and goals. But then you have to trust. In fact, in the end, management doesn't change culture. Management invites the workforce itself to change the culture," says Gerstner. "Frankly, if I could have chosen not to tackle the IBM culture head-on, I probably wouldn't have."

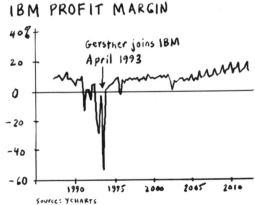

IBM PROFIT MARGIN

Gerstner joins IBM
April 1993

Source: YCHARTS

Luckily, he did tackle it, and persistent effort paid off. Between 1990 and 1993, when Gerstner took over, IBM lost $16 billion. In his first year, he rescued IBM from its steep dive and returned it to profitability. The company has grown steadily ever since.

WHEN IN DOUBT, GET IN TOUCH WITH YOUR CUSTOMERS

Name a company you love, a company you are loyal to, a company you buy things from all the time, and you will inevitably find a company that's connected to its customers, that knows who they are and what they care about.

Focusing on customers doesn't mean trying to please everyone. It's about getting a deep sense of who your customers are and what they care about. Walmart dominates retail by relentlessly focusing on price-sensitive customers. Everything in Walmart's culture is focused on squeezing one more penny of cost out of their operations, and sharing those cost savings with customers. Much smaller retailer Nordstrom has only 2% of Walmart's revenue, but generates higher profits by focusing on customers who prefer excellent service and selection over price. Walmart and Nordstrom focus on two profitable but distinct market segments, while other retailers who try to be too many things to too many people, like Sears and JC Penney, get squeezed.

Some things customers care about won't change.

The world is constantly changing, and so are customers. Customers won't always want any one product or service. They won't always want iPads.

But some things won't change. There will always be customers who want great experiences, great service, convenience, selection, low prices, and fast delivery. A customer-focused company knows what its customers care about and builds capabilities and strategies that reinforce its advantages over time.

GE, IBM, and Starbucks turned their companies around by focusing on customers. Kodak continues to struggle—the company's latest bet is using its patent portfolio to finance a line of cheap inkjet printers it hopes will save the company. Kodak investors are understandably skeptical, and the company's stock today is trading at all-time lows.

There's an old adage about making difficult decisions: "When in doubt, go towards the fear."

When you are facing a difficult decision, more often than not you know deep down what direction you need to take. But when that direction is risky, or difficult, or otherwise scary, people look for reasons to avoid the difficult road. So lurking within most difficult decisions is trepidation and fear about the road you must take.

We can only imagine what the decision makers at Kodak must have felt when they realized the future of photos was filmless. The fear must have been palpable. But at the same time the imperative must also have been evident: start getting out of film and preparing for the digital world.

Unfortunately, we can all too easily imagine the meetings and memos that rationalized away the fears, the people hanging on to near-term retirement, the desperate hope that by some miracle, the world would not evolve.

When in doubt, don't look inside your company for answers. Turn around and face the market. Get back in touch with your customers.

NOTES FOR CHAPTER FIVE

"XEROX HAS BEEN INFESTED"
Malcolm Gladwell, "Creation Myth: Xerox PARC, Apple, and the truth about innovation," *The New Yorker*, May 16, 2011.

FIRST DIGITAL CAMERA
Steve Sasson, "We Had No Idea," Kodak's *Plugged In* (blog) , October 16, 2007.

If change is happening on the outside faster than on the inside the end is in sight.

—*Jack Welch, former CEO, GE*

CHAPTER SIX

Structural change is necessary

Growth and evolution leads to increasing specialization, which limits a company's ability to adapt and evolve. If your company is at or near peak effectiveness for a particular purpose, and the environment around you is shifting, you may need to undergo fundamental structural change in order to become adaptive.

HOW DID WE GET HERE?

Dividing labor and standardizing work is a good thing. Right?

DIVIDING WORK

Division of labor, as Adam Smith pointed out in the 1700s, has the potential to increase productivity. But division of labor also leads to interdependency: every worker relies more heavily on others in order to be able to do the job, and as the number of handoffs increases, so does the potential for dropped balls. As the number of divisions grows, so grows the interdependence.

This interdependence creates a need to synchronize and coordinate the work. Traditionally, this has been the job of management and bureaucracy. They coordinate the work through measurement and control.

As you increase the number of divisions, you also increase complexity—especially from a management perspective—because you have more stuff that needs to be coordinated. And so, if something can be automated, you automate it. If you can't automate it, you constrain it to the minimum possible variation. Dividing labor makes work more efficient, more consistent, more predictable and reliable: more idiot-proof.

Of course, the more idiot-proof the system, the more behavior is constrained, forcing people to act like idiots even when it's against their better judgment. Even when your employees know there's a better way to do something, they will often be constrained by policies and procedures that were designed to reduce variety in the system. If your system needs to solve problems that you can't anticipate, then it's going to fail, because automated systems and employees who are treated like idiots can't solve problems.

THE MORE IDIOT-PROOF THE SYSTEM, THE MORE PEOPLE WILL ACT LIKE IDIOTS.

How many times have you heard someone say, "I don't know the reason for it, and I know it doesn't make sense, but it's our policy"?

In addition, although dividing work may make the system more efficient, by dividing work into ever-more specialized tasks, we also disconnect people from the meaning and purpose of what they are doing. From their small, constrained box, people can't see the big picture, so they must make decisions and act with a very limited perspective.

INTERCHANGEABLE PARTS

Another core idea from the age of the industrial revolution is the concept of interchangeable parts.

Standardization does make it easier to mass-produce quality products. We run into problems, though, when we try to apply standards to things that inherently have a high degree of variety—for example, a customer service call. Customer problems come in all shapes and sizes, and even problems that might seem very similar on the surface can be subject to a lot of variability based on the context.

We have gotten so used to the idea of standards as a good thing that we tend to apply them in the wrong places. For example, consider the idea of a "best practice." The concept of a best practice assumes that there is one "best way" to solve a problem. It assumes that every problem can be isolated from its context, and a single best way of solving it can be described and shared. Unfortunately, this has caused a lot of problems in the business world, because it's impossible to isolate problems from their contexts.

A system is not just the sum of its parts. What makes a system work is not the parts in isolation, but the interactions between them, and the inherent tradeoffs that must be made to achieve different kinds of system performance. Standardization is something you apply to the parts of a system, not a whole. A best practice from one company, or from one part of a company, cannot necessarily be applied successfully elsewhere.

Systems expert Russell Ackoff points out that, "If we have a system of improvement that is directed at the parts, taken separately, you can be absolutely sure that the performance of the whole will not be improved."

Ackoff illustrates his point with the following example:

> I read in *The New York Times* that 487 kinds of automobiles are available in the United States. Let's buy one of each and bring them into a large garage. Let's then hire 200 of the best automotive engineers in the world and ask them to determine which car has the best engine. Suppose they come back and say the Rolls Royce has the best engine. Make a note of it. 'Which one has the best transmission?' we ask them, and they go over and test and they come back and say the Mercedes does. 'Which one has the best battery?' They come back and say the Buick does. And one by one, for every part required for an automobile, they tell us which is the best one available. Now we take that list, give it back to them and say, 'Now remove those parts from those cars, and put them together into the best possible automobile, because now we'll have an automobile consisting of all the best parts.' What do we get? You don't even get an automobile, for the obvious reason that the parts don't fit. The performance of a system depends on how the parts fit, not how they act taken separately.

What's true for the fit of the parts of a system is also true of the fit between a service and the context within which the service is delivered. Every interaction with a customer is different—sometimes in subtle ways, and sometimes in profound ways.

Two interactions that look similar on the surface may be dramatically different, in ways that are hard to predict. Consider a customer who has already been bumped from two flights and whose luggage has been lost, walking up to an airline counter. These previous interactions will have a major effect on the context of the current one.

Managers think that standardization is a good thing to do. If we standardize, goes the idea, our costs will go down. But if your interactions are highly variable, as most service interactions are, then the opposite will happen. Attempts to standardize the work will make costs go up, not down. This is because standardizing the work reduces the ability of your system to absorb variety. We try to cage variety into nice neat swim lanes—for example, voice menus in an automated voice system. But when there is a lot of variety in your environment, these kinds of control systems are exactly the way to make things not work.

CONFLICTING CONSTRAINTS LEAD TO RIGIDITY

Growth and change in business requires constant tradeoff between conflicting constraints. Every new change could potentially cause conflicts with some element of the existing business. So companies must continually weigh potential gains in one area against the potential problems they might cause elsewhere.

Optimization starts with the division of labor. The modern corporation is a great big machine that divides up the work and coordinates it so everyone can specialize and optimize for a particular piece of the work. As companies divide the work, they bump into conflicts.

This is just as true in nature as it is in business. If you want to be strong, then your bones need to be massive enough to support your muscles and resist breaking. If you want to fly, then you are going to have to deal with having light and fragile bones. So there's a tradeoff there. In a co-evolving world, you need to make these kinds of tradeoffs to get ahead.

For example, a small, five-person company has no trouble coordinating its activities. But as it grows to 20, 30, 40 people, it becomes more difficult to coordinate the work. So the company initiates a Monday morning "all-hands" meeting, where everybody shares what they are working on and their plan for the coming week. As more people join the company, the Monday meeting becomes overly lengthy, and people become frustrated because they spend so much time talking about work that they don't have enough time to complete their projects.

In other words, the Monday meeting solves one problem: the problem of coordinating the work. But at the same time it causes another problem: less time to do the work.

The company must make a tradeoff between talking and doing, between coordinating and executing. If it spends too much time coordinating, people will have perfect knowledge but won't get any work done. If it spends too much time executing, it will find itself working at cross-purposes.

One common conflict often arises between sales and operations. Sales is measured on the revenue it generates, while operations is measured on profitability. Under pressure to sell more projects, the sales team offers price discounts to customers. The discounted price makes it more difficult for operations to make the profit numbers.

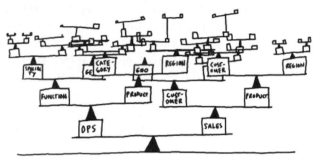

CONFLICTING CONSTRAINTS ACCUMULATE OVER TIME

There are tradeoffs everywhere you look, in every organization: between efficiency and service, efficiency and innovation, high reliability/security and cost, predictability and flexibility, and so on. And constraints build on top of other constraints.

For example, even if you solve the conflicts between sales and operations, how are you going to divide the labor in sales—by product or by customer? If you divide by product, salespeople can develop expertise in a product area. But then you get customers who are frustrated because they have a new salesperson calling on them every week, and none of them knows what the others are doing. If you organize by customer, so you can provide one sales person who has an integrated understanding of what the customer needs, then the salesperson can't answer the product questions because he is spread too thin. You could pull product people into the sales team, but that would pull them away from operations and hurt your profit margins.

And so on and so on.

This never ends. Compromise after compromise, tradeoff after tradeoff, you build your optimization machine and you refine the system.

When adaptive moves in one area cause changes in another area, we can say that the areas are linked, or *coupled*. Two units that are coupled are interdependent: changes in one affect the other. As organizations try to optimize across more and more functional areas and groups, the couplings and interdependencies increase. At some point, as the company continues to optimize, the number of interdependencies becomes so large and the system becomes so complex that it is difficult to understand or predict the effects of change.

Thus, as interdependency increases, the organization becomes more and more inflexible, since a small change in one area might have complex and unpredictable cascading effects elsewhere.

For example, imagine that a company decides it wants to scan items in a warehouse electronically instead of counting them by hand and recording them on paper. This may seem at first like a simple change. But it means that all items going into the warehouse must be coded so they can be read by the scanner. Warehouse staff must be trained on the scanners and their proper use. The people who receive the reports and read the data must now learn to use an electronic system instead of paper.

It's not hard to see that the larger the organization, the more likely it is to have coupled systems and interdependencies. And as interdependencies increase, so does the pain and effort involved in change.

The more tradeoff decisions you make, the more complex the whole structure becomes, until you get to a point where you can't make any more changes without causing damage somewhere else in the organization. Over time, the structure gets more rigid and inflexible.

NOTES FOR CHAPTER SIX

THE PERFORMANCE OF A SYSTEM
"Systems Thinking" talk by Russell Ackoff, at The Learning and Legacy of Dr. W. Edwards Deming (event), 1994.

Everything that we are making, we are making more and more complex.

—*Kevin Kelly, Cofounder,* Wired Magazine

CHAPTER SEVEN

Complexity changes the game

The complexity of the new networked, interdependent economy creates an ambiguous, uncertain, competitive landscape. Companies must be flexible enough to rapidly respond to changes in their environments, or risk extinction.

RETURN ON ASSETS IS DWINDLING

In *The Power of Pull: How Small Moves, Smartly Made, Can Set Big Things in Motion* (Basic Books), John Hagel and John Seely Brown observe that return on assets—the measure of how efficiently a company can use its assets to generate profits—has steadily dwindled to almost a quarter of what it was in 1965.

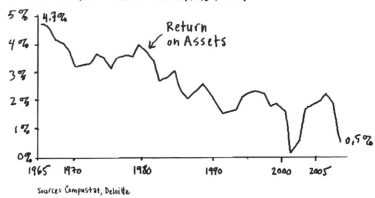

ECONOMY-WIDE ASSET PROFITABILITY

Source: Compustat, Deloitte

FEWER AND FEWER COMPANIES ARE SURVIVING IN THE LONG TERM

The S&P 500 has fewer and fewer long-term survivors. New entrants aren't faring much better. The average life expectancy of a company in the S&P 500 has dropped from 75 years (in 1937) to 15 years in a more recent study.

Turnover in the Fortune 1,000 is also increasing. If your company is in the Fortune 1,000, the chance that you will still be there in ten years is diminishing rapidly.

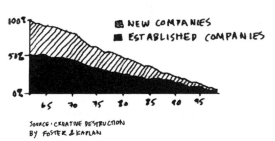

LONG-TERM SURVIVORS
PERCENT OF THE S&P 500

SOURCE: CREATIVE DESTRUCTION BY FOSTER & KAPLAN

WHAT IS CAUSING THIS INCREASE IN DEATH RATES?

FASTER CHANGE

First, the pace of technological change is accelerating. Things are getting smaller, faster, and cheaper. And since information technology affects every other industry, the entire economy is vulnerable to disruptive change. The faster the rate of change, the more the uncertain the environment becomes.

As long as this rapid technological change continues, it is an ever-present threat—as well as an opportunity for those with the insight and ability to take advantage of it.

COMPETITION

Second, global competition is heating up. For customers, Google offers a continually updated global directory of goods and services in just about any category. For companies, access to those customers is as simple as a 50-cent text ad that appears next to the search results. The pressure is on, and companies are feeling the pain.

The more companies that compete for customers, the more intense the competition becomes, and the more difficult it becomes to make a profit. This is simply a matter of supply and demand. There are only so many customers and only so much money to go around.

INCREASING COMPLEXITY

Faster change and increased competition lead to a third challenge: greater overall complexity.

It's not only that technology makes everything better, smarter, faster, and cheaper, or that more competitors are entering the fray. In addition, everything is getting networked—being connected to everything else—at the same time. So while technology increases the rate of change, and new entrants increase the competitive pressure, the networking of everything simultaneously increases complexity.

When simple things are connected, they become more elaborate. An individual ant or bee is a simple organism—in fact, so simple that it will die on its own—and each individual's behavior, seen on its own, is simple. But when they are connected, they exhibit very complex behavior.

Complexity can stem not only from connection but also from division. Any business niche that is successful will sooner or later attract competitors. As more competitors enter the niche, one company will begin to dominate, forcing others to specialize so they can differentiate and attract customers. Thus every competitive niche has a tendency to split into more niches as competition increases. The greater the competition and the faster the business cycles, the more niches will be created. As more niches are created, the overall diversity in the system will increase. Greater diversity means more kinds of interactions. More interactions means more complexity.

Complexity is a function of three things: the number of unique nodes (in this case, companies); the number of connections and potential connections (not just competitors but partners and other allies); and the rate of change in the system. Taken together, these three change forces create a highly volatile, uncertain environment, where advantages are short-lived and the competitive landscape is constantly shifting.

We're moving down an ever-accelerating path toward faster change, more competition, and more complexity at the same time, which is like a triple-whammy.

No wonder organizations are having a tough time of it.

THE RED QUEEN RACE: IF YOU'RE NOT RUNNING, YOU'RE FALLING BEHIND

Complexity begets complexity. The more that companies adapt to a rapidly changing environment, the more others need to adapt just to keep up.

THE RED QUEEN RACE

This kind of accelerating hypercompetition is known as a Red Queen race, named for the Red Queen in Lewis Carroll's *Alice in Wonderland*:

> "...in our country," said Alice, still panting a little, "you'd generally get to somewhere else—if you run very fast for a long time, as we've been doing."
> "A slow sort of country!" said the Queen. "Now, here, you see, it takes all the running you can do, to keep in the same place. If you want to get somewhere else, you must run at least twice as fast as that!"

The challenge of a Red Queen race is that as you evolve, the other organisms in the system, including the environment itself, are also evolving. And the greater the number of coevolving organisms, the faster the rate of change, so you need to run faster and faster just to hold your place. Says complexity theorist Bill McKelvey: "The Red Queen race can only be won by speeding up co-evolutionary processes."

WHAT IS A COEVOLUTIONARY PROCESS?

Every time you adapt to a situation, you change it, compelling others to respond in order to remain competitive. In business and in nature, this ongoing process of adaptive moves and countermoves by multiple parties is called *coevolution*. Every move has both intended and unintended consequences, and whether those changes are good or bad depends on what others are doing.

Coevolution can get very complex. Sometimes species compete, sometimes they cooperate. The more diversity there is in the system, the more complex the interrelationships.

EVERY ADAPTIVE MOVE BY ONE ORGANIZATION AFFECTS OTHERS

Adaptive moves change things. When one organization makes a move, others respond. Consider the monarch butterfly, which is toxic to birds. The monarch has evolved a distinctive color pattern to signal its toxicity to birds, who avoid it. The viceroy butterfly, which is not toxic, has evolved to mimic the monarch, so birds avoid eating it also.

Flowers require pollinators in order to reproduce, and so flowers must compete to attract pollinators (much like companies must compete for customers). Certain flowers have co-evolved by changing their shape and color to attract hummingbirds: their tubular shapes force the hummingbird to orient its head a certain way while extracting nectar, allowing pollen to rub off on the bird, and their red color sends a strong signal to the hummingbird, due to its high sensitivity to color at the red end of the spectrum.

Plants develop spines, bristles, and thorns to make them less attractive to predators. The predators must develop in response, with stronger teeth, thicker skin, longer beaks, and so on.

What is true in nature is also true in strategy. Strategies don't evolve in a vacuum. They coevolve, as organizations interact with each other and with their environments. Consider insurgency and counter-insurgency in Iraq. In response to rapidly innovating insurgent weapons and tactics, like improvised explosives that can be set off with cell phones by innocuous-looking civilians, the US military now emphasizes rapid learning and design as a core element of military strategy.

The effect that Walmart has had on local communities is well known. When Walmart moves in, the community is changed forever. Small businesses must improve their game or it's likely they will go out of business. Target has responded to Walmart with a design strategy that emphasizes not only low prices but also design excellence.

ADAPTIVE MOVES CAN BE COMPETITIVE—AND COOPERATIVE

Cows and other herbivores have bacteria in their intestines that help them digest the grasses they eat. The bacteria get a steady flow of nutrients supplied by the cow, and the cow benefits with improved digestion.

In a similar collaboration, Walmart and consumer goods giant P&G have teamed up to share data. P&G has deep expertise in market research and new product development, while Walmart has voluminous data on in-store buying patterns and behavior.

Walmart's deep customer data gives P&G insights into customer behavior and actual, on-the-ground demand. Since P&G also develops new products continually, this allows the companies to work together to improve the number of winners and reduce the number of losers on Walmart's shelves, boosting sales by 32.5%.

They use joint scorecards and technology to streamline their logistics and share data to generate insights about customers, leading to improved sales. Walmart has also suggested innovations to P&G products, like adding a longer pole to the floor-cleaning Swiffer duster so it can clean hard-to-reach things like blinds and ceiling fans.

Sharing information improves the competitive advantage of both companies and allows them to work together to reduce costs and grow revenue. Since P&G initiated a dedicated Walmart team, they have grown their Walmart business from $375 million to more than $4 billion.

WALMART AND P&G TEAM UP TO SHARE DATA

Fred Mosser, who came to online shoe retailer Zappos from Nordstrom to head up merchandising, soon realized that with an online catalog, Zappos would be managing so many brands and styles that they would never be able to staff enough buyers to manage them adequately. So they engaged vendors to help them.

Zappos opened up their data and gave vendors the same access to information that their buyers had. Since the average buyer works with 50 brands, by making their buyer data transparent, Zappos multiplies the thinking power of each buyer by 50.

Vendors can see inventory levels, prices, and profitability. They can suggest orders to buyers and communicate with Zappos creative teams about marketing and make changes to their brand boutique on the Zappos website.

Usually, retailers hide their profits so they can demand lower prices from vendors. But for Zappos, cooperating with vendors means more merchandising expertise, and brand representatives spend more time working with Zappos than they do their other accounts. When a hot item is scarce, Zappos has access to inventory that its competitors lack.

ADAPTIVE MOVES CAN CREATE OPPORTUNITIES FOR OTHERS

Sometimes one species creates benefits for another as an unintended byproduct of its natural behavior. When horses and cattle graze in a field, they stir up insects, so egrets have learned to follow the herds. Army ants on a raid also stir up insects, so birds have learned to follow them.

This fast-follower strategy is common both in nature and in business. McDonald's uses sophisticated market research when deciding to open a new store. But competitor Burger King simply watches McDonalds' moves and opens new locations nearby. Adaptive moves can also change the environment in which firms operate.

For example, when Amazon opened an online store, it changed the operating environment for other retailers: as customers shifted their behavior, becoming more familiar and comfortable with online purchases, many brick-and-mortar retailers found themselves operating a high-cost Amazon showroom, as customers came into their stores to check out products and then ordered them online at a lower cost.

When Netflix offered DVDs as a mail-based subscription service, it changed the business model for movie watching. Instead of renting films one at a time, customers could pay a flat fee and keep movies as long as they wanted. When Redbox partnered with Walgreens, McDonald's, and other commonly visited locations such as grocery stores to place video game and DVD rental kiosks inside and outside stores, they further shifted the competitive environment.

Each competitive move offers customers more options: greater convenience, lower prices, more choices.

Changes in one environment can also impact adjacent environments. When the entertainment industry lobbied for and supported a bill to stop online piracy (The Stop Online Piracy Act, or SOPA), this threatened the business models of many online service providers such as search engine companies, sparking a battle for the hearts and minds of US politicians as well as the general population.

COEVOLUTIONARY RELATIONSHIPS CAN BE VERY COMPLEX

Ants discovered agriculture about 50 million years ago, long before humans even existed. Leaf-cutter ants in the Amazon grow gardens of fungi for food on shredded leaves in underground chambers. Not only have the ants coevolved with the fungi—much the way humans have domesticated many plants and animals—but they have also coevolved with pests and even an antibiotic bacteria that fights the pests. The ants' fungal crop is sometimes attacked by a parasitic mold called Escovopsis. Leaf-cutter ants carry an antibacterial fungus around with them by letting it grow in patches on their bodies. This is an example of four different species coevolving together: three mutually beneficial and one parasite.

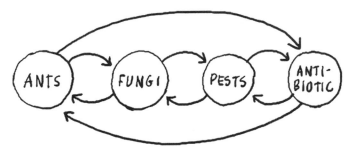

There are similar complex coevolutionary relationships in technology ecosystems, where devices, operating systems, and applications must coexist in a fragile balance. When Microsoft or Apple upgrade their operating systems, application providers must adapt by upgrading their software.

Think of how the technology ecosystem works: if you start with a PC, then the PC needs software to run on it, so sooner or later you get an ecosystem of software companies that all need to coevolve with the PC company and each other. Then you get browsers, which need to coevolve with the PC and the software. Then web apps start to pop up, and the web apps need to make sure they work on all the browsers, which have to be sure they work on all the operating systems. Then you get plug-ins and add-ons that have to cooperate with all the apps. Then you get apps that need to work on multiple devices and multiple device operating systems. Since everything is dependent on other things, pretty soon you have a complex web of coevolving companies all running as fast as they can just to keep up.

Netflix, for example, wants to offer a seamless streaming service that you can access on any device, from your phone to your computer to your game console. Netflix's user interface coevolves with more than 400 different devices.

Dropbox is another company that needs to coevolve with a lot of other systems. The point of Dropbox is to sync your files across all your devices. So Dropbox works on Windows, Mac, and Linux as well as mobile operating systems like iOS (iPad and iPhone), Android, and Blackberry.

OPTIMIZATION IS A JOURNEY THAT LEADS TO A FEW FITNESS PEAKS

Evolutionary biologists use something called a fitness landscape to represent the journey that organisms and organizations make as they negotiate tradeoffs betweenconflicting constraints and coevolve, trying to achieve optimal fitness for their environment. The journey is called an *adaptive walk*. As organisms make adaptive moves and countermoves, trading off one functional trait for another, they move upward on the landscape, toward an optimum fit. But with every move, those tradeoffs make it more and more difficult to go anywhere else but up toward the top of that particular peak. Eventually, you reach a point where you can't go any farther up—or, you will have to go downhill before you can scale another peak. And that means that before you can get better, you will need to get worse.

This adaptive walk toward fitness peaks is another way to visualize the experience curve and its diminishing returns. As you move upward toward an optimum—or peak—efficiency, there are fewer and fewer choices that will take you higher on the landscape, until you reach the top. And once you have reached a peak, moving in any direction will take you downhill.

If you are at the top of a fitness peak and the landscape starts changing, it can really throw you off. Companies doing the right thing at the time—making the right moves for their situation, trying to optimize their production lines to squeeze out all the costs and inefficiencies so they can run lean and mean operations—may later find that they have optimized for a business environment that no longer exists.

WE ARE REACHING A COMPLEXITY TIPPING POINT

When the environment is shifting around you, peak effectiveness is more of a liability than an asset, precisely because of the tradeoffs you made on your way to efficient specialization. By selecting and advancing toward a particular fitness peak, you have reduced the number of options available to you.

Every coevolutionary move, whether it's by a friend or foe, changes the terrain. The fitness landscape today looks less like solid rock and more like shifting sands or rolling waves.

Moreover, complexity and change show no signs of abating or slowing down. Rather, they are speeding up. Many companies will find that change in their competitive environment is accelerating faster than they are able to adapt. This pressure will only increase.

Rapid change, along with increasing competition and complexity, set the stage for a coevolutionary Red Queen race. The faster things change, the faster you need to run just to stay in the same place. Red Queen races can only be won by increasing the speed of your coevolutionary processes: increasing the rate at which you can make adaptive moves. Every adaptive move changes the landscape, requiring more adaptive moves in a never-ending cycle.

Jack Welch once said, "I've always believed that when the rate of change inside an institution becomes slower than the rate of change outside, the end is in sight. The only question is when."

To win in a Red Queen race, organizations will have to detect, respond, and adapt on many fronts simultaneously, something most of today's organizations are not designed to do. Some companies will find ways to do this. Those that can't will not survive.

Darwin said, "It is not the strongest of the species that survives, nor the most intelligent, but the one most responsive to change." When the world is *constantly* changing, the speed at which you can learn is the only thing that can give you a long-term, sustainable advantage. The problem is that while today's companies are very good at processing information and producing outputs, they don't know how to learn.

THE FUTURE IS CONNECTEDNESS

Today's customers are more connected than ever. The rate of change in society is accelerating, as whole families—kids, parents, and grandparents—join online social networks to keep up with each other and with friends, to share their interests and connect with new people. Social networks are where the people are going; that's where the customers are. But most companies are slow to adopt these new, connected technologies.

Why? In some cases they don't understand how social networks will impact the business. They can't see a clear path or understand the implications. In most companies, there are a few people who do understand. But bureaucracy, corporate culture, blind spots, fear, and risk-avoidant behaviors stand in their way.

Connecting your company with customers will require ongoing, continuous feedback between your company and customers. Without that continuous dialogue, it's inevitable that you will drift apart over time. If you want to stay close to your customers, you will need to become a connected company.

NOTES FOR CHAPTER SEVEN

COEVOLUTION
Bill McKelvey, "Managing Coevolutionary Dynamics," *http://billmckelvey.org/documents/Managing Coevolutionary.pdf*, July, 2002.

WALMART AND P&G
Michael Grean and Michael J. Shaw, "Supply-Chain Integration through Information-Sharing: Channel Partnership between Wal-Mart and Procter & Gamble," *http://citebm.business.illinois.edu/it_cases/graen-shaw-pg.pdf*.

SOPA
Sarah McBride and Lisa Richwine, "Epic Clash: Silicon Valley blindsides Hollywood on piracy," *Reuters*, January 22, 2012.

NETFLIX
Ben Galbraith, "Coping with Over Four Hundred Devices: How Netflix Uses HTML5 to Deliver Amazing User Interfaces," *FunctionSource*, 2011, *http://functionsource.com/post/netflix-feature*.

PART TWO

What is a connected company?

To adapt, companies must operate not as machines but as learning organisms, purposefully interacting with their environment and continuously improving, based on experiments and feedback.

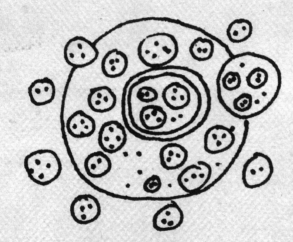

THE CONNECTED COMPANY

If you can run the company a bit more collaboratively, you get a better result, because you have more bandwidth and checking and balancing going on.

—*Larry Page, Cofounder, Google*

CHAPTER EIGHT

Connected companies learn

We are accustomed to thinking of companies as machines. But machines can't learn, and therefore they can't adapt. Learning is a property of organisms.

THE COMPANY AS A MACHINE

Historically, we have thought of companies as machines, and we have designed them like we design machines. A machine typically has the following characteristics:

1. It's designed to be controlled by a driver or operator.

2. It needs to be maintained, and when it breaks down, you fix it.

3. A machine pretty much works in the same way its entire life. Eventually, things change, or the machine wears out, and you need to build or buy a new one.

A car is a perfect example of machine design. It's controlled by a driver. Mechanics perform routine maintenance and fix it when it breaks down. Eventually, the car wears out, or your needs change, so you sell the car and buy a new one.

We tend to design companies the way we design machines. We think we need the company to perform a certain function, so we design and build it to perform that function.

The machine view is very successful in a stable environment. If there is a steady, predictable demand for a standard, uniform product, then machines are very efficient and productive. In such conditions, a machine-like company can profit by producing uniform items in large lots.

But over time, things change. The company grows beyond a certain point. New systems are needed. Demand changes. Customers want different products and services. So we need to redesign and rebuild the machine to serve the new functions.

This kind of rebuilding goes by many names, including reorganization, reengineering, right-sizing, flattening, and so on. The problem with this kind of thinking is that the nature of a machine is to remain static, while the nature of a company is to grow. This conflict causes all kinds of problems, because you have to constantly redesign and rebuild the company while you also need to operate it. Ironically, the process of improving efficiency is often very inefficient.

And the faster things change, the more of a problem this becomes, because companies are not really machines so much as complex, dynamic, growing systems. After all, companies are really just groups of people who have banded together to achieve some kind of purpose, and people are organic.

For a machine, purpose is simple. A machine's purpose is designed into its structure. Once a machine's purpose has been set, it does what it has been designed to do. But if the environment changes, a machine does not have a way to become aware of the change and adjust to the new situation. It just becomes obsolete.

While a machine does whatever it was designed to do, organisms control themselves. An organism's purpose does not come from an outside designer or controller, but from within. An organism strives over time to realize its goals in the world. As conditions in the environment change, an organism responds by adjusting its behavior to improve its performance. In other words, it learns.

For many years, the machine view has prevailed, and many companies are designed as information-processing and production machines. But information processing is not learning. Production is not learning. Learning is a creative process, not a mechanical one.

Inherent in the mechanical view is the idea that all knowledge is explicit, and can be represented in manuals, documentation, and quantitative metrics. This is a behaviorist concept that harkens back to Frederick Taylor, the father of *scientific management*, a theory of management that was based on measuring and analyzing work with the idea of reorganizing it to make it more efficient.

The focus in scientific management is on defining and measuring work in the form of words, charts, and numbers. In other words, what can be seen and recorded is the only thing that matters. Results are achieved by administering positive and negative reinforcement—rewards and punishments—to individuals, based on how well they are able to meet performance measures. This way of inducing behavior is called *operant conditioning* and comes from the behaviorist school of psychology, which, like scientific management, focused exclusively on observable phenomena. What this behaviorist philosophy fails to take into account is that many important drivers of success cannot be easily observed, counted, documented, or measured.

FREDERICK TAYLOR

INTRINSIC REWARDS DRIVE PRODUCTIVITY

Certainly people respond to punishments and rewards. The threat of jail keeps most of the population decent, and most of us go to work so we can earn money and buy things. But this is an extremely crude and unsophisticated way to encourage performance. It fails to take into account of the joy of learning and mastering new skills; the power of passion and voluntary commitment to a cause, the value of teamwork, of understanding how a system works and where you fit; and the satisfaction that comes from a job well done. It does not consider that people like making other people happy, or that people feel good about themselves when they are appreciated and respected by others. It fails to account for the added motivation that comes from being in control of your own work, and from achieving a level of expertise where your opinion is sought after and respected.

People work harder when they are passionate about their work and committed to success. People are motivated to perform when they are connected to the purpose of the work, when they understand the system—how all the pieces and parts fit together—and when they have the power to improve it.

PEOPLE RESIST BEING CONTROLLED

We all like to believe that we are in control of our lives. We don't like being told what to do. It's only natural. So when workers become subject to a formal, hierarchical, and authoritarian power structure, they naturally resist.

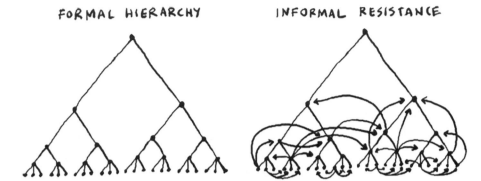

FORMAL HIERARCHY   INFORMAL RESISTANCE

EVERY FORMAL HIERARCHY IS RESISTED BY AN INFORMAL ORGANIZATION THAT SUBVERTS IT.

Every authoritarian hierarchy is resisted by an informal organization that opposes and subverts the formal organization. The informal organization arises as a natural consequence of the formal one. Sometimes the resistance is explicit, in the form of unions or outspoken protests. More often it is subtle, and exists within the cracks. It shows up in the executive who makes her numbers at the expense of the organization, the workers who don't like their boss and set him up to fail, or the manager who tries to make himself stand out by gossiping about peers or making them look bad.

WHAT DRIVES GROWTH?

In addition to those internal intangibles, there are also many external factors that cannot be easily measured or controlled, but which nevertheless have a vital impact.

For example, what is the lifetime value of a happy customer? What is the multiplying effect of a happy customer who shares her positive experiences with friends, colleagues, and family? What is the value of an authentic smile, as opposed to a fake one, when greeting a customer? What is the value of a hundred or a thousand people who genuinely and enthusiastically connect with customers on a daily basis?

Especially in a service economy, the most important things—like authenticity, trust, and connection—are often the most difficult to measure. And they certainly can't be controlled by traditional methods, such as supervisors, policies, scripts, and procedures. Imagine trying to measure something like authenticity. You can force people to say, "Have a nice day." You can't force them to mean it.

This brings us to the topic of closed and open systems.

CLOSED AND OPEN SYSTEMS

Most natural systems are open systems. An open system is simply a system that exchanges information with its environment. For example, you breathe in air, which provides your cells with oxygen, and exhale carbon dioxide. You drink water and eat food to survive, and expel what you don't need. Companies are open systems, too, because they exchange information with customers and suppliers.

A closed system is self-contained and isolated from its external environment. Most machines are designed as closed systems, with a hard shell to protect their delicate insides from the surrounding environment. For example, a watch has a hard case that protects its inner workings from the outside world. A watch can operate efficiently as long as that case is not violated. A factory works in a similar way. Like the inner workings of a watch, its internal processes are isolated from the outside world.

Because it is isolated from its environment, a closed system is easier to control. Performance is easier to measure because the environment inside the shell or system boundary is stable.

In contrast, an open system is continually exchanging energy with its environment, taking in information and adjusting based on feedback. This constant flux makes open systems more difficult to measure and control.

Auto manufacturers in the US have traditionally focused on building factories to efficiently produce cars in large quantities. These factories are closed systems: as long as they get a constant volume of input, they produce a constant volume of cars. But the auto industry as a whole is an open system, subject to things like customer demand, which the companies cannot control. The auto industry has outsourced the "open" part of their system to networks of dealers. The result is that auto makers continue to push cars out of their factories even when demand drops. When this happens, the market becomes glutted with new cars and prices fall. Dealers can't sell the cars, and manufacturers are forced to offer incentives and sell cars at a loss just so they can keep the factories running.

The auto industry's focus on formal systems of control has also resulted in an equal and opposing force, organized labor, which rose naturally as a counterbalance to top-down, machine-like control systems. Labor relations in the auto industry are some of the most contentious you will find anywhere.

A CLOSED SYSTEM   AN OPEN SYSTEM

While parts of an organization can sometimes be isolated and treated as closed systems, all organizations are fundamentally organic, open systems, constantly exchanging energy and information with the outside world. Unlike machines, which can be controlled, organisms control themselves. Organisms are open systems.

Companies are made up of people, who have wills of their own. People can be guided and governed, but they don't like to be controlled. They prefer to have control over their work, and if you push them too hard, they push back.

COMPLEX ADAPTIVE SYSTEMS

Complex adaptive systems are a special class of open systems, characterized by dynamic networks of agents interacting with each other and their environments. Complex adaptive systems are continuously evolving and shifting. Examples of complex adaptive systems include ant and bee colonies, the stock market, and biological ecosystems, as well as human organizations like political parties, companies, and cities. One trait of complex adaptive systems is that the behavior of the whole cannot be predicted by analyzing the parts in isolation.

So what happens if we rethink the modern company—if we stop thinking of it as a machine and start thinking of it as a complex adaptive system, one that operates within a larger complex adaptive system? What happens if we think of a company less like a machine and more like an organism?

One possibility is to compare the traditional organization with other large-scale complex systems, especially human systems, like cities.

Cities are large, complex adaptive systems, but we don't really try to control them. In Stephen B. Johnson's book *Emergence: The Connected Lives of Ants, Brains, Cities, and Software* (Scribner), he quotes complexity pioneer John Holland:

> Cities have no central planning commissions that solve the problem of purchasing and distributing supplies…How do these cities avoid devastating swings between shortage and glut, year after year, decade after decade?

A COMPLEX ADAPTIVE SYSTEM

No, we don't try to control cities, but we can manage them well, and for many purposes, cities seem to be able to organize themselves to get things done, without central planners or managers.

Yes, cities have planners and managers, but they don't try to control the activities in the city the way that managers try to control companies. What they do is manage the support systems—the infrastructure and essential services—rather than trying to direct the activity of every citizen. For good reason. Cities are far too complex, and have so many connections and interactions that it would be impossible to manage them in a top-down way.

If we start to look at companies as complex systems instead of machines, we can design and manage them for productivity instead of collapse.

Cities are more productive than their corporate counterparts. In fact, the rules governing city productivity stand in stark contrast to the "3/2 rule" that applies to company productivity. As companies add people, productivity shrinks. But as cities add people, productivity actually grows.

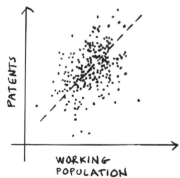

Sources: CYBEA Journal, Federal Reserve Bank of Philadelphia study

A study by the Federal Reserve Bank of Philadelphia found that as the working population in a given area doubles, productivity (measured in this case by the rate of invention) goes up by 20%. This finding is shown in study after study. If you're interested in going deeper, take a look at this recent *New York Times* article, "A Physicist Solves the City."

Okay, you say, but cities are fundamentally different than companies. Just because this works for cities doesn't mean that it will work for companies. Right?

THE LONG-LIVED COMPANY

Back in the early 1980s, right after the revolution in Iran, Shell Oil was concerned about the future of the oil industry. What might Shell look like after oil, they wondered? So they commissioned a study with some very interesting parameters:

1. First, they looked only at large companies with relative dominance in their industries, such as Shell had.

2. Second, they looked only at companies with very long lifespans—100 years or more.

3. Third, they looked at companies that had made a major shift from one industry or product category to another.

In other words, they looked at the immortals: the companies that didn't die. The study was never published, but the findings were detailed in a book called *The Living Company* (Harvard Business Review Press) by Shell executive Arie de Geus. Shell studied 40 large, long-lived companies, some of which had survived for more than 400 years.

Interestingly, these companies had a lot in common with large cities.

Distributed control: Long-lived companies were decentralized. They tolerated eccentric activities at the margins. They were very active in partnerships and joint ventures. The boundaries of the company were less clearly delineated, and local groups had more autonomy over their decisions, than you would expect in the typical global corporation.

Strong identity: Although the organization was loosely controlled, long-lived companies were connected by a strong, shared culture. Everyone in the company understood the company's values. These companies tended to promote from within in order to keep that culture strong. (Cities also share this common identity: think of the difference between a New Yorker and a Los Angelino, or a Parisian, for example.)

Feedback loops: Longlived companies had their eyes and ears focused on the world around them, and were constantly seeking opportunities. Because of their decentralized nature and strong shared culture, it was easier for them to spot opportunities in the changing world and act—proactively and decisively—to capitalize on them.

DESIGN BY DIVISION

Historically, we have designed companies like machines, by division. We constructed the org chart to divide the big chunks of work and separate them from each other—Finance, Sales, Operations. We designed the workflows that process inputs into outputs: raw materials into products, prospects into customers, complaints into resolutions.

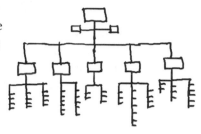

As we design this kind of company—the divided company—we need to separate functions, which means people may not always have a sense of the larger thing they are working on. They get very good at one of the tasks, but lose touch with the bigger picture. They become disconnected from customers and the larger purpose of the organization. We have to design rigid policies and procedures so people will function efficiently and so they won't interfere with each other's work.

The problem comes with scale. As the number of employees grows, the profit per employee shrinks. It's a game of diminishing returns. Efficiencies of scale are balanced by the burdens of bureaucracy. Divisions become silos, disconnected from each other. Overhead costs increase with size. Eventually, the company reaches a point where the costs of control exceed the benefits of further growth, or the company becomes too internally focused and loses touch with the market.

DESIGN FOR CONNECTION

A connected company is a complex, adaptive system that functions more like an organism than a machine. To design connected companies, we must think of the company as a complex set of connections and potential connections: a distributed organism with brains, eyes, and ears everywhere, whether they are employees, partners, customers, or suppliers. Design for conn-ection is design for companies that are made out of people. It's design for complexity, for productivity, and for longevity.

Most importantly, a connected company must be able to respond dynamically to change—to learn and adapt in an uncertain, ambiguous, and constantly evolving environment. A connected company is a learning company.

NOTES FOR CHAPTER EIGHT

FEDERAL RESERVE
Gerald A. Carlino, Satyajit Chatterjee, and Robert M. Hunt, "Urban Density and the Rate of Invention," by the Federal Reserve Bank of Philadephia, Working Paper, 2006, *http://www.phil.frb.org/research-and-data/publications/working-papers/2006/wp06-14.pdf.*

PRODUCTIVITY
Jonah Lehrer, "A Physicist Solves the City," *The New York Times*, December 17, 2010.

Maximizing shareholder value
is the dumbest idea in the world.

—Jack Welch, former CEO, GE

CHAPTER NINE

Connected companies have a purpose

Learning happens in the context of a goal, an attempt to do something or to make something happen. Without a purpose to drive learning, it is haphazard—not much more useful than blind flailing about. The purpose of a company is to do something for customers while making a profit.

PURPOSE ACCELERATES AND FOCUSES LEARNING

Sometimes you learn things by accident. For example, when a child puts her hand on a hot stove, she learns not to touch it. You can learn more by exposing yourself to a lot of different environments and by trying a lot of things. And certainly this kind of serendipitous learning can be very valuable. But while accidents can create a lot of opportunities, you will learn more, and have more happy accidents, if you are pursuing a goal.

Think about learning to swim. If you get into the water without a goal, you may enjoy yourself, but you won't learn much. Most learning happens by trial and error: you try something, and then based on your success or failure, you learn and improve over time. Purpose gives learning energy and direction, and therefore accelerates and focuses it.

If your goal is to learn to swim, you will know you're making progress by comparing the current state to your goal. If you sink, you're not making progress. If you are able to float, you are making a step in the right direction. And if you are able to propel yourself in a given direction, that's real progress.

But without a goal in mind, you will simply be flailing about.

Machines and organisms both have purposes. But it's not necessary—nor is it possible—for a machine to be consciously aware of its purpose. It's the operator who has the understanding of the purpose; the machine itself does not need to be aware. In a machine-like company, senior executives can fiddle with the controls, and individuals need only focus on their functions—since they are cogs in the machine, they don't need to understand the machine's higher purpose.

But a living organism by nature has a purpose; it has things it wants to do in the world. An organism that is unaware of its purpose operates without intention. An organism needs to know where it's going.

If you are self-aware, you can learn and adjust based on external feedback: you can adjust your performance relative to a goal. But that's not all you can do. You might encounter unexpected opportunities along the way.

For example, Amazon's goal was to be the store with the world's biggest selection. Along the way to achieving that goal, they built one of the most robust IT infrastructures on the planet. This new capability gave rise to a new, parallel goal: as long as Amazon was building such a powerful infrastructure, why not rent it to other companies as a service? It's like buying a building for yourself and renting out the additional space to other companies.

A MACHINE IS NOT AWARE OF ITS PURPOSE.

Command intent is a style of management used by the US Military when a situation is too complex or uncertain to give detailed orders. Command intent is a set of goals and a vision for possible methods of achieving those goals. It's sufficiently high-level that it can be broadcast widely to everyone in the system, and front-line troops can then interpret how those goals apply to their front-line situation.

WHAT IS THE PURPOSE OF A COMPANY?

People band together into organizations for all kinds of reasons. Some organizations are temporary, like people who come together to help offer relief during crises like Hurricane Katrina in New Orleans or the 2010 earthquake in Haiti. For those organizations, the purpose is clear: help people out. And when the crisis is over, the organization disbands.

But most organizations that persist over the long term fulfill a number of purposes, not just for their customers but for other constituents like shareholders and employees. For customers, companies provide a service; for shareholders, they are an investment; and for employees, they provide a livelihood.

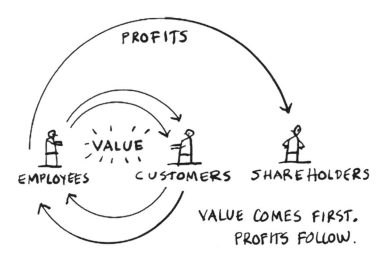

The relationship between these constituencies is important to understand. This is a bit of a simplification, but at a high level, customers care about service, shareholders care about profit, and employees care about pay and work conditions. These things are dependent on one another. Some are causes—drivers of value—and some are effects.

Customer demand for services, and those services provided well, is the primary driver of value for any organization. It is the cause of growth, profits, and shareholder value.

Employee pay and work conditions, profits, and returns to shareholders are all effects—things that result from the primary driver of delivering value to customers.

Many companies get this backwards. Company executives focus on pleasing shareholders, because it's the shareholders that drive the stock price of a company.

It's easy to understand why this is the case. It goes back to the historical focus on explicit measures. Many people consider a company's stock price the primary indicator of the value of a company. And it's true in one sense, because if you own stock and you sell it, you can realize that value.

But stock price is only an indicator of shareholder perceptions, and shareholders have a very limited view of what's happening in the company. They can only see lagging indicators like revenue, profits, and growth rates, reported on a quarterly basis. These kinds of numbers are useful for investors, because they make for easy comparisons between companies and industries. An investor can compare an oil company, a pharmaceutical company, and a retailer by looking at things like price-to-earnings ratios, revenue growth, dividend yields, and so on.

But while these numbers are useful, they don't offer any insight to the inner workings of the company, or the activities that are creating that value in the first place. Shareholders rarely get a deep sense of the company's value as perceived by customers: how satisfied they are with a service, whether they recommend it to friends, and so on. Shareholders don't have a window into customer loyalty.

SHAREHOLDERS HAVE A LIMITED VIEW
OF WHAT HAPPENS INSIDE A COMPANY.

Customers who like a service, use it often, and recommend it to other customers are leading indicators. They are the things that cause growth and profits. But shareholders can only see the results.

HOW PROFITS CAN DESTROY YOUR COMPANY

Profits are the lifeblood of any business. But not all profits are created equal. Loyalty expert and management consultant Fred Reichheld makes a distinction between good profits and bad profits in his book *The Ultimate Question: How Net-Promoter Companies Thrive in a Customer-Driven World* (Harvard Business Review Press).

Good profits come from creating value for customers. Bad profits come at the expense of happy customers and long-term sustainable growth. Bad profits come from customers who are locked in, who feel trapped or abused. Bad profits come from nuisance fees, like airlines charging extra for checked baggage, car rental companies charging $10 per day for a GPS unit that cost them $100, or banks charging $15 to $25 for a bounced check that costs the bank less than $3. Bad profits maximize transaction value, but they destroy relationships in the process.

And bad profits are addictive. Once you have started down the bad-profit road, it can be hard to turn back. In retail banking, up to a third of earnings comes from bad profits. In mobile and telecom, as much as 40% of profits come from relationship-destroying activities.

Profits in and of themselves should never be a goal. A company can show profit increases, sometimes for a long period of time, when the actions that generate those profits eat away at the company from within, like a cancer, destroying customer relationships and the company's reputation in the process.

Lou Gerstner, an IBM customer when he was CEO at American Express (he later became CEO of IBM and transformed the company), recalls one such relationship-destroying incident:

BAD PROFITS COME FROM CUSTOMERS WHO FEEL TRAPPED OR ABUSED.

> I'll never forget the day one of my division managers called and said that he had recently installed an Amdahl computer in a large data center that had historically been 100% IBM equipped. He said that his IBM representative had arrived that morning and told him that IBM was withdrawing all support for his massive data processing center as a result of the Amdahl decision. I was flabbergasted. Given that American Express was at that time one of IBM's largest customers, I could not believe that a vendor had reacted with this degree of arrogance. I placed a call immediately to the office of the chief executive of IBM to ask if he knew about and condoned this behavior. I was unable to reach him and was shunted off to an AA (administrative assistant) who took my message and said he would pass it on. Cooler (or, should I say, smarter) heads prevailed at IBM and the incident passed. Nevertheless, it did not go out of my memory.

Profits are not a cause of success, they are an effect. They are a result. And looking at a result tells us very little about the causes that led to that result. Quality pioneer W. Edwards Deming once said:

> The thermometer might read 108 degrees Fahrenheit. Blistering hot. But the thermometer does not do anything about it...We focus on visible figures only, with no consideration of figures that are unknown... Where are the figures? What is the multiplying effect of a happy customer? What is the multiplying effect of an unhappy customer? *Where are the figures?*

The causes of success are never revenue, cost, profit, or other financial measures; these are lagging indicators or effects. A profit number by itself tells you nothing about the long-term value of a company. What matters are the activities that generate the profits: are they activities that create long-term value? Or are they activities that destroy value?

When companies focus on pleasing shareholders first, it gives them an incentive to maximize the numbers, even though they might be destroying value in the long run. Executives tend to be compensated for things like profits and stock price. This sounds reasonable. But it's not hard to show profits in the short term while destroying long-term value. For example, you can cut costs by reducing the quality of materials or cutting support services that are important to customers. In the short term, you will show a profit, but in the long term, you are destroying the very thing that drives long-term success: strong relationships with customers.

Unfortunately, most pay-for-performance incentives are focused on the short-term transactions that show up on the balance sheet immediately. Sadly, what often suffer are the things that drive value and make the company sustainable in the long run. By focusing on short-term profits, companies stop investing for the future, because investments in the future don't show up on the balance sheet today. Critical sources of long-term value, which in many cases took years or even decades to build, can be destroyed in a few short years. Hard-to-count intangibles like customer relationships and loyalty, investments in support systems, and innovation initiatives are often invisible or discounted by investors.

When CEOs destroy long-term value to please shareholders, they aren't pleasing shareholders at all. In fact, they are ripping them off. What shareholders really want is an asset that appreciates in value over time.

But the thing is, the intangible soft stuff does lead to hard numbers like growth and profit improvement. In *Jack: Straight from the Gut*, Jack Welch remembers his first speech to shareholders as the new CEO of GE:

> The analysts arrived that day expecting to hear the financial results...they expected a detailed breakdown of the financial numbers. They could then plug those numbers into their models and crank out estimates of our earnings by business segment...As I moved into "soft" issues like reality, quality, excellence, and the "human element," I could tell I was losing them...I pressed on, not letting their blank stares discourage me...This "human element" would foster an environment where people would dare to try new things, where they would feel assured in knowing that "only the limits of their creativity and drive would be the ceiling on how far and how fast they would move."...At the end, the reaction in the room made it clear that the crowd thought they were getting more hot air than substance. One of our staffers overheard one analyst moan "We don't know what the hell he's talking about.

As early as 1981, Welch was describing his vision for a learning organization, one that could evolve along with customers and keep up with competitors. Investors may have been confused in the short run, but in the long run, they were very happy indeed. During Welch's tenure, GE shareholders who reinvested all their dividends saw their investment appreciate by 6,220%—more than 20% per year.

Of course, profits are important. And measurement is important. What gets measured gets done. If you only measure profits, then that's what you'll get. But the wrong kind of profits will kill your company. Traditional accounting tells you nothing about the quality of your relationships with customers. And happy, loyal customers are the only driver that will yield success in the long term.

While a company serves multiple purposes for different people, as an investment, a place of work, a paycheck, and so on, by far the most important purpose of a company is the job it does for customers. Companies that neglect or forget this fact have lost their way.

PURPOSE SETS THE CONTEXT FOR ORGANIZATIONS TO LEARN

Cybernetics pioneer Stafford Beer said, "The purpose of a system is what it does." The purpose of a company is what it does for customers.

Clayton Christensen calls this "the job to be done." He points out that while technologies and methods change over time, the job doesn't change that much. For example, the service provided by FedEx—get something from here to there, as quickly as possible, with perfect certainty—is something Julius Caesar could have used.

He also notes that while understanding and empathizing with customers can be

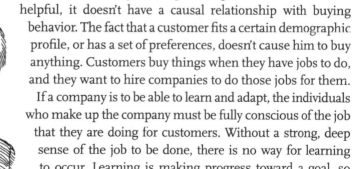

helpful, it doesn't have a causal relationship with buying behavior. The fact that a customer fits a certain demographic profile, or has a set of preferences, doesn't cause him to buy anything. Customers buy things when they have jobs to do, and they want to hire companies to do those jobs for them.

If a company is to be able to learn and adapt, the individuals who make up the company must be fully conscious of the job that they are doing for customers. Without a strong, deep sense of the job to be done, there is no way for learning to occur. Learning is making progress toward a goal, so people need to know what they are shooting for. Otherwise, they are just performing a function, like cogs in a machine.

AKIO MORITA

It's not always easy to understand what customers really need. Sony founder Akio Morita encouraged his designers to watch what people were trying to do in their lives and try to find ways to do those things better, easier, and cheaper. Focusing on the jobs customers are trying to do will help you understand what you are competing against from the customer's point of view.

A company's purpose often includes not just a job to be done but also a way of doing it. For example, Ritz-Carlton Hotel employees pledge to provide personal service and a warm, relaxed, yet refined ambiance, exemplified by their motto: "Ladies and gentlemen serving ladies and gentlemen." Employees are committed to fulfill even the unexpressed wishes and needs of their guest. For a Ritz-Carlton employee, there can be no doubts about the job to be done.

A clear purpose opens the door for learning and improvement. Learning is driven by questions and hypotheses. In the case of Ritz-Carlton, the purpose suggests questions like, "How might we discover the unexpressed wishes of our guests?"

This question led to the development of a sophisticated system for tracking customer preferences, described by James Heskett and W. Earl Sasser in their book *The Service Profit Chain* (Free Press):

> At the Ritz-Carlton, the staff is trained to listen for guest preferences, not always stated in the form of direct inquiries. A preference can be for something as incidental as a certain brand of bottled water with a meal or a down pillow on the bed. When a guest preference becomes known, it is noted on a Guest Preference Form by any frontline service person. Guest preferences are then entered into a computerized file called the Guest History at each hotel. Each night the file is downloaded into the chain data base, so that a guest staying at two different Ritz-Carlton hotels will be sure to have preferences honored at both. Each morning, the list of reservations at a particular hotel is then used to query the file for guest preferences so that the staff can take whatever action is necessary to prepare for guest arrivals.

Walmart's purpose is different but equally clear: "Always low prices." Every single employee at Walmart understands the job they are doing for customers with crystal clarity. From the motley collection of headquarters office furniture, scrounged from manufacturer's display models, to executives sharing hotel rooms when they are on the road, the company's culture of thrift is evident in everything they do.

PURPOSE IS A MOVING TARGET

Getting a package from here to there in two months might have sufficed for Julius Caesar, but if he were alive now, he'd definitely want the same job done in a day.

Continuous improvement is natural and satisfying. If you're learning and improving at work, there's much more to it than just showing up and doing your job. There's joy in performance improvement, the deep satisfaction that comes from being at the top of your game, the best in class. It's no different than an athlete who is continually honing and improving her game, looking forward to the next challenge as an opportunity to test her mettle.

But as you and your competitors give customers what they want, their expectations will increase. What made customers happy a few years ago won't necessarily make them happy today. In other words, if you're not learning and evolving, you're falling behind.

NOTES FOR CHAPTER NINE

"CUSTOMERS BUY THINGS WHEN THEY HAVE JOBS TO DO"
Clayton M. Christensen, Scott Cook, and Taddy Hall, "What Customers Want from Your Products," Harvard Business School Working Knowledge, January 16, 2006, *http://hbswk.hbs.edu/item/5170.html.*

The more you engage with customers, the clearer things become, and the easier it is to determine what you should be doing.

—*John Russell, former Vice President, Harley Davidson*

CHAPTER TEN

Connected companies get customer feedback

Learning requires feedback in order for performance to improve. The most important judge of service quality is the customer. Therefore, the most important feedback is customer feedback.

PERFORMANCE IS HOW WELL YOU ARE DOING

Purpose gives you the context for learning by orienting you toward a goal. You can't learn if you don't understand the purpose. But once you are pointed in the right direction, you need a way to track your progress. You need feedback.

Companies typically track performance over time. They compare current performance to past performance and look for improvements. Most workers get the majority of their feedback from supervisors and managers, based on internal controls and metrics. But usually, and especially in times of rapid change, front-line workers know more about the context and requirements of the work than their bosses do.

Also, just because you are doing "better than before" does not mean you are doing well enough. It could be that even though you are making progress, you are not doing it fast enough to keep up with customer expectations. Customers not only compare your service to what you have done in the past, but they also compare it to their other alternatives, or even similar experiences in entirely different domains.

For example, once customers have gotten used to online banking and bill pay, they are more likely to become irritated when your company won't accept online payments. What was perfectly acceptable a few years ago has now become a nuisance.

THE ONE JUDGE OF SERVICE QUALITY

Only one person can judge service quality: the customer. Customers come to you with a purpose: they have a job they need to do, and they want you to help them do it.

Service quality is the difference between that purpose (what customers expect) and your performance (what they get). If customers get exactly what they expect, then the service is successful. If you exceed their expectations, customers may be delighted. If they get less than they expect, your service falls short.

Therefore, there are two ways to improve service quality: improve your performance on the things customers care about, or get your customers to reduce their expectations to better match what you can reliably deliver.

Marketing's job is to make realistic promises that help set customer expectations. It's the job of the rest of the organization to deliver on that promise. It's all about the match. A company that promises more than it can deliver will disappoint customers, and that's very dangerous, because today's customers have the tools to tell the world about their poor service experiences.

A good service is one that can perfectly match customer purposes with the company's promises and performance. For example, if you go to Amazon, search for a book, click "Buy," and the book is delivered as promised, then the service succeeded.

BALANCING PROMISE, PURPOSE, AND PERFORMANCE

Here's how it's supposed to work: Your promise sets the expectation. When a customer has a purpose that matches your promise, they come to you with that job to do. If you can perform in such a way that you meet the customer's expectations, you win. To succeed in services, companies must align promise, purpose, and performance as closely as possible.

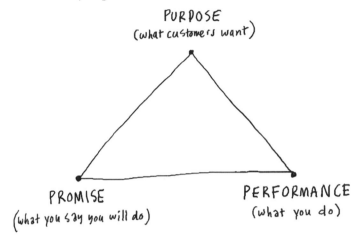

Think of a service provider you're happy with (I know, it might take a while), and you will find a good match among that company's promise, your purpose, and their performance.

Consider Southwest Airlines. The company's promise is to deliver cheap flights within the US and to make that no-frills flying experience as fun as possible. Customers come to Southwest with the purpose of getting from here to there as cheaply as possible. And Southwest delivers on its promises.

How do they do it? Southwest must coordinate a whole bunch of activities to support that simple promise. To take just one example, in order for Southwest to make the flying experience fun, they must have cheerful workers. In order to have cheerful workers, they must have great relationships with employees.

Southwest is 85% unionized, but leaders at the highest level are committed to good employee relationships, and consequently the company has very little labor strife. Employees, spouses, and dependent children fly free on Southwest and enjoy discounts on other airlines. Employees can also earn up to four "buddy passes" per quarter so friends can fly free, too. Employees share in the company's profits (yes, an airline with profits! Southwest has been profitable 38 years running), and enjoy excellent health benefits including vision and dental.

Southwest employees feel valued by the company, and it shows. It's not hard for any customer to see that they enjoy their jobs more than most other airline workers.

SERVICE QUALITY IS A MOVING TARGET

Products can always be measured against a template, which means that you can control the quality of a product with a supervisor or internal inspector. You can simply compare the output of the factory with the product template. You make sure it matches the specifications, and you have done your job. It's a quality product.

Services are a different story, because services are judged by customers, and they are not necessarily consistent. Services by their very nature are variable. Customers often don't want services to be delivered consistently. They want customization—services that are personalized to them.

PROMOTERS AND DETRACTORS

In *Human Sigma: Managing the Employee-Customer Encounter* (Gallup Press), John Fleming and Jim Asplund found that fully engaged customers—those who promote your business to friends and colleagues—represent a 23% premium over average customers in share of wallet, profitability, revenue, and relationship growth, while detractors—customers who are actively disengaged, and who talk about it—are worth 13% less than the average. In most cases, detractors actually cost you money. One Bain study found that each detractor cost Dell $57, while each promoter generated $328 for the company.

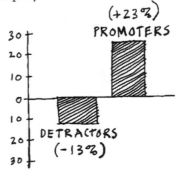

A satisfied customer tells five others, on average, while a dissatisfied customer tells ten or more. The internet amplifies these effects. In a connected era, the amplifying effect of an angry customer is something you don't need.

Promoters are less price sensitive, they increase their spending faster, they accelerate your growth, and they have a positive lifetime value to your business. Detractors defect at higher rates, complain more, and cost more to serve. They are a drag on growth and have a negative lifetime value to your business.

New customers referred by promoters are more likely to become promoters themselves. Another study found that improving your client retention rate by 5% boosts profits from 25 to 100%.

Through in-depth customer research, Harrah's Hotels and Casinos discovered that 26% of their customers generated 82% of the revenues. To their surprise, these customers were not high rollers. They were middle-aged and senior adults with discretionary time and income who enjoyed playing slots. Many lived near the casinos they visited regularly, so they didn't want free rooms. The rewards they wanted the most were free chips they could spend in the slot machines. Harrah's found that if they could improve a customer's rating of their service from a B to an A, the result would be a 12% increase in revenue.

BUILDING LONG-TERM RELATIONSHIPS WITH CUSTOMERS

Many customers are abused today. They want to be heard. They want to be seen. They want to be appreciated and understood.

One way that leading service companies show their appreciation is by trusting their customers to do the right thing. One Amazon customer told the following story: "I got a confirmation saying that a package had been delivered, but either it had not been delivered or perhaps it was stolen from my porch. I contacted Amazon and within two hours they credited my account, no questions asked."

Lands' End offers an unconditional guarantee. You can return any item at any time for a full refund. Nordstrom does the same. These companies trust their customers, and their trust is rewarded with loyalty. All three companies are rated very highly by customers and have a high percentage of promoters. Building strong relationships with customers will require a major shift for most organizations, from practices that are convenient for the business—like internal cost efficiency—to practices that are convenient for customers.

How well do you understand your customers and what they want? What you need is a way to let customers pull you toward the things they need and want most. You need a way for the market to pull you in the right direction.

If you want customers to help you measure quality, you will need their consent. If you want customers to serve as quality inspectors, they will need to agree to enter into that relationship with you.

And for the most part, customers who like your service are willing to get involved to help you make it better. Actually, the customers who hate your service are also often willing to chime in, if they think you're listening. It's the people in the middle, who really don't care one way or the other, that probably won't get actively involved.

THE NET PROMOTER SCORE

The Net Promoter Score (NPS), developed by Fred Reichheld of Bain & Company, measures the customer perception of quality with a single question: "On a 0 to 10 scale, how likely are you to recommend us to a friend or colleague?" The Net Promoter Score gives you an unambiguous number that can be used to quantify the value you are delivering to customers.

Customers fall into three well-defined categories, each of which exhibits a distinct kind of behavior.

Promoters, who respond with a nine or a ten, are your most loyal customers and your biggest fans. They make repeat purchases and spend more than other customers. They recommend you to others. They also contribute more, by taking the time to give constructive feedback and suggestions.

Passives, who respond with a seven or eight, are not loyal to you. They are likely to defect if another company comes up with a better offer. They rarely recommend you to others, and if they do, the recommendation is likely to be qualified or unenthusiastic.

Detractors are customers who give you a score of six or lower. They feel that their lives have been diminished by interactions with you. They are likely to badmouth you to anyone who will listen. They complain and they drive up your costs.

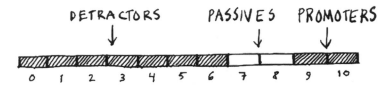

"ON A ZERO-TO-TEN SCALE, HOW LIKELY ARE YOU TO RECOMMEND US TO A FRIEND OR COLLEAGUE?"

Reichheld also recommends a follow-up question: "What is the primary reason for your score?" This question serves as a diagnostic, to help you determine which of your practices have the most impact on customers, for good or ill. It's a request for feedback about how you can do better.

The Net Promoter Score is calculated by subtracting the percentage of customer detractors from the percentage of promoters (you throw out the passives). In 10 years of research, Reichheld and his colleagues have found that companies with high Net Promoter Scores gain more market share, spend less on marketing, and make more in profits than their peers. No other question correlated more strongly with sales and profits.

NET PROMOTER AT ENTERPRISE

One of the pioneers of the net promoter approach is Enterprise Rent-A-Car, who introduced a version of NPS called the Enterprise Service Quality Index, or ESQi, in the summer of 1994. The top question on the survey was: "Overall, how satisfied were you with your recent car rental from Enterprise?" Customers could answer by checking one of five boxes, from "completely satisfied" to "completely dissatisfied." Sixty percent of customers checked the "completely satisfied" box, or "top box," as it came to be known. Scores across the company ranged from 50 to 80%.

One of the most profitable regions came in with one of the lowest scores—54%. Not surprisingly, low-scoring regions criticized the metric, questioning whether the numbers had anything to do with growing the company. Enterprise checked the numbers and did the due diligence. Researchers called customers who had taken the survey to ask whether they had made any referrals or come back to Enterprise. They found that the top question on their survey correlated strongly with repurchases and referrals. Customers who answered "completely satisfied" were three times more likely to return to Enterprise, and generated 90% of positive referrals. Over time, Enterprise dropped all of the other questions on the survey to focus on this single question that tied so strongly with results.

These findings gave CEO Andy Taylor the resolve to push forward. He didn't just want a measure of customer satisfaction—he wanted feedback so the company could improve. After all, what use is an average number when you want to learn? You need to know specifics: what you're doing right and what you're doing wrong. For customer satisfaction to be a true operating metric, feedback loops would need to be consistent, as well as granular and timely enough that employees and managers could make the links between customer feedback and the specific practices and behaviors they needed to improve. The measures would also need to be taken seriously throughout the company as a true operating metric, as important as profit.

CONSISTENT

Enterprise decided to poll at least 25 customers per month at every branch. Since Enterprise had 1,800 branches at the time, this meant the company would get feedback from at least 45,000 customers every month.

ENTERPRISE POLLS 45,000 CUSTOMERS EVERY MONTH.

GRANULAR AND TIMELY

To make feedback as timely as possible, the company switched from mail to phone surveys. An independent research firm called customers and asked them how satisfied they were with their most recent rental. If the customer was not satisfied, the caller asked if they would accept a call from the branch manager. If the customer said yes, their number was forwarded to the branch manager for follow up. Branch managers were expected to call right away, apologize, and ask questions to find the root of the problem so they could fix it.

Customers seem to appreciate the feedback loop. Since the survey is so short— only one question—95% of the people who answer the phone complete the survey. And of those who are dissatisfied, 90% agree to a follow-up call.

SERIOUS

To emphasize the importance of ESQi, anyone from a branch or region whose ESQi scores were below average would not be eligible for the company's annual President's Award. More importantly, nobody from a group with a below-average score would be eligible for promotion. This became known as "ESQi jail." And monthly operating reports included ESQi scores, listing every branch's score right next to its profit number.

Since Enterprise implemented ESQi scores in 1994, detractors have dropped from 12% to 5%. Enterprise has been rated number one in customer satisfaction for the car rental industry for seven out of the last eight years. In 2007, Enterprise acquired National and Alamo and instituted ESQi scoring at both companies. Both have risen in customer satisfaction rankings since. Competitor Hertz has caught on, rolling out NPS globally in 2007. Competitive intensity is heating up, and customer satisfaction is rising in the rental car industry as a whole.

NET PROMOTER AT APPLE

Apple rolled out Net Promoter Scores to its retail stores in 2007. At that time, Apple had about 163 stores, and as the first numbers came in, they found that their average score was 58%. Not bad—average scores in retail are about 46%, and in computer hardware averages are 32%—but not world-leading, where Apple felt it needed to be.

From the beginning, Apple wanted to innovate in retail, just as they had with computer products, to create an "insanely great" retail experience. Ron Johnson, who joined Apple from Target to launch Apple Retail, started asking people about the best service experiences they had ever had. The majority of people spoke of hotel experiences. So Apple patterned its stores on the hotel experience, including a bar—the Genius Bar. "Instead of dispensing alcohol, we dispense advice," says Johnson. While most companies are moving customer support to overseas call centers, Apple is bringing real face-to-face support to your neighborhood.

In the early stages, Apple recruited managers from the hospitality industry, most notably from service leader Ritz-Carlton. Each manager spent a week in Cupertino for specialized training. Managers were steeped in the Apple philosophy of service. Salespeople did not work on commission, and were encouraged to focus on connecting with customers, getting to know them and their needs, and helping them make good decisions. Early stores were seeded with high-end support people from Apple who were paid to relocate.

But this approach did not easily scale, and as the retail store concept took off, Apple needed a more reliable system for managing its customer-centered approach. In 2007, they implemented Net Promoter Scores. There were a few glitches at first.

One problem was that Apple wasn't measuring the scores consistently across all touch points. For example, a customer with a computer problem would be surveyed after a Genius Bar appointment, but not when service was completed. So a manager trying to optimize scores might encourage geniuses to make promises that the store could not realistically deliver. If Apple wasn't measuring that touch point, the store would still get a high score, even if the customer was dissatisfied at the end of his experience. At some stores, a kind of Whack-A-Mole game ensued: As managers reacted to solve problems in one area, they would pop up elsewhere. Managers were simply moving customer dissatisfaction from one area to another.

Another problem was that many things that dissatisfied customers were not things that individual employees could easily control. For example, in a busy, crowded retail store, customers might be frustrated waiting for service at a relatively small Genius Bar. Geniuses spoke of the "circle of anger" that surrounded them at such busy times. They would finish serving a customer and look up to a circle of frustrated faces waiting for their turn at the crowded bar. Such problems can be fixed in the longer term, but imagine the frustration of an individual employee, getting consistently low scores because of something he could not directly control.

Apple has worked out the glitches, and Net Promoter has resulted in some system-wide innovations that have greatly improved the customer experience, giving employees more time and latitude to focus on customer service. For example, the circle of anger dissipated when Apple launched an internal system that automatically populates digital forms with device information that they used to have to enter manually. The same customer management system that used to tether them to the Genius Bar itself can now work over local wifi networks, so if the Genius Bar is crowded, a genius can take a customer to another part of the store, or even the coffee shop next door. Today, every salesperson has an iPod touch that can be used to enter the details of customer transactions, take payments, and email the customer a receipt.

A portion of customers get an NPS survey, and emoticon-coded responses with verbatim customer comments are automatically routed to store managers. If a customer registers dissatisfaction, one click brings up the transaction details, and with another click, Apple can call the customer directly. All dissatisfied customers are contacted within 24 hours. In follow-up research, Apple has calculated that every hour of time spent calling detractors results in an incremental $1,000 of revenue.

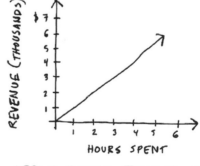

APPLE FOUND THAT EVERY HOUR SPENT TALKING TO DETRACTORS RESULTED IN A THOUSAND DOLLAR REVENUE INCREASE.

Apple's NPS has risen from 58% in 2007 to 78% today, leading the pack in consumer electronics (42 points higher than second-ranked Toshiba) and close to the top in retail.

NET PROMOTER AT LOGITECH

Since Net Promoter is primarily a service measure, you might not expect it to be adopted by a product-oriented company. But consider Logitech, which makes just about everything you might want to attach to your computer: webcams, keyboards, mice, trackballs, headsets, microphones, speakers, and so on, launching more than 100 new products every year. Look around your desktop and chances are, you'll see something made by Logitech.

The company has a reputation for making easy-to-use, reliable, high-performing products. Fans say things like, "You can close your eyes and buy anything from Logitech, and you will be happy with it." If you search for Logitech on Amazon.com, you will find hundreds of products, but you will have a hard time finding a review that's three stars or lower.

Logitech has always focused on customer experience and easy-to-use products, but collecting meaningful feedback was a challenge. Due to the company's fast-paced product development cycle—it launches a new product every week—by the time customer complaints had been collected, they were often out of date. And most products were sold through resellers, making it hard to collect feedback.

In 2007, Logitech started using the Net Promoter Score to understand how customers felt about their products.

They introduced a new stage in the production process called "Gate X," in which new products are tested with users before being approved for mass production. Users are asked to rate their satisfaction, and Net Promoter Scores are calculated. Every new product has a target release date, retail price, and Net Promoter Score. If a product does not meet its target NPS threshold, it goes back to the product team for redesign. Logitech has found that the customer feedback from NPS also helps resolve disagreements among engineering teams about how to prioritize designs.

Logitech surveys 40,000 customers per quarter, and the rankings are available to everyone on a common dashboard. They have also changed their call center support metrics to measure NPS instead of industry standards like call times and volume.

Logitech tracks NPS alongside revenue in each product category. Every product has a Net Promoter Score and products can be rank-ordered by score. And NPS translates directly into business results: products that are number one in the company's NPS rankings are consistently number one in revenue.

ENGINEERS AT LOGITECH USE NPS SCORES TO PRIORITIZE DESIGNS.

The best way to acquire new customers is to engage existing customers. A connected company is not only connected internally, but it is also connected to customers and the market.

NOTES FOR CHAPTER TEN

DELL DETRACTORS AND PROMOTERS
Detailed discussion: Word-of-mouth economics at Dell, 2006–2011, *http://www.theultimatequestion.com/theultimatequestion/company_example_dell.asp.*

CLIENT RETENTION RATE AND PROFITS
Frederick F. Reichheld and W. Earl Sasser Jr., "Zero Defections: Quality Comes to Services," *Harvard Business Review,* September 1990.

We want to be a company that is
constantly renewing itself, shedding
the past, adapting to change.

—*Jack Welch, former CEO, GE*

CHAPTER ELEVEN

Connected companies experiment

When the environment is variable with many unknowns, it is impossible to know in advance what kind of performance will be needed or what kind of learning will occur. If people are to learn, they must be free to experiment and try new things.

MOMENTS OF TRUTH

Jan Carlzon, former CEO of SAS Airlines (Skandinavian Airlines), pointed out in his book *Moments of Truth* (HarperBusiness) that a service company's performance is contingent on its ability to deliver in critical time periods when they have an opportunity to deliver a customer impression. That impression can be positive, if the company can respond quickly and decisively, or it can be negative, if the company fails to deliver. Either way, in these kinds of moments, emotions run high and will leave a lasting impression.

The thing is, moments of truth come in so many varieties that it's impossible to predict every situation and plan for it in advance. Even if you could, the manual of procedures would be so thick that front-stage workers could never look up the procedures in time.

For people to be effective in such situations, they need to understand the company's purpose, its stance. A moment of truth at Nordstrom and a moment of truth at Southwest Airlines will require different kinds of responses, because the companies do different jobs.

But even if employees understand their company's purpose, they can only respond effectively if they have the freedom to do so. Most companies don't give their workers the freedom and autonomy to act decisively and proactively to address customer needs.

THE PROBLEM WITH PROCEDURES

In many companies today, the people at the top try to design processes with rules and procedures that will predictably and reliably solve any problem that should arise. But processes are brittle. A new process breaks a lot. And when a process breaks, we usually fix it by changing it, or adding a few more rules to handle exceptions. Over time, most processes become rigid, bureaucratic, and bloated with rules, regulations, and procedures for handling this or that.

The purpose of all these procedures and rules is to ensure that the rank-and-file employee doesn't have to make decisions. The rules are designed to reflect the decisions that top management would presumably make given the same situation. The big idea is that for every problem, there is one optimal solution that balances the needs of the company with the needs of the customer, and smart people can figure out that optimal solution and roll that information out to the rest of the company in the form of rules.

However, this requires that all possible problems be defined in advance. So there's a lot of work that has to go in to identifying and solving problems that don't exist yet and may never exist.

And the more problems and solutions we define in advance, the more difficult it becomes for employees to understand or even find the rules that apply in a given situation.

But imagine a company that trusts every employee to use her best judgment and act in the best interests of the customer and the company. A company where employees have all the information they need to make good decisions. A company where most of the policies and procedures that constrain and limit employees are unnecessary, because every worker is fully authorized to act as a representative of the company, to make decisions, and to authorize expenses when necessary. If you can imagine these things, then you are imagining a learning company.

THE FRONT LINE IS NOT A PRODUCTION LINE

No plan survives contact with the enemy. – *Helmuth von Moltke*

In a service-driven marketplace, the focus needs to shift from the production line to the front line. The line of production is a one-way arrow, starting with raw materials and suppliers and ending with the customer who buys the product.

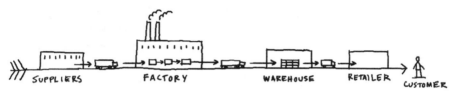

But the front line is not a one-way arrow so much as a boundary, like the cold front in a weather pattern: it's the edge of the organization, the interface where customers and the company interact.

Optimizing for the production line and optimizing for the front line require fundamentally different kinds of organization. A production line requires efficiency. Inputs can be standardized, and environments and processes can be internally controlled. But a front line requires optionality. Front-line people deal with environments and circumstances that cannot be predicted. What they need are support systems that they can access as needed, like "call a friend" on "Who Wants to be a Millionaire."

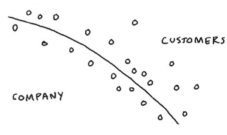

A company that's organized for production can measure quality internally and objectively. Product quality can be defined by the degree to which a physical object conforms to, or varies from, a standard template. But a company organized to provide services has no physical product to measure. Services are experiences, and the only quality measure that matters is subjective: how the customer perceives the experience.

Thus, most service companies are focusing on the wrong things: they are doing the wrong things, and they are measuring the wrong things. No wonder customers are frustrated.

THE LAW OF REQUISITE VARIETY

Since customer needs come in all shapes and sizes, variety is a fact of life in any service business.

The Law of Requisite Variety, also known as *Ashby's Law*, states that any control system must be capable of variety that's greater than or equal to the variety in the system to be controlled.

In other words, if there is variety in the environment, you need enough variety in your system to absorb it effectively. Imagine you are throwing balls at a juggler and the juggler is trying to keep them all in the air. No matter how skilled the juggler, there will always be a point at which there are too many possible states for the juggler's mind and hands to maintain control. At some point, you will either need to reduce the number of balls, or you will need more jugglers.

There are two ways to deal with variety. You can reduce variety by standardizing inputs and controlling the environment as much as possible (fewer balls), or you can design a system that's capable of absorbing more variety (more jugglers).

REDUCING VARIETY

Reducing variety is a factory approach to service design. This works when you can successfully constrain your inputs to a small number of possible states and control the environment in which the service is delivered.

McDonald's is an example of a service company that succeeds because it is able to reduce variety. Consider the McDonald's drive-through experience: as a customer, your orders are limited by what you can see on the menu. You order some quantity of menu items, which triggers a factory-like production process behind the scenes, while you pay at a payment window. You pick up your food at a delivery window. Purpose matches performance. Service delivered.

As a customer, you are a willing participant in the factory experience. Your car is an item in an assembly line, and you can be sure that the time between your order and the delivery of your food is carefully monitored by the company.

This works for McDonald's because they have organized their promise around something that can be consistently and reliably delivered in a factory-like way. For this to work, customers must follow the process as prescribed. If you walk in to a McDonald's restaurant, you don't expect the kind of service you would get in a sit-down restaurant. If you sat down at a table and waited to be served, you would be waiting a long time. McDonald's works more like a giant vending machine. You wait in line until you get to the machine interface, you put in your order and your money, and the food comes out of the slot. This works for McDonald's because they have narrowed customer expectations to match a factory-like service.

McDonald's is an excellent service provider in their niche, not so much because they are excellent at service delivery, but rather because they have reduced their promise to a very narrow window, reducing variety in their inputs and controlling the environment as much as possible. There is a cost to this approach, however. People in such tightly controlled systems don't have a lot of autonomy, and they have few opportunities to exercise creativity at work. So when a McDonald's employee says, "Have a nice day," you might feel like it came from a robot. Because when people are treated like robots, they act like robots.

ABSORBING VARIETY

Most services cannot reduce the variety of their inputs and control their environment as easily as fast-food restaurants. Customer demand is not usually so easily standardized and regulated. Customers have many problems to solve in their lives. They have many jobs that need doing, and only a few of them can be easily reduced to a small set of standard inputs.

Customers have a tendency to resist standardization. The more you try to standardize their service requests, the more you will anger them. Not a good recipe for customer satisfaction or long-term business growth.

ABSORB VARIETY

The real world throws a lot of variety at you. It's bound to throw things at you that you didn't prepare for, plan for, or anticipate. In most cases, service providers must reorganize to absorb variety rather than reduce or contain it. Online shoe store Zappos' call centers are designed to absorb variety. Most call centers look at customer support as a cost. After all, if you have already been paid for a product and delivered it, then you already have your money and any additional effort on your part will only cost you money, right? Zappos looks at the equation differently.

Zappos knows that a customer call probably represents a very tiny fraction of their total interactions with the company. Unlike most online retailers, Zappos encourages person-to-person contact. Zappos publishes its 1-800 number on every page of its site. Online stores don't get a lot of chances for real human contact with customers, and Zappos does everything it can to turn customer calls into positive human experiences that customers will remember. Its number-one goal is to deliver experiences that are so great they are worth talking about.

The first step in creating a great customer experience is hiring the right people. After four weeks of training, Zappos call center reps are offered $3,000 to quit immediately. Remember, this is for an $11-an-hour job. By offering people money to quit, Zappos ensures that the people they hire are really excited about working there.

At Zappos, there are no "customer service scripts" or pre-set time limits for customer support calls. Reps are encouraged to take as much time as necessary to solve the customer's problem, and their mission is to provide the best customer service possible. Zappos has a 100% satisfaction guaranteed return policy. After the call, service reps follow up and keep their promises, and they send a personal note as part of their follow up.

Good customers are profitable customers. Zappos treats frequent customers well, with surprises like upgrades from standard ground shipping to next-day air. Making customers happy, says CEO Tony Hsieh, leads to cost savings elsewhere, like marketing. "We let our customers do our marketing," he says.

By making sure they get the right people and giving them the autonomy and authority they need to serve customers, Zappos call centers are designed to absorb variety, not contain it.

FREEDOM TO EXPERIMENT

Service leaders like Southwest Airlines, Nordstrom, and Ritz-Carlton give employees wide latitude to resolve issues for customers. At Southwest Airlines, employees are expected to act immediately to take care of customers and to check with a supervisor only if a customer asks for something that makes them feel uncomfortable. At Nordstrom, employees are told to use their best judgment in all situations. If a customer at a Ritz-Carlton hotel has a problem, any employee has the authority to spend up to $2,000 to resolve it immediately, without checking with a supervisor.

One study found that employees who are given more latitude are more effective and learn faster than their peers. The thing is, you can't learn in a box. Learning requires the freedom to experiment, to try new things, to step outside the lines. People learn through an ongoing process of trial and error. They learn by doing things. (You learn to read and write by reading and writing. You learn math by solving math problems. You learn to ride a bike by riding a bike, to swim by swimming, and so on.)

Learning is fundamentally different than training. Training is when a company teaches people how to do stuff that the company already knows how to do. Learning is a way to deal with new, uncertain, and ambiguous situations, a process of exploration by which you come to find and discover new things.

It's hard to imagine a more complex operation than an aircraft carrier. An aircraft carrier is a floating city with a population of 6,000 people, with an airport on the roof. It turns over 100% of its population every four years and must operate reliably in any kind of weather.

On aircraft carriers, control is distributed differently, depending on the context. The US Navy's "operating system" transforms from a centralized control hierarchy to a flexible, migrating decision structure, depending on the circumstances.

When the situation is stable, predictable, and well-understood, traditional hierarchy prevails. But when decisions need to be made quickly, decisions migrate to the edge, where people can sense and respond to situations in real time.

For example, any individual involved in a landing can abort the landing at any time. Although the decision may be examined (in the same way that sports teams review game films in order to improve) individuals will never be punished for making a wrong decision.

People at the edge, therefore, have a lot of autonomy, and they tend to make more accurate decisions and take them more seriously as a result. When people who are accountable for decisions encounter uncertainty, they will rely on the more experienced members of the crew, regardless of rank.

The Navy even has rules about when to break rules. For example, "Never break a rule unless safety will be jeopardized by following the rule."

AN AIRCRAFT CARRIER IS A CONTINUALLY-LEARNING ORGANIZATION THAT IS GREATER THAN THE SUM OF ITS PARTS.

Due to the high rate of rotation on an aircraft carrier, everyone on board is doing one thing, learning another, and teaching something else, all at the same time. The result is a continually learning organization that is greater than the sum of its parts.

At one point, it was proposed that the US might be able to park a few aircraft carriers for a while in order to reduce costs and bring them back into service when they were needed. But they ended up determining that there was no way that you can park an aircraft carrier, because there is no manual for it. The only manual for an aircraft carrier is the carrier itself in operation. If you stopped running it, you couldn't start it up again very easily at all.

Learning is happening constantly. There are always people rotating in, so they are always asking questions: "Why do we do it that way? Why don't we do it this way instead?" There's this constant churn that, while it does make the whole organization less efficient in the short term, in the long term creates a learning, adaptive organization.

To the degree that your business environment is uncertain and variable, it's impossible to know in advance what kinds of actions will constitute good performance. There is no way to specify behaviors in advance when you don't know what kind of behavior will be required. Creative solutions must be generated by people thinking creatively within the context of their situation.

In *The Nordstrom Way: The Inside Story of America's #1 Customer Service Company*, (Wiley) Robert Spector and Patrick McCarthy clearly point out the secret of Nordstom's success: "Nordstrom gives its employees the freedom to make decisions. And Nordstrom management is willing to live with those decisions. Everything else flows from that premise."

Giving employees this kind of freedom requires a great deal of trust. But without this kind of latitude, they won't be able to learn and improve.

NOTES FOR CHAPTER ELEVEN

EMPLOYEE LATITUDE AND LEARNING
"The Learning Effects of Monitoring," by Dennis Campbell, Mark Epstein, and F. Asis Martinez-Jerez, Harvard Business School Working Paper, November 2010, *http://hbswk.hbs.edu/item/6582.html.*

How does a connected company work?

A connected company learns and adapts by distributing control to the points of interaction with customers, where semi-autonomous pods pursue a common purpose supported by platforms that help them organize and coordinate their activities.

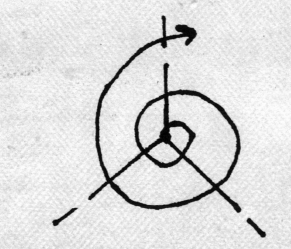

THE GROWTH SPIRAL

Agility means that you are faster than your competition. Agile time frames are measured in weeks and months, not years.

—*Michael Hugos, CIO, Center for Systems Innovation*

CHAPTER TWELVE

Wrangling complexity

The good news is that many of the problems
of addressing complexity and change have
already been solved by the very people who
started the complexity problems in the
first place: technologists. They solved these
problems because they had to.

THE COMPLEXITY ISSUE

Technologists started wrestling with complexity before anyone else. The wave of complexity, change, and coevolution that is now cresting across the business world first appeared in the technology domain, as computer scientists tackled software design problems and struggled to interweave multiple systems into large-scale "systems of systems."

Since the 1950s, technologists have adopted new approaches that allow them to better address complexity and ongoing change. One, called *agile development*, is a different way of doing work. The other, called *service orientation*, is more focused on how bits of work are connected to other bits. Both of these approaches emphasize continuous learning, adaptation, and distributed control—rather than planning, prediction, and central control. They are specifically designed for managing work in fast-changing, uncertain environments.

These approaches function like complex adaptive systems, where the parts of the system can learn, adapt, and coevolve like a biological community.

AGILE DEVELOPMENT

As early as the 1950s, IBM programmers were working on software for things like submarine-control systems and missile-tracking systems, which were so complex that they could not be conceived of and built in one go. Programmers had to evolve them over time, like cities, starting with a simple working system that could be tested by users (sometimes called the minimum viable product or MVP), and then gradually adding more function and detail in iterative cycles that took one to six months to complete. In a 1969 IBM internal report called simply, "The Programming Process," IBM computer scientist M.M. Lehman described the approach:

> The design process is...seeded by a formal definition of the system, which provides a first, executable, functional model. It is tested and further expanded through a sequence of models, that develop an increasing amount of function and an increasing amount of detail as to how that function is to be executed. Ultimately, the model becomes the system.

This iterative approach to software development—where programmers start by creating a simple, working seed system and expand it in subsequent cycles of user testing and development—has become a common approach in software design, known under a variety of names such as iterative development, successive approximation, integration engineering, the spiral model, and many others. But in 2001, a group of prominent developers codified the core principles in a document they called the Agile Manifesto, and the name "agile" seems to have stuck.

ITERATIVE DEVELOPMENT

Agile development is about small teams that deliver real, working software at all times, get meaningful feedback from users as early as possible, and improve the product over time in iterative development cycles. Developing software in an agile way allows developers to respond rapidly to changing requirements. Agile developers believe that where uncertainty is high, there is no such thing as a perfect plan, and the farther ahead you plan, the more likely you are to be wrong.

SERVICE ORIENTATION

Early computer programs were written as sets of instructions, like recipes: first do this, then that; if the user does this, then do this—otherwise, do that; and so on. This worked just fine for simple programs. But software tends to get more complex over time. When programs reached about a million lines of code, they hit a complexity ceiling and started to break. And as software and systems were connected with other systems, the number of dependencies and interconnections increased to the point where the tangled web of interdependent functions was impossible to modify or adjust in one place without breaking something somewhere else.

In the 1960s, computer researchers started to code modular, reusable building blocks instead of procedural instructions. Computer pioneer Alan Kay named the approach, calling it *object-oriented programming*. "I thought of objects being like biological cells...only able to communicate with messages," he later explained.

Object orientation allowed programmers to design software as a system of interacting objects instead of a list of instructions. They could modify a single object without worrying about complex interdependencies. Each object could be seen as an independent machine with its own roles and responsibilities within a larger system.

Object-oriented programming was primarily used inside large enterprises, and not so much for interactions between companies. But the advent of the internet added another layer of challenge and complexity—as well as opportunity. Suddenly it was feasible for software to exchange information not only within a business, but between the business and its partners, suppliers, and customers.

The next phase in programming's evolution, service orientation, emerged to solve this problem. It provided a way for software objects to interconnect with one other over the Internet at massive scale.

Software services are very similar to software objects. They are modular functional units that can operate independently and interact with other services using an agreed-upon set of common standards. The big move forward comes from the way that they interact with the larger world. In service orientation, technologists have now agreed to a set of standards that allow any service to interact with any other service, regardless of the service's underlying technology.

Services can be made available over the Web or any other network. They can be made available to the general public, or to a defined set of authorized users. The power of a service-oriented architecture is that each service can learn, adapt, and coevolve without wreaking havoc on the overall system, just like species coevolve in a biological community.

Three principles at the core of service-oriented design are service contracts, composability, and loose coupling.

SERVICE CONTRACTS

A service contract is a simple description of the service, including what the service provider needs from customers, what it will do for them, and any rules about how the service provider and customer will interact. Like any business contract, it represents an agreement.

Business examples abound. The contract doesn't need to be specified in writing as long as both parties understand the agreement. For example, the service contract of a fast-food restaurant is different than that of a sit-down restaurant. The agreement is that customers will stand in line and order by number in exchange for faster service. If you sit down at a table in a fast-food restaurant and wait for a server to come and take your order, you will be waiting a long time. The reason fast food works is that providers and customers both understand the promise of the service and agree to work together in a certain way.

A service contract specifies *what* the provider will do, but it doesn't specify *how* the work will be done. The advantage of this is that a service can hide its internal complexity, and even change the way it operates, as long as it continues to keep the promise of its contract. This is important because it allows the service to independently evolve and improve its operations without affecting customers or other services. A service can be as complex as it likes internally, so long as it provides a simple contract describing what it does and how it will interact with its customers.

SERVICE ORIENTATION

SERVICE CONTRACTS

LOOSE COUPLING

COMPOSABILITY

Most services have some kind of complexity that is invisible to customers. For example, the kitchen and dishwashers in a restaurant are not usually visible to diners, and most stores have areas such as storerooms and shipping/receiving docks that are not obvious to customers. Amazon customers don't have to know anything about Amazon's warehouses or distribution systems. They just order on the website and sign for the package when it arrives. The iOS operating system that powers iPhones and iPads hides a lot of internal complexity. There is no desktop filing system—there are only apps that you access to do things.

As Steve Jobs once said, "Put complexity where it belongs."

The reason to hide complexity is that it makes a service easier to understand and use. Since customers see only the things they can act on, make decisions about, or buy, they can make better, faster choices.

COMPOSABILITY

Most services are combinations of other services. For example, any kind of food service, from a vending machine to a five-star restaurant, must provide a few core services. It must be able to take orders. It must be able to take payments. It must be able to store food and deliver it to customers. Every food service must make decisions about how it will do each of these things, and how it will combine these services with other services to deliver value to customers.

Common standards make services more useful by making them connectable and composable so they can be easily combined into larger services.

For example, consider a restaurant with a bar and a kitchen. When they use a common ordering system, they can work together more effectively. Waitstaff can easily access both the bar and kitchen services, and the total charge can show up on one bill. This means the larger service works better, and it's more convenient for the customer. At the same time, the bar and kitchen services are separate in the sense that they are not dependent on one other—they can exchange information, but each can also operate independently of the other. If the bar shuts down, people can still order food, and vice versa.

LOOSE COUPLING

Loose coupling simply means that services agree to use a common set of rules about how to connect. So as long as a service follows the rules, it can update, change, or modify itself without having to worry about the impact on other services in the system.

Web pages, for example, are loosely coupled, because one web page can link to another without knowing anything about the other page beyond its address and the rules for connection (which in this case is HTTP, the protocol common to most web pages).

The opposite of loose coupling is tight coupling, where elements on both sides must be designed to complement and fit one another. For example, many mobile phone companies have a unique interface for attaching the charger to the phone. There's really no benefit to customers in this. The primary reason is so they can sell more chargers. This is why you have a drawer full of perfectly good chargers that are useless to you or anyone else.

But there can be good reasons for tight coupling. Things that are designed to work closely together can deliver better performance, and more efficiently. For example, most of the components of your car are tightly coupled, because each part is designed to fit and integrate smoothly with every other part. You can't take a door or an engine out of a Honda and attach it to a Ford—at least, not easily.

But your car is loosely coupled with many other elements in the road-and-car system, and for good reason. For example, when you pull into a gas station to fill up your tank, you don't have to worry about whether the pump nozzle will fit, because there is a standard for that. If you need to put air in your tires, you don't have to worry about whether the air hose will fit your tires, because there is a standard for that. Cars are tightly coupled internally but loosely coupled with the overall system in which they operate.

Service-oriented architecture works in the same way. Internally, a service can be as complex or tightly coupled as it wants to be, just like your car. But when it needs to interoperate with the larger system, it follows a common set of standards.

Standards can be proprietary and closed, such as Apple's iOS, Microsoft's Windows, and Facebook's application development platform, which are provided and managed by a single company; or they can be open, like HTTP and TCP/IP (which govern web interactions) and the electrical sockets in your home. Open standards are defined and managed by technical communities. Sometimes, though, they just evolve naturally over time, like the standard for the width of cars and roads, which can be traced back to the width of Roman roads, which was determined by the width of the two horses it took to pull a Roman chariot.

Regardless of whether the standards are open or closed, it is the number of people and businesses that have adopted them that make them valuable. The more people and businesses that adopt the standard, the more valuable it is.

Service contracts make services simple, modular, understandable, and easy to access, like building blocks. Composability makes services combinable and connectable. Loose coupling is the standardized interfaces and connections that make it all work.

ORGANIZING FOR AGILITY

Agile and service-oriented approaches are designed for complex, uncertain, fast-changing environments. They are proven methods for organizing systems and work. And the same approaches that solved complex software problems can also work in business.

Taken together, agile teams, service contracts, composability, and loose coupling allow the creation of complex service clusters and networks that operate in a peer-to-peer, city-like way. In fact, these kinds of "service cities" can sometimes be so complex that the only way to manage them is to not manage them. Instead, the company focuses on creating an environment within which they can thrive.

NETFLIX, A CITY OF SERVICES

Netflix, the DVD and streaming movie subscription service, operates more like a city than a typical company, especially in its streaming division.

Small two- and three-person teams are responsible for various aspects of the streaming service. Each team is responsible for continuously improving its service as an independent, autonomous unit.

For example, there's a team that manages the algorithm that recommends movies based on your tastes. In many cases, it's a single engineer that's responsible for a service (although any engineer with a single service has a "buddy" who understands the service well enough to serve as backup if the primary engineer gets sick or goes on vacation). Altogether, there are 200 to 300 services constantly running and interacting with one another, managed by about 700 engineers.

In the early days, Netflix engineers worked together to build the software in one piece, on a regular schedule with deadlines. But as the company got bigger, this became more and more complex and difficult to manage. Netflix Cloud Architect Adrian Cockcroft explains:

> What we had was one monolithic application talking to several monolithic databases...The problem was that it worked when there were a handful of engineers, because they were just trying to get stuff done. When it got to tons of engineers it started to creak a bit because people were breaking each other's code. We had these big scrambles trying to figure out who had broken whose code, and we were emailing every engineer in the company to dive in and see what happened and it stopped scaling.

Netflix gave up trying to organize its software as one large monolithic application and broke it down into independent services that can manage their interactions in a peer-to-peer way, like companies in a city:

> We gave up trying to make a readable map of our infrastructure. We have several hundred services, several thousand systems. That's just the one region in the U.S. and then there's another thousand in Europe that are connected in various ways. It's actually a bit cleaner and easier to figure out but it's still quite complex. Every team is throwing out new versions asynchronously and managing it and what you end up with is this chaotic system that's actually quite resilient.

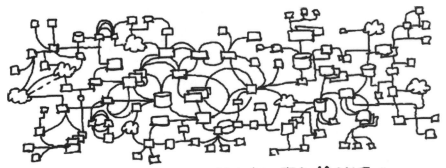

NETFLIX GAVE UP TRYING TO MAKE A
READABLE MAP OF THEIR INFRASTRUCTURE

Unlike many business processes that are designed to be efficient, closed systems, complex systems like Netflix's are designed to be resilient. This means they continue to work even when many of the parts are broken.

If a wheel falls off of your car, you can't keep going. You have to stop. But when a Netflix service breaks, the system as a whole continues to function without that part, because the system is designed to be failure tolerant.

The web is another good example of a resilient system. When a link to a web page breaks, your browser doesn't crash, you just get a notification that it found a broken link. It's as if you tried to deliver something to a city address, but the recipient doesn't live there anymore. The system itself continues to function.

So in a complex system of interacting services, how does Netflix manage quality? Like a city does, with building codes and inspectors who check up on people to make sure they are following the rules. Netflix has a kind of digital "building inspector" they call the chaos monkey. Says Cockcroft:

> The chaos monkey...goes around killing things, killing services. The chaos monkey is the building inspector that makes sure that you followed the planning department's advice and you built a safe building that won't burn down. If you build something that's fireproof, it doesn't matter how much fire there is. It's fireproof. The chaos monkey is our pet arsonist.

If you build a service that doesn't meet the building code, the chaos monkey will burn it down.

Like a city, Netflix's system seems chaotic, but it works much better than if you tried to manage it in a top-down way. When asked about the company's org chart, Cockcroft simply says, "It's fluid and it's ambiguous and strange things appear and nobody really cares."

WHOLE FOODS, AN AGILE TEAM OF AGILE TEAMS

Another example is Whole Foods Market, where small, agile teams run everything in the company, from store departments all the way up to the senior executive team.

Small, agile, autonomous teams: Each store is an autonomous profit center made up of about 10 self-managed teams that direct various aspects of the store, like produce, deli, and so on. Teams determine their own staffing levels and manage their own parts of the store. Teams are responsible for all operating decisions within their group, including pricing, orders, and point-of-sale promotion. Teams buy locally and stock the things they feel will be most interesting to local customers.

New hires are subject to peer review: after a one-month trial, team members vote, and a two-thirds majority is required to keep the person on the team.

Service contracts: Each team is bound by a service contract that specifies what it is accountable for, how it is measured, and how performance will be rewarded.

Each team is measured and managed as its own profit center. Every four weeks, the company calculates profitability for every team in every store. Teams get bonuses when they meet or exceed profit targets.

Ten times a year, a regional leader or executive from company headquarters conducts a surprise inspection and gives the store a report card that rates it on 300 items. Once a year, the company does a survey to probe for employee morale issues.

Composability: The teams are also composable. On average, 10 teams make up a store, and each team's leader participates in a higher-level team that manages the store. The team leaders of each store in a region make up a regional team, and the six regional presidents make up the team that manages the company.

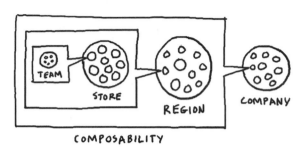

COMPOSABILITY

Loose coupling: Each Whole Foods team operates as an autonomous unit that has control over its own fate. Performance data is available to all the teams, so they can compare their performance against other teams in their store, similar teams in other stores, or against their own team's historical performance.

Teams also have access to detailed financial data, like product costs, profits per store, and even one another's compensation and bonus information. They can look up the best-selling items at other stores and compare them to their own. Employees at Whole Foods are so well informed that the SEC has designated all employees "insiders" for stock trading purposes.

This data transparency both builds trust and fuels a spirit of intense competition between teams and stores, since every team can compare itself with every other team and try to rise through the ranks.

Whole Foods has created a platform that makes it possible for the company's stores and teams to compete with each other, so they can tune and improve their performance over time. At the same time, each team has the autonomy to make local decisions as they see fit to improve their performance. So every Whole Foods store carries a unique mix that is tailored by self-managed teams for that particular location. Whole Foods' agile, team-based strategy allows it to target extremely small locations with customized stores. They are starting to open small stores in suburbs and college towns where rents are lower and competition less fierce.

Customers like the system. The industry average sales per square foot is about $350, and Whole Foods is one of the top 10 retailers in the US, with sales of about $900 per square foot—higher than Best Buy and Zales Jewelers. Not bad for a grocery store.

Employees like it, too. Whole Foods has made *Fortune*'s "100 best places to work" list every year since the list was started in 1998.

MOST COMPANIES ARE NOT BUILT FOR AGILITY

Most businesses today are not designed with agility in mind. Their systems are tightly coupled, because their growth has been driven by a desire for efficiency rather than flexibility.

Consider the difference between a car on a road and a train on a train track. The car and the road are loosely coupled, so the car is capable of independent action. It's more agile. It can do more complex things. The train and track are tightly coupled, highly optimized for a particular purpose and very efficient at moving stuff from here to there—as long as you want to get on and off where the train wants to stop. But the train has fewer options: forward and back. If something is blocking the track, the train can't just go around it. It's efficient but not very flexible.

TRAINS ARE EFFICIENT...

... BUT CARS HAVE MORE OPTIONS.

Many business systems are tightly coupled, like trains on a track, in order to maximize control and efficiency. But what the business environment requires today is not efficiency but flexibility.

We have these tightly coupled systems in which the rails are not pointing in the right directions. And changing the rails, although we feel it is necessary, is complex and expensive to do. So we sit in these business meetings, setting goals and making our strategic plans, arguing about which way the rails should be pointing, when what we really need is to get off the train altogether and embrace a completely different system and approach.

This seems simple when you think about it. But it's difficult to do. It's hard to even think about it, especially when you are sitting on a business train that's going a hundred miles an hour headed in the wrong direction.

NOTES FOR CHAPTER TWELVE

THE PROGRAMMING PROCESS
"The Programming Process," by M. M. Lehman, IBM Res. Rep. RC 2722, IBM Research Centre (Yorktown Heights, New York), September 1969.

THE AGILE MANIFESTO
"Manifesto for Agile Software Development," *http://agilemanifesto.org.*

OBJECT-ORIENTED PROGRAMMING
Explained via email to Stefan Ram in 2003, canonical URL: *http://userpage.fu-berlin.de/~ram/pub/pub_jf47ht81Ht/doc_kay_oop_en.*

SCALING NETFLIX
Interview with the author, 2011.

WHOLE FOODS SALES PER SQUARE FOOT
"Ranking U.S. Chains by Retail Sales per Square Foot," *RetailSails*, August 21, 2011, *http://retailsails.com/2011/08/23/retailsails-exclusive-ranking-u-s-chains-by-retail-sales-per-square-foot/.*

Big companies are inevitably slow and cumbersome; small companies are quick and responsive. Therefore, break big companies into the smallest pieces possible.

—*Lou Gerstner, former CEO, IBM*

CHAPTER THIRTEEN

The future is podular

Connected companies are not hierarchies, fractured into unthinking, functional parts, but holarchies: complex systems in which each part is also a fully-functional whole in its own right. A holarchy is a different kind of template than the modern, multidivisional organization. It's podular.

THE PARABLE OF THE WATCHMAKERS

Small, autonomous teams are the service teams of the future, the fundamental unit of an organization that makes a learning organization possible. The next challenge is putting them together into a cohesive organization that is able to function as a single entity.

In 1967, in a book called *The Ghost in the Machine* (Penguin Books), Arthur Koestler coined the term "holarchy" to describe systems in which each part was also a whole in its own right. The concept was inspired by a story told by systems theorist Herbert Simon, called the Parable of the Watchmakers:

> There once were two watchmakers, named Hora and Tempus, who manufactured very fine watches. Both of them were highly regarded, and the phones in their workshops rang frequently. New customers were constantly calling them. However, Hora prospered, while Tempus became poorer and poorer and finally lost his shop. What was the reason?

> The watches the men made consisted of about 1,000 parts each. Tempus had so constructed his that if he had one partly assembled and had to put it down—to answer the phone say—it immediately fell to pieces and had to be reassembled from the elements. The better the customers liked his watches, the more they phoned him, the more difficult it became for him to find enough uninterrupted time to finish his watch.

> The watches that Hora made were no less complex than those of Tempus. But he had designed them so that he could put together subassemblies of about ten elements each. Ten of these subassemblies, again, could be put together into a larger subassembly; and a system of ten of the latter subassemblies constituted the whole watch. Hence, when Hora had to put down a partly assembled watch in order to answer the phone, he lost only a small part of his work, and he assembled his watches in only a fraction of the man-hours it took Tempus.

Wherever you go in a connected company, you encounter autonomous units that are connected to the whole, yet are able to operate and evolve independently of other units. It's not a hierarchy but a holarchy, in which every part is also a whole.

THE PODULAR ORGANIZATION

This is a different kind of template than the modern multidivisional organization, which most companies have adopted and which is the model taught in most business schools today. The multidivisional form, first realized by General Motors in 1920, is phenomenally effective in some ways, but also has significant weaknesses when it comes to innovation.

There are things that seem "obvious" about organization design that are in fact not so obvious at all. Some things that we take for granted as fundamental are in fact only optional. We tend to design organizations by splitting them into divisions. We divide the business—and the labor—in order to do work more efficiently. We put the software developers together so they can focus on software; we put the salespeople together so they can focus on selling and learn from each other; and so on. Sounds obvious, yes? And it's very efficient. But as we move into a world where efficiency leads to commoditization, and where value will increasingly be driven by innovation, efficiency is no longer the overarching goal.

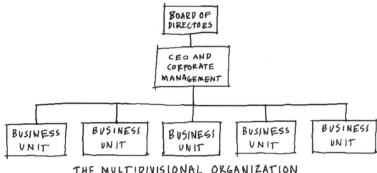

THE MULTIDIVISIONAL ORGANIZATION

How can you divide the labor in your organization to optimize for innovation rather than efficiency? The answer is to supplement divisional thinking with another approach: podular organization.

In a divisional organization (the kind we are all familiar with), you divide the labor into functions and specialties. As you continue to divide an organization in this way, you increase efficiency, but as a side effect, you also disconnect people from the overall purpose of the business. People in a functional group tend to identify with one another more than they identify with the purpose of the organization.

In a podular organization, you divide labor into "businesses within the business," each of which can function as a complete service in its own right. Since each pod functions as a small business, its focus remains outside the pod, on its customers. Those customers might be inside or outside the organization as a whole, but each pod delivers a complete service. A podular approach allows a large company to act as if it were a flock or swarm of small companies; it gives the whole a level of flexibility and adaptiveness that would never be possible in a divisional organization.

A podular organization is a fractal organization: every pod is an autonomous fractal unit that represents, and can function on behalf of, the business as a whole.

PODULAR ORGANIZATION

Does this sound strange? How is this possible? Let's look at four examples from four different industries: a food processing company, a retailer, a software company, and a conglomerate.

MORNING STAR'S SELF-ORGANIZING MARKETPLACE

Morning Star, a privately held company, was started in 1970 as a one-truck owner-operator, hauling tomatoes. Today, the company is the world's largest tomato processor, with revenues of $700 million a year.

At Morning Star, workers manage themselves and report only to each other. The company provides a system and marketplace that allows workers to coordinate their activities. Every worker has suppliers and customers—and personal relationships—to consider as they go about their work.

Every employee writes a personal mission statement that describes how they will contribute to the company's goal and is responsible for the training, resources, and cooperation he needs to achieve it. Every employee also creates a yearly Colleague Letter of Understanding (CLOU), describing his promises and expectations for the coming year, negotiated in face-to-face meetings with peers. All the agreements, taken together, describe about 3,000 peer-to-peer relationships that comprise the activities of the entire organization. Each Morning Star business unit negotiates agreements with other units in a similar way.

If a worker needs something, he can issue a purchase order. If someone needs help or identifies a new role that's needed to do the job better, he can start the hiring process. The bigger the dollar amount, of course, the more important it is to lobby peers and get their buy-in for the purchase, because the unit will sink or swim together. Over

MORNING STAR: A MARKETPLACE OF MUTUAL ACCOUNTABILITY

time, workers tend to move from simpler to more complex roles, hiring people to fill the roles they need to support them. There's no competition for management jobs because there are no management jobs. To get ahead, workers must find better and more valuable ways to serve their peers.

The discipline at Morning Star comes from a strong sense of mutual accountability. Problems are settled through mediation. If mediation can't settle it, a panel of peers is convened. If that doesn't work, a dispute will go to the president for a final decision. If the problem is serious or sustained enough, the worker(s) may be fired. But while people can be fired, nobody has a boss hovering over them. What they do have is customers.

Every two weeks, the company publishes detailed reports of finances and other measures that are transparent and available to everyone.

Business units are ranked by performance, and those at the bottom of the list can expect a tough conversation. In yearly planning meetings, business units present their plans to the entire company, and workers invest using a virtual currency, which then informs the budgets for the year. Workers elect compensation committees to evaluate performance and set pay levels based on performance.

Morning Star is a marketplace, where every worker is a business within the business. You can read more about Morning Star on their website, or in the excellent *HBR* article by Gary Hamel, "First, Let's Fire All the Managers."

THE NORDSTROM WAY

Nordstrom is a publicly traded, high-end retailer known for excellent service, with revenues of about $9 billion a year.

Nordstrom's employee handbook is so short and simple that it can fit on an index card. It states: "Use your best judgment in all situations. There will be no other rules."

Nordstrom salespeople are free to make their own decisions, although Nordstrom's strong culture of putting the customer first provides a guiding light for all to steer by.

That customer service culture is at the core of Nordstrom's success. The entire system is organized in order to support the salespeople on the Nordstrom floor to help them deliver the best possible customer service. If Nordstrom stocks something, they will make every effort to stock it in every size available—they don't want to disappoint a customer by not having something in their size.

Salespeople aren't chained to a department like they are in other stores. If a salesperson wants to walk through the whole store to help her customer pick out clothes, shoes, cologne, and anything else, she can do that. A Nordstrom salesperson might stay in touch with customers by Twitter, email, or whatever else is convenient. The message to customers is: however you want to buy it, however you want to interact with us, we can do it that way.

Customers are encouraged to take things home and try them, and bring them back at any time. If you ask, "How long can I bring it back?" the answer you will hear is, "forever." And they mean it.

One Nordstrom customer said, "What I love about Nordstrom is that if I want to browse by myself that's fine, and if I want help people are there and happy to assist me."

As you can imagine, customers love it. In *The Nordstrom Way: The Insider Story of America's #1 Customer Service Company* (Wiley), Robert Spector and Patrick D. McCarthy write:

> Nordstrom has the faith and trust in its frontline people to push decision-making responsibilities down to the sales floor, the Nordstrom shopping experience is "as close to working with the owner of a small business as a customer can get," said Harry Mullikin, chairman emeritus of Westin Hotels. Nordstrom salespeople "can make any decision that needs to be made. It's like dealing with a one-person shop."

Nordstrom culture demands that the employee put the customer before company or profit in all decisions. Nordstrom provides a platform—the store—and each employee is treated as an entrepreneur who can set up a business on the platform. With commissions, Nordstrom salespeople can make six figures yearly on a base wage as low as $11 an hour. One worker stated:

> The way I saw it, the Nordstroms were taking all of the risks and providing all of the ingredients—the nice stores, the ambiance, the high-quality merchandise—to make it work. All I had to do was arrive every morning prepared to give an honest day's work, and to value and honor the customer.

Nordstrom employees can offer the best service in the industry because every Nordstrom salesperson operates a business within the business, backed by the full support and resources of a Fortune 500 company.

SELF-ORGANIZING TEAMS AT RATIONAL SOFTWARE

Rational Software was founded in 1981 to provide tools for software engineers. Rational was acquired by IBM for $2.1 billion in 2003. (Because Rational has been acquired, I will describe the company in the past tense, although it may operate similarly today as a group within IBM.)

Rational's goal was very transparent to everyone in the company: "Make customers successful." Customers were served by small, autonomous pods known as field teams. Each field team operated as a fully functional, standalone unit, with technical and business experts working closely together. The same team that sold a product or project was also responsible for delivering it. Resources were distributed to teams based on their performances.

Rational's team-based approach permeated the culture at all levels. "If you weren't team oriented, you wouldn't survive," says Jerry Rudisin, Rational's VP of Marketing from 1991 to 1999. Rational put team orientation first even when it hurt the bottom line in the short term.

"When I was a district manager, I fired the top sales rep more than once," says Kevin Kernan, who worked at Rational in a variety of roles for 17 years. "We had zero tolerance for people who didn't exhibit team behavior—that was just poisonous to our culture."

The cross-functional teams at Rational were a great way to build entrepreneurial skills within the company, because every team member understood every aspect of the business. Team members worked closely together and learned from each other constantly. As the company grew, many technologists grew into new careers in sales, fielding their own teams in new territories. Many went on to start companies of their own.

Rational management focused on managing the teams as if they were a portfolio of companies. Teams were evaluated on five things:

1. **Customer success:** Did the team help customers succeed in achieving their goals?

2. **Revenue:** Did the team make or beat its revenue targets?

3. **Team development:** Was the team optimizing for the career growth of each team member as well as the team?

RATIONAL: SELF-ORGANIZING TEAMS

4. **Territory growth:** Was the team growing in reach as well as revenue?

5. **Business basics:** Did the team play well with other teams? Did they spend money as if it was their own?

"You could have a team that did poorly in their overall ranking even though they made their revenue target, because their customers weren't successful in achieving their goals," says Kernan. One year, a new sales rep in a seven-person team was fired because he didn't treat his team well and had filed some paperwork that was misleading, even though the deals he made with customers were all solid and his sales accounted for 25% of the company's revenue.

Top-down intervention in team dynamics was rarely necessary. When a team member wasn't performing, the greatest pressure for improvement came from the team itself. "When I was a district manager I had 25 direct reports, but I rarely intervened. The teams basically managed themselves," says Kernan.

Teams made their own hiring decisions, and hired outside consultants or traded resources with other teams when necessary. "You had to be careful when you brought on a new member," says Ray LaDriere, who worked in one of the Rational sales pods. "If you hired someone and they didn't pull their weight, the deal was that we had to carry them for a full year." Since one poor performer could hurt the performance of the whole team, people were very careful in their hiring decisions.

"It was an amazing experience for 17 years, and I would be surprised if you found anyone who worked at Rational for any significant period of time that didn't feel the same way," says Kernan. "Our goal was to change the world by changing the way people design, build, and deploy software. And we did it."

DEMOCRATIC MANAGEMENT AT SEMCO

Semco is a Brazilian conglomerate that specializes in complex technologies and services like manufacturing liquids, powders, and pastes for a variety of industries; refrigeration; logistics and information processing systems; real estate, inventory, and asset management; and biofuels. Semco's revenues are around $200 million a year.

Semco is a self-managed company. There is no HR department. Workers at Semco choose what they do as well as where and when they do it. They even choose their own salaries. Subordinates review their supervisors and elect corporate leadership. They also initiate moves into new businesses and out of old ones. The company is run like a democracy.

Says CEO Ricardo Semler, "I'm often asked: How do you control a system like this? Answer: I don't. I let the system work for itself."

Semco is organized around the belief that employees who can participate in a company's important decisions will be more motivated and make better choices than people receiving orders from bosses. Workers in each business unit are represented by an elected committee that meets with top managers regularly to discuss any and all workplace issues. And on important decisions, such as plant relocations, every employee gets a vote.

Workers at Semco choose their own hours. CEO Semler recalls that when he first proposed the idea, managers were convinced this wouldn't work, especially when it came to factory work. But Semler was confident. "Don't you think they know how to manage their own work?" he asked. Turns out they did, and they do.

Semler says simply, "If you want people to act like adults, you need to treat them like adults."

Things do take longer than they do in a traditional, hierarchically managed company. Semler elaborates in his book *Maverick: The Success Story Behind the World's Most Unusual Workplace* (Grand Central Publishing):

> Dissent and democracy go hand in hand. It's also good management technique. What traditional executives don't consider is that decisions arising from debate are implemented much more quickly because explanations, alternatives, objections, and uncertainties have already been aired.

One of the principles underlying Semco's success is the idea that every business should be small enough that each worker can comprehend it as a whole system. If a business grows to more than 150 people, Semco will split it into two.

Another principle is transparency and trust. "The only source of power in an organization is information, and withholding, filtering, or retaining information only serves those who want to accumulate power through hoarding," says Semler.

Once a month, Semco holds open meetings for the employees of each unit, where all the numbers in the business are presented for open examination and discussion. The company also offers courses to help employees better understand financial reports such as balance sheets, profit-and-loss reports, and cash flow statements.

What about profits? In his book, *The Seven-Day Weekend: Changing the Way Work Works*, Semler writes:

SEMCO: FINANCIAL TRANPARENCY

> Profit is highly important to us at Semco, and we're as avid about it as a general is about his supplies. If provisions run out, his soldiers will die. If a company ceases to make money, it too will die. But armies are not created to feed soldiers, just as companies don't generate income just so they can hire more employees. Food fuels the soldiers and keeps them going. Yet to serve as more than mere gun fodder, they must have a higher purpose, a reason for going through boot camp and charging the enemy in battle This is where profit and purpose meet and, unfortunately for most organizations, it's a head-on Humvee wreck.

Nearly a quarter of Semco's profits go to employees, but the company doesn't decide how to distribute it. Each quarter, the profit contribution of each unit is calculated, and 23% of profits go to that unit's employees, who can distribute it however they wish. So far, they have always decided to distribute that money evenly to everyone.

Employees who are particularly confident can choose to put up to 25% of their pay "at risk." If the company does well, they get a bonus raising their compensation to 150% of normal; if the company does poorly, they are stuck with 75% of their pay.

Does it work? Semco's growth from $4 million in 1980 to more than $200 million today seems to point in that direction.

CAN YOUR COMPANY GO PODULAR?

Although each company has done it differently, Morning Star, Nordstrom, Rational, and Semco have all found success by organizing in a podular way.

This kind of design won't make sense for every situation, or for every division. It's a model designed to be flexible and resilient, as opposed to predictable and efficient. But it's not a new model. It's been done a lot of times, in a lot of industries, in a lot of ways.

At its heart, podular design is a kind of franchise model, and franchises are one of the most common and scalable models in the business world. Franchises operate like cities in many ways: they provide a core infrastructure, support systems, and services that allow clusters of entrepreneurial people to succeed. They extract "taxes" in the form of franchise fees. And they enable motivated people to form a business within the business.

NOTES FOR CHAPTER THIRTEEN

PARABLE OF THE WATCHMAKERS

Herbert A. Simon, "The Architecture of Complexity," *Proceedings of the American Philosophical Society*, 106, no. 6 (1962): 467–482.

MORNING STAR

Gary Hamel, "First, Let's Fire All the Managers," *Harvard Business Review*, December 2011.

RATIONAL

Based on interviews conducted by the author in 2011.

The strength of the team is each individual member. The strength of each member is the team.

—*Phil Jackson, former NBA coach*

CHAPTER FOURTEEN

Pods have control of their own fate

The core building block of a podular organization is the pod: a small, autonomous unit that is authorized to represent the company and deliver results to customers. Pods are flexible, fast, scalable, and resilient.

WHAT IS A POD?

A podular organization is designed so that decisions and changes can be made as quickly and as close to customers as possible. There is no way for people to respond and adapt quickly if they have to get permission before they can do anything.

If you want an adaptive company, you will need to unleash the creative forces in your organization, so employees have the freedom to deliver value to customers and respond to their needs more dynamically. One way to do this is by enabling small, autonomous units that can act and react quickly and easily, without fear of disrupting other business activities: pods.

A pod is a small, autonomous unit that is enabled and empowered to deliver the things that customers value.

PROCESS TO POD

Traditionally, it's been the job of managers to coordinate activity across divisions or lines of business, because processes are usually complex and interdependent. Making changes in one part of the process might solve a problem for that unit but cause problems for others.

The goal of podular design is to reduce that interdependency by enabling autonomous teams to focus on clear outcomes that deliver value to customers.

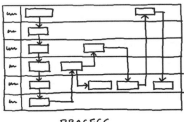

PROCESS

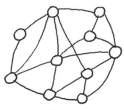

PODS

CHAINS VERSUS NETS

You can think of any business process as a chain: a series of steps that people go through to get things done. Processes don't depend on the intelligence or creativity of the people who run them, so much as their consistency and ability to perform a specialized task. The manager of the process is responsible for the intelligence of the system.

A process is like a recipe. Recipes are fine as long as you want to achieve the same result every time. But recipes are also very inflexible when it comes to change and innovation. If you are responsible for a part of a complex process, it's hard to try something new.

If you get one step wrong, there is a cascading effect, and everything downstream from that change is affected. Small changes at the beginning of a process can have devastating effects elsewhere in the system.

A chain, as the saying goes, is only as strong as its weakest link. Break one link and the whole chain fails.

A podular system is like a net. It distributes the workload across a wider area by allowing each pod to focus on goals rather than on steps or stages. If one strand breaks, the system can still carry the load.

CHAIN

In a podular system, the burden of creativity and intelligence is on the people in each pod. In a pod, your focus is on solving problems and delivering value rather than on executing predefined steps. You can no longer just pull the levers, move the dials, and say you did your job even though the customer didn't get what he wanted. Giving the customer what he wants *is* your job.

NET

If processes are *fool proof*, then pods are *fail proof.*

PODS ARE FLEXIBLE, PODS ARE FAST

When pods are autonomous, they can try new things without worrying about a "ripple effect" that will disrupt the activities of other units. They can adopt new tools and practices quickly, without having to ask permission. They can be flexible in the ways that they choose to respond to customer requests. This means that each pod can be free to innovate, try new things, adjust its work process, and so on.

PODS CAN FAIL

When a step in a complex process fails, the entire process comes to a halt. In a Toyota plant, each worker has the power to stop the entire process when she sees a problem or opportunity. This is great, in the sense that it enables a process to continually improve, but it doesn't solve the problem of interdependency—the whole process still must stop in order to accommodate the change.

In a podular system, however, each pod can make adjustments without disrupting its neighbors, and even when a pod fails, there is enough redundancy in the system that those services can most likely be found elsewhere.

PODS CAN SCALE UP FAST

Since pods are inherently modular, it's easier to scale them up to meet increases in demand. There's a huge amount of tacit experience in each pod, because each pod is like a tiny fractal snapshot of the entire business—focused on customer value instead of a specialized task or functional process step.

This means that when it's time to scale up a particular service, a pod that has, for example, seven people, can reproduce itself by dividing into two pods, each of which can bring on new members with minimal growing pains.

REPRODUCTION

WHAT KINDS OF COMPANIES HAVE BEEN SUCCESSFUL WITH A PODULAR APPROACH?

Xerox, Procter and Gamble, AT&T, and many other companies have credited self-directed teams with having a marked impact on their operations, including improvements in customer service, manufacturing, inventory management, and other productivity gains. Let's look at three highly effective podular systems: one old-school company, one new-school company, and one old-school industry that's reinventing itself.

3M IS PODULAR

Although they are known for innovation, 3M was incorporated in 1902, making it more than a hundred years old.

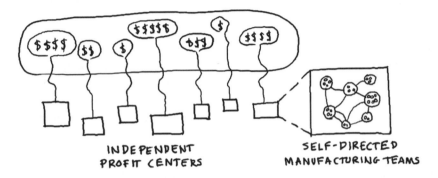

INDEPENDENT
PROFIT CENTERS

SELF-DIRECTED
MANUFACTURING TEAMS

Big pods: 3M has roughly 100 autonomous profit centers, each of which operates like a separate company. As operations grow, profit centers divide in order to keep each group small and agile. 3M's R&D teams are integrated with business units to keep them close to buyers and markets.

Small pods: In the 1990s, 3M implemented "self-directed work teams" in their manufacturing operations. The teams did their work as a group and managed themselves. Managers in this system were freed up to become coaches and teachers—essentially full-time trainers. Self-directed teams were not a top-down directive at 3M. Initial self-direction efforts arose out of manufacturing, where complexity in the operations made traditional management cumbersome. Productivity soared.

AMAZON IS PODULAR

Amazon is still a teenager, but it's one of the biggest retailers in the world.

Amazon is an ecosystem: Legend has it that Jeff Bezos named his company Amazon after the world's largest river to give the impression of size, or to ensure that it showed up high in Yahoo's alphabetical listings. But there may be a deeper, more strategic concept underlying the name. The Amazon rainforest is one of the richest ecosystems in the world, and Amazon the company has been very deliberately organized like a complex, customer-centered ecosystem.

Rapid change: Just like animals coevolving in a complex ecosystem, small teams at Amazon develop features in parallel. It's a probabilistic approach, oriented toward fast failure and recovery rather than failure avoidance. Teams are self-organizing, self-repairing, and self-managed.

Data Darwinism: New features are tested on a small portion of the overall population and compared against the original—an approach known as *A/B testing.* The fittest designs survive and are rolled out to the larger system. What you want to do as a company is maximize the number of experiments you can do per unit of time, said Bezos in a 2007 interview with the *Harvard Business Review.*

Amazon is built around self-managed teams: In 2004, Bezos talked to *Fast Company* about connecting technological advancements to customer happiness:

> We have this weirdness in our business...The raw ingredients that make our business—things like CPU processing power, bandwidth, and disk space—get twice as cheap every 12 to 18 months. Disk space is 30 times cheaper today than it was five years ago. Thirty times cheaper! So the real question becomes, What can you do with 30 times as much disk space, 20 times as much computing power, and 30 times as much bandwidth? All right, how are you going to make customers happy with that? It turns out that these are not easy questions to answer.

Bezos does have an answer, though: break big problems down into small ones. Distribute authority, design, creativity, and decision making to the smallest possible units, and set them free to innovate. Small teams focus on small, measurable components that customers value.

MASSIVELY PARALLEL
PRODUCT DEVELOPMENT

One example is a team that decided to focus on finding phrases that are unique to a particular book. Says Amazon CTO Werner Vogels:

> The Statistically-Improbable Phrases service...turns out to be a mechanism that brings very remarkable collections together... Remember that most of our developers are in the loop with customers, so they have a rather good understanding about what our customers like, what they do not like, and what is still missing.

Teams are limited in size to about 8–10 people. At Amazon, they call them *two-pizza teams:* if you can't feed a team with two pizzas, it's too large.

What keeps the teams close to customers? Three things:

1. Each team has a fitness function—a number they are focusing on—and organizes its work in any way it pleases to improve that number. Such data is critical for organizing autonomous pods. "Fact-based decisions overrule the hierarchy," says Bezos. Since each team focuses on a small part of the ecosystem, the company gets closer and closer to the data, tightening up feedback loops and helping the whole system evolve faster.

2. Teams work backwards from customer value to service or product. They start with a press release describing their intended features, and start collecting feedback before they have built a thing.

3. Every two years, each Amazon employee is required to spend a couple of days interacting directly with customers at a call center or other facility.

Amazon's approach is supported by a strong platform that allows the whole Amazon website to be developed in a massively parallel fashion by podular teams. When you visit an Amazon page, you might be accessing a hundred or more web services that are orchestrated to give you a personalized experience. Behind the scenes is a sophisticated, service-oriented architecture that allows Amazon's podular teams to access common data and functionality without having to worry about interdependency and conflict. "Any algorithm that requires agreement will eventually become a bottleneck...each node should be able to make decisions based on the local state," says Vogels. Because of the architecture, services can evolve in parallel without affecting each other.

A PODULAR SYSTEM TRADES FLEXIBILITY FOR CONSISTENCY

Pods don't answer every business problem. Like any other strategic decision, the choice to go podular involves inherent risks and tradeoffs. A podular system is certainly not the most efficient or consistent way to conduct business. There is more redundancy in this kind of system, which usually means greater cost. When units are autonomous, activity will also be more variable, which means it will be less consistent.

The bet you are making with a podular strategy is that the increase in value to customers, paired with increased resiliency in your operations, will more than offset the increases in costs. It's a fundamental tradeoff and thus a design decision: the more flexible and adaptive you are, the less consistent your behavior will be. The benefit, though, is that you free people to bring more of their intelligence, passion, creative energy, and expertise to their work.

The self-empowered team concept is not new. In fact, it precedes the Industrial Age altogether. In an age where passion and creativity is increasingly important, we need to take another look at organizational forms that play to natural human strengths, like ingenuity, curiosity, and the joy of making a clear and recognizable impact on the world.

WHY AREN'T MORE COMPANIES GOING PODULAR?

Pods—also known as self-directed work teams—are 30 to 50% more effective than their traditional counterparts. A survey of senior line managers offers some of the benefits they have derived from self-directed teams:

- Improved quality, productivity, and service
- Greater flexibility
- Reduced operating costs
- Faster response to technological change
- Fewer, simpler job classifications
- Better response to workers' values
- Increased employee commitment to the organization
- Ability to attract and retain the best people

So if it's such a great idea to go podular, then why aren't more companies doing it? Podular design is a concept that focuses on modularizing work: making units more independent, adaptive, linkable, and swappable. But the environment that surrounds the pods is equally critical to the success or failure of a podular system. Modular components are a critical element of a connected company. But to take advantage of pods, you also need a business that is designed to support them.

NOTES FOR CHAPTER FOURTEEN

A/B TESTING
"Institutional Yes: The HBR Interview with Jeff Bezos, by Jeff Bezos, Julia Kirby, and Thomas A. Stewart," *Harvard Business Review*, October 2007.

"WE HAVE THIS WEIRDNESS IN OUR BUSINESS"
Alan Deutschman, "Inside the Mind of Jeff Bezos," *Fast Company*, August 1, 2004.

THE STATISTICALLY-IMPROBABLE PHRASES SERVICE
Jim Gray, "A Conversation with Werner Vogels: Learning from the Amazon Technology Platform," Association for Computing Machinery, May 1, 2006.

POD EFFECTIVENESS
Self-Directed Work Teams, the New American Challenge, by Jack D. Orsburn, Linda Moran, Ed Musselwhite, and John H. Zenger, New York: McGraw-Hill, 1990.

What we need to do is learn to work in the system, by which I mean that everybody, every team, every platform, every division, every component is there not for individual competitive profit or recognition, but for contribution to the system as a whole on a win-win basis.

—*W. Edwards Deming, statistician & educator*

CHAPTER FIFTEEN

Pods need platforms

A podular organization requires support
structures that network the pods together
so they can coordinate their activities,
share learning, and increase the company's
overall effectiveness. Platforms are support
structures that increase the effectiveness
of a community.

WHAT IS A PLATFORM?

A platform is a support structure that increases the effectiveness of a community. Some platforms are public. For example, a local farmers' market or swap meet clusters sellers together so they can attract more buyers. Like local swap meets, eBay and Craigslist provide platforms for people to buy and sell used goods or unique items. Amazon's Mechanical Turk provides a marketplace for buyers and sellers of human labor at a micro scale—tiny bits of work for tiny bits of money. The Internet is another public platform. So is the Global Positioning System (GPS) that allows you to track your location by satellite.

A PLATFORM IS A SUPPORT STRUCTURE THAT INCREASES THE EFFECTIVENESS OF A COMMUNITY

Companies can provide platforms that are more restricted in their use. For example, platforms may be available only to employees. Nordstrom provides a platform for salespeople who share their high-touch, high-service approach to retail. Whole Foods provides a platform for people who share their mission to help the world eat healthier, and who like the team-based, performance-oriented approach of that company.

Platforms may be available for a fee. Microsoft charges for its Office suite of applications. Shopping malls and other landlords, like Amazon Marketplace, extract rents for businesses that want to access their platforms. Other platforms, such as Google, Facebook, and Craigslist, are free for users but not for advertisers. Telecom, cable, and Internet service providers charge for access to their networks.

Platforms may be codeveloped by a community as a shared resource. When he was 21, Linus Torvalds released a very basic operating system he was working on as a hobby. Over time, an army of developers joined the project, and Linux now powers not only tablet computers, mobile phones, and game consoles, but also some of the fastest supercomputers on the planet. Wikipedia started as a side project that complemented a more traditional online encyclopedia, called Nupedia. But contributors preferred Wikipedia's less bureaucratic structure, and it quickly overshadowed its parent. When Nupedia was shut down in 2003, it had published only 24 articles. Meanwhile, Wikipedia had published more than 20,000 articles and was available in 46 languages.

Everything in business is built on platforms of one kind or another. At the most basic level, companies need to speak the same language as customers. They need some form of currency, and a system for exchanging money with customers and suppliers. They need laws and regulations to ensure they get paid and that their money is worth something. At a higher level, they need infrastructure, like electricity, telephone service, internet access, access to transportation, and so on. And at a still higher level, they need hardware, software, and applications—things like email, word processing, and spreadsheets.

You can get just about anything you want in a city, yet very few of the services available in cities are provided by the cities themselves. The city generally provides a platform: the basic infrastructure and services that everything else is built on, such as roads, electricity, gas, traffic signals, police and fire services, trash collection, and so on. Everything else is created by the population themselves.

Consider Facebook, which is growing so fast that it's impossible to keep up with the figures. By the time this book comes out, it will have exceeded 1 billion members. Fifty percent of Facebook users log on every day. In the US, the average Internet user spends more time on Facebook than on any other site. And Facebook provides zero content. Zero. All of Facebook's content is provided by users. Facebook concentrates on providing a platform for all of its users to interact, start businesses, advertise, and exchange information. Facebook is a city, more than 20 times the size of Tokyo.

WHAT IS THE VALUE OF A PLATFORM?

Pods are more powerful when they are networked together. A platform supports the work of the pods and gives them a way to coordinate their activities in a peer-to-peer way. Platforms reduce friction, increase cohesion, and allow a community or organization to scale in an exponential fashion.

A network of pods is a form of distributed intelligence, a massively parallel processing system. As pods are out in the field, interacting with customers in different contexts and environments, a shared platform allows them to compare their experiences, learn together, and keep track of information they all need to do their work.

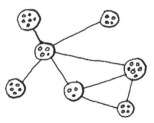

PODS ARE MORE POWERFUL WHEN THEY ARE NETWORKED

What city-like organizations like Facebook and Amazon have done is create platforms that provide a common backbone that provides consistency and order, without squelching innovation.

Amazon merchants can sell whatever they like as long as they abide by some basic policies and treat customers well. Like any good shopping mall or district,

Amazon provides the basic infrastructure needed to manage a store: site hosting, payment services, customer rating and ranking, and so on. For those who want even more service, Amazon will store a merchant's products in their warehouse, and also handle shipping and returns.

The shared infrastructure offers many benefits:

1. Traffic brings customers. Amazon's voluminous traffic is a rising tide that lifts all the boats in the store. More traffic means more business for everyone. This is a basic characteristic of any high-traffic shopping area, in the physical world or on the Web.

2. Infrastructure allows focus on differentiators. The shared common infrastructure and common standards allow companies to focus on the things that truly differentiate them, like customer service or unique products.

3. Rules bring trust. The rules that Amazon enforces with all merchants raises the overall quality of all the stores. Merchants that treat customers poorly or fail to deliver on their promises are shut down. So customer confidence goes up because Amazon, just like any regulator or police force, has made the marketplace safe for people to do business in.

A PLATFORM IS A GOVERNMENT

Most companies are structured like kingdoms, with subjects to be ruled. Platforms are more like governments, where power comes from the consent of the governed.

Like any government, a platform must carefully weigh individual freedoms against the common good. It's a balancing act. But platforms are different than traditional management structures. They are about support, not control. This is a fundamental difference that turns traditional management structures and paradigms upside-down. Platforms require a completely different approach.

STANDARDS

Even without a traditional command-and-control hierarchy, autonomous pods still need to make decisions and coordinate their activity in order to deliver value to customers. The secret of coordination is to make those exchanges as frictionless as possible.

Technical standards are simply interfaces that allow you to connect things at will. For example, the electrical socket in your wall uses a common standard that allows you to get electricity when you plug in a device. When your electrician installed that socket in the wall, you didn't have to know in advance what you might want to plug in to it. And device makers can be confident that if their plugs follow a common standard, you will be able to plug them into your wall.

TECHNICAL STANDARDS

Those of us who travel a lot wish that the world had a common electrical standard, but alas, it does not. And, sadly, these kinds of standards are not as common in business as you might think. But things have come a long way in the last 10 years or so.

We've already discussed how Service-Oriented Architecture (SOA) allows companies to bundle small pieces of functionality into podular services that anyone can access. PayPal, for example, handles payments securely and quickly via standard connections with other companies. Any web service or company can easily link into PayPal for payment processing, which means they don't have to build that function themselves. But even something as simple as a standard protocol for email

CULTURAL
STANDARDS

addresses (first initial, last name, for example) can help people connect with less friction.

Cultural standards, put simply, are the kind of values and behaviors you can expect in a given company. Like clarity and constancy of purpose, a strong culture reduces the friction in making decisions and connections.

Decisions: If you're in a pod and you need to make a decision, common purpose and values can help you make that decision promptly, without the need to check with superiors. This means you can act more quickly than competitors who need to check with the boss before they can proceed. Common cultural standards give you confidence that your behavior will be consistent with that of other units.

Connections: If your pod needs to connect with other pods, it's easier to link up and collaborate when you know what kinds of behavior to expect when you speak the same language and work in the same way. Pattern languages are collections of common standards that allow teams to more easily connect and collaborate, without being overly prescriptive. They are guidelines, not rulebooks. Gamestorming, for example, is a pattern language for cross-disciplinary design.

Culture can be as simple as a set of shared values, or it can be codified in rules and policies. The important thing is that the values and rules are understood and the behavior is consistent with them. If the culture says everyone is equal, then the CEO better not have a reserved parking spot. Culture is built by establishing behaviors that the whole organization can and will adhere to consistently.

For a podular system to work, cultural and technical standards are imperative. This means that a pod's autonomy cannot extend to everything. Shared standards and protocols lose their value if they are not, well, shared. This kind of system needs a strong backbone that clearly articulates those standards and provides a way to evolve them when necessary.

A PODULAR SYSTEM NEEDS A BACKBONE

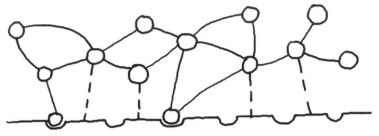

For small and large companies alike, the most advantageous standards are those that are most widely adopted, because those standards will allow you to plug in more easily to the big wide world, and the big wide world *always* offers more functionality—better and more cheaply than you can build it yourself. Backbone activities are about coordination and consistency, so the best way to organize them may not be podular. When it comes to language, protocols, culture, and values, you don't want variability, you want consistency. Having shared values is one of the best ways to ensure consistent behavior when you lack a formal hierarchy. Consistency in standards is an absolute requirement if you want to enable autonomous units.

ATTRACTORS

Why should someone join your platform? What motivates her to learn, improve, and perform at a high level over time?

Is it easy to join? Whole Foods' platform is available only to employees, so in effect, they are paid to join and use the platform, and their livelihood depends on it.

But not all platforms serve employees only. Many companies have found ways to extend their platforms to engage a wider community. For example, Amazon created a platform where people can make money by linking to Amazon products from their blogs and web pages. It's easy to join—signing up as an Amazon affiliate takes only a few minutes.

Shopping malls will offer very low rents to attract "anchor stores" that will help attract shoppers and other tenants to the mall.

What's the incentive to perform? As Adam Smith wrote in *The Wealth of Nations,* "It is not from the benevolence of the butcher, the brewer, or the baker, that we expect our dinner, but from their regard to their own interest."

Some platforms are only available to paid employees. Some are open to qualified parties like suppliers, partners, or franchisees. Others are open to anyone who wants to join. But in every case, the benefits of the platform must exceed the cost, whether you measure that cost in money, time, or hassle factor.

A strong common purpose can be a powerful motivator. Whole Foods workers are committed to creating a healthier, more sustainable world. But money helps, too. For example, Whole Foods employees get a bonus when profits exceed their targets. Amazon affiliates get a commission for sales that they generate. Franchisees get a percentage of profits.

SUPPORT

A platform is a support structure. It needs to make life easier for the pods.

What kind of support do you offer? McDonald's provides training for franchisees at Hamburger University, which graduates more than 5,000 people each year, and the McDonalds operations manual is legendary for its thoroughness.

Everything about Nordstrom's platform is designed to support and enable that salesperson on the retail floor. Nordstrom's customer-oriented, high-touch service culture is the core of the platform.

Can people get the information they need to do their work? The more information that's available in the platform, the better teams can self-organize to coordinate their work.

Think about the information available to Whole Foods employees on demand: they can look up any store on the platform and see the best-selling items in the store. They can rank stores by sales, growth, or profitability. If they want to look for the best cutting-edge practices, they know exactly where to look and whom to talk to.

To maintain a shared awareness of customer issues and concerns, Vanguard Mutual Funds collects customer feedback through multiple channels like surveys, focus groups, comments on the website, customers conversations with phone associates, and so on. The customer feedback is aggregated and published to the entire company in a daily email called Voice of the Client (or VOC for short), so everyone can see the actual things that customers are saying, in their own words, on a daily basis.

GOVERNANCE

What are the rules and how are they enforced? How tight or loose are the parameters? How do you balance the needs of different constituents? It's a balancing act.

Drawing boundaries. The tighter the parameters, the less room there will be for creativity and experimentation. But as you loosen parameters, there's a danger of losing cohesion.

At the loose end of the spectrum is the venture capital (VC) firm, which makes investments in a portfolio of companies and influences those companies by advising them or taking a board seat. VC firms may have an investment strategy that concentrates on a particular industry or technology, but the companies in the portfolio usually don't function as a cohesive whole.

At the tight end of the spectrum is a company like McDonalds, with rigid requirements for who is allowed to operate a franchise and strict rules about how each store must be operated. A tightly-controlled platform like McDonalds' ensures consistency but limits innovation at the store level.

In between is a wide band of possible models, where operators have varying degrees of autonomy and control.

"Thou shalt" versus "thou shalt not." A "thou shalt" platform like the one McDonald's provides to franchisees is very prescriptive. There is a big fat operations manual laying down the company's policies and procedures, covering everything from how long to toast a bun (17 seconds) to how much sanitizer to use when cleaning the shake machine (1 packet in 2.5 gallons of water). And owners have a calendar that lays out a schedule—some kind of maintenance is scheduled for every day of the year.

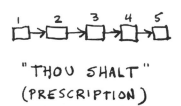

"THOU SHALT"
(PRESCRIPTION)

"THOU SHALT NOT"
(FREEDOM WITHIN BOUNDARIES)

A "thou shalt not" platform is one like Amazon Marketplace, which is more like a zoned shopping district. Amazon merchants can sell just about anything except those things that are prohibited, like alcoholic beverages, pets, livestock, guns, and ammunition. Merchants must abide by certain policies that make Amazon Marketplace a safe and reliable place for shoppers.

BALANCING THE NEEDS OF CONSTITUENTS

Platform providers often must balance the needs and demands of multiple parties. The needs of one constituency may be in conflict with the needs of another, and how the platform provider chooses to strike a balance sets the tone for the platform.

For example, Google must balance the needs of users and advertisers. Users have a need to quickly find information, while advertisers want to influence users and sell them a product or service. Google has chosen to favor users, prioritizing those ads that are the most useful to customers.

First and most obviously, search is free, whereas advertisers must pay for ads. Second, Google places ads that are as relevant as possible to a user's search, increasing the chances that ads will be seen as a benefit. (After all, users are often searching in order to buy something.) Third, Google avoids image-based ads in favor of less-obtrusive text advertising. And fourth, Google algorithms do their best to ensure that the most popular ads are displayed most frequently.

Advertisers are not ignored. They have access to deep analytics showing how and when their ads are viewed, and they pay only for ads that are clicked on. However, both Google and advertisers understand that Google's strategy is dependent on a never-ending river of customers quickly finding what they want through search, and advertising priorities are never allowed to compromise that experience.

CUSTOMERS   ADVERTISERS

PLATFORM PROVIDERS MUST BALANCE THE NEEDS OF CONSTITUENTS

Amazon also must balance the needs of sellers and buyers. Allowing negative reviews of products is often not popular with publishers, but like Google, Amazon is focused on long-term customer loyalty, not short-term profits. Amazon's opinion, which is embedded in their selling platform, is that helping your customers make good buying decisions is more important than making any one particular sale.

Backbone decisions can be dictated from above (for example, the way Apple dictates standards for its App Store) or agreed upon by consensus (for example, the way web standards are developed). What's most important about backbone decisions is that they focus on the connections *between* pods rather than *within* pods. In other words, a pod can do what it likes internally, but when it shares or receives information, it needs to speak the same language as other pods.

To truly enable pods, backbones should be as lightweight as possible. Consider this: the US military will be using standard Internet protocol as the backbone for its net-centric warfare strategy, a podular approach to military operations. If Internet protocol is secure enough for the US military, it's probably secure enough for you.

YOU DON'T HAVE TO BE BIG

You don't have to be a big company to create a powerful platform. You just have to create something that's valuable and supports people in their work.

37signals is a small software company with fewer than 30 full-time employees. In 2003, David Heinemeier Hansson of 37signals was working on the company's core software product, Basecamp, a web-based project-management application. He was writing code in a language called Ruby, first created in Japan in the early 1990s. As he worked, Heinemeier Hansson developed a series of libraries and frameworks that made it easier for him to do the work. At some point about halfway through the project, he realized that the tools he had created constituted a work environment that made it much easier to program web applications. So he decided to share it with other developers.

He open-sourced the framework and called it Ruby on Rails. Rails was an immediate hit with programmers, because it allowed them to do more work more elegantly and efficiently than they could in any other language.

The developer community that rallied around Rails helped build out and improve the framework, adding new functionality, fixing bugs, adding patches, and so on. By sharing the Rails platform with a developer community, 37signals was able to recruit an army of developers that collectively extended and strengthened it in ways that the company never could have done by itself. And giving the code away cost them nothing. Says Heinemeier Hansson:

> I'm going to be no poorer because I shared this open source software that I developed anyway. I needed it already. So if I give it away after it's already done, what am I losing? Exactly nothing. I'm gaining a ton of stuff though. I'm putting this into a wonderful, beautiful commons and everybody else is doing the same thing and all the actors walk away from that richer.

It also turned out to be a great way to attract new talent. Many prominent figures in the open source Rails developer community have since become employees at 37signals.

37signals doesn't sell services or commercial licenses for the framework. They simply share it and use it themselves to get work done. All of their software is built on Rails, and thanks to the worldwide development community, their software is better, faster, and stronger than anything they could have accomplished on their own.

Because Rails was ready to go, it made it much easier for web developers to get new applications up and running quickly. Its popularity grew rapidly. In 2007, Apple shipped Rails with its Mac OS. The Rails platform has become one of the most common development platforms in the web world today, used by Twitter, Hulu, Shopify, and other web-based service providers, large and small, all over the world.

In a *Chicago Tribune* interview, Heienemeier Hansson's partner Jason Fried said, "That's one way to stay small, let other people do your work for you. I think people who think about proprietary technologies are thinking in the Old World."

WELL-DESIGNED PLATFORMS ABSORB VARIETY

Amazon realized they would never be able to stock everything on the planet all by themselves. That was why they created Amazon Marketplace, a platform that allows anyone to sell their stuff on Amazon. They made it so simple that anyone can do it. By creating a platform and supporting this huge network of dealers, they can absorb a huge amount of complexity, and they can scale that indefinitely (or until they run out of merchants). They are moving complexity from inside the company to outside, and they are distributing local control to their merchant partners.

Google does the same thing with Adwords. They created a simple system that allows anyone to create an ad. They basically created a way for their customers to do their own work and manage their own campaigns. Again, they are shifting complexity, putting the control in the hands of customers and creating a platform on which they can do the work.

Apple has simplified its devices and operating system and outsourced the work of building apps and content to a network of developers.

Facebook has done the same. They focus on the core set of social networking services and let others do the rest. Customers create the content by updating their status, liking things, uploading photos, and so on. App developers create the applications. Advertisers develop and deploy their own ads. Facebook makes it super easy to do all these things. And once again, they have distributed control of the system to customers and partners so those folks can manage the complexity of the system.

With this kind of approach, a company can avoid many of the conflicting constraints that come with growth. Complexity can be managed locally and doesn't have to be controlled by the organization.

NOTES FOR CHAPTER FIFTEEN

US MILITARY INTERNET PROTOCOL
Next-Generation Internet Protocol to Enable Net-Centric Operations, US Department of Defense, news release no. 413–03, June 13, 2003.

RUBY ON RAILS
David Heinemeier Hansson, "Good Programming is Like Good Writing," *BigThink*, August 3, 2010, *http://bigthink.com/ideas/21598*.

PROPRIETARY TECHNOLOGIES
Miriah Meyer, "Gamer cracks code, finds jewel," *The Chicago Tribune*, August 28, 2006.

You can't make a recipe for something as complicated as surgery. Instead, you can make a recipe for how to have a team that's prepared for the unexpected.

—*Atul Gawande, physician & journalist*

CHAPTER SIXTEEN

How connected companies learn

Connected companies grow and learn over time. Like all life forms and complex systems, their growth is governed by natural rhythms and patterns. As individuals and teams learn, they must find ways to share their knowledge with the larger community. As communities learn, platforms must learn how to support them.

THE GROWTH SPIRAL

All learning and improvement begins with action. For example, as a child, you might touch a hot stove. Action leads to feedback and discovery: in this case, you discover that the action led to pain, burning, and discomfort. Based on this feedback, you start thinking about new ways of interacting with your environment. Based on your reflection, you start to do things differently. Over time, this leads you closer and closer to your ideal relationship with your surroundings.

The entire process is a growth spiral called *successive approximation*. Successive approximation is the secret sauce that makes methods like agile programming work so well. It's the same process that is at work when you have a conversation.

Successive approximation works because—unlike many business thinking, planning, and execution activities—it's easy and natural. We do it instinctively.

The same process is at work in all learning and at all levels, from a child learning to walk to a scientist exploring the laws of the universe.

Organizational learning is an emergent property that manifests itself when growth spirals are happening at all levels.

LEVEL ONE: HOW ENTREPRENEURS LEARN

"The best way to predict the future is to invent it." – *Alan Kay*

People are naturally creative. It's the nature of our species to invent. But many people, especially in large organizations, have had the creativity trained out of them. If you want an organization that is capable of learning and growth, you will have to find ways to unleash the inherent creativity and innovative potential of your people. You need entrepreneurs.

Entrepreneurs are one of the most important engines of economic growth, and yet they are one of the least-studied aspects of business and management.

One difficulty in studying entrepreneurial success is the challenge of revisionist history. Many entrepreneurs are natural storytellers, and while this is certainly one of the reasons for their success, they also have a tendency to look at the past through rose-colored glasses. As Steve Jobs said in his famous speech to Stanford graduates, it's much easier to connect the dots looking backward than it is to connect them looking forward. Whether entrepreneurs are telling a success story or a failure story, they tend to introduce a lot of bias.

Management researcher Saras Sarasvathy, recognizing this problem, found a unique way to understand how entrepreneurs tick. Instead of asking them to tell her about their past successes and failures, she presented them with new situations that represented the kinds of challenges entrepreneurs are likely to face in creating and growing a business. She asked them questions and asked them to think out loud about how they would tackle those challenges.

What she found was very different from traditional assumptions about entrepreneurs. Entrepreneurs do exactly the opposite of what is taught in most management courses and business schools.

Traditional business approaches emphasize market research, predictions, capital investment, and return on investment over time. They focus on first creating goals, and then building the capabilities to achieve those goals. In the traditional management model, entrepreneurs develop an idea and then "pitch" it to investors to get the funding they need to make that idea a reality. This is kind of like asking mom and dad for money instead of getting a job and earning the money for yourself.

SARAS SARASVATHY

Entrepreneurs hate asking mom and dad for money, and they only do it as a last resort.

Instead, entrepreneurs focus on the capabilities they have and ask the question: "Given what is currently under my control, what kinds of things could I do in the world?" Instead of looking for money, they focus on the means they have at hand and what they can afford to lose.

PLAN ⟶ O GOAL

causal reasoning

MEANS ⟶ O POSSIBLE GOALS

effectual reasoning

Sarasvathy has summarized her research into something she calls the entrepreneurial method. It works like this:

1. Expert entrepreneurs do not start with predictions. They start with what they care about, what they know, and who they know. They initiate a process of learning by interacting with people, showing them prototypes, and asking them questions.

2. As they interact with people, they seek commitment. Some of the people will be interested enough in the idea to get involved—either joining the project or committing resources to it in some way.

3. As people get involved, the project gains momentum, new capabilities, and new people who have goals of their own. The entrepreneur will adjust the goals of the project based on the new people and their goals and capabilities.

4. As resources accumulate, this constellation of capabilities and goals begins to coalesce into a working model, and possibly a new and innovative offering.

The bottom line is that entrepreneurs focus on things that are within their direct control and try to make things happen. If life gives you lemons, you make lemonade.

We have a tradition of making heroes out of entrepreneurs: people like Richard Branson of Virgin Media, Steve Jobs of Apple, and Jeff Bezos of Amazon. And indeed, they are amazing people. But they can also be intimidating. The deification of entrepreneurs can lead to a feeling of helplessness, the idea that we as individuals aren't smart enough or visionary enough to pull it off.

But the powerful message here is that anyone can be an entrepreneur. An entrepreneur isn't a kind of person; it's a method that anyone can follow. It's a way of looking at the world, a way of being. And we can all do it.

It doesn't take a genius. What it takes is a bias for action, a willingness to work with what you've got, to experiment, and to engage people in collective action.

The logic of innovation is simple: work with what you have, seek commitments from others, evolve goals from individual to mutual, grow, and gain momentum. If you fail, move on.

LEVEL TWO: HOW ORGANIZATIONS LEARN

All group learning starts at the level of the individual. Individual knowledge is highly personal, based on concrete actions within a particular context. But knowledge cannot be shared unless it can be amplified at the group or organizational level. For learning to be shared, it must somehow make the leap from the individual who first learned it to others in the group.

TACIT AND EXPLICIT KNOWLEDGE

Knowledge can be classified into two categories: *explicit knowledge*, which can be counted, quantified, documented, and easily shared, and *tacit knowledge*, which includes things that are difficult to measure and share, like expertise, technical know-how, informal relationships, intuition, mental models, beliefs, and trust. It is tacit knowledge that constitutes our understanding of reality, and tacit knowledge makes up the bulk of the knowledge in most organizations. As the saying goes, the company's intellectual property walks out the door every evening.

The learning challenge for the company comes from the dynamic relationship between the two forms of knowledge. Tacit knowledge is where the action is, and in most cases, it's the people with the tacit knowledge that deliver the results. But the only way tacit knowledge can be broadly shared is by translating it into explicit knowledge—a very difficult task that very few companies have mastered.

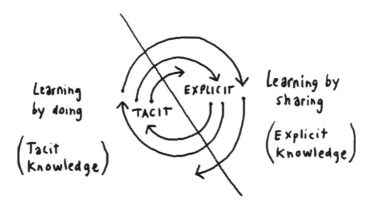

One way to solve this problem is apprenticeship. Consider the newspaper business: when a rookie journalist is assigned a story, she will go out, do the legwork, and come up with a first draft. Then she will sit down with an editor (a former journalist) who goes through the story, line by line—usually at the same terminal at the same time—asking questions that he feels are unanswered by the story. The editor then rewrites the story while the reporter watches (and, hopefully, learns). If there are still unanswered questions, the reporter must go back to the original sources and get those questions answered. Journalists learn slowly over long periods of time, in numerous learning loops of action, feedback, and reflection. Since the process at a newspaper is repeated every day, there are a lot of opportunities to practice, and people learn quickly.

However, the process at work here is not just the cycle of action, feedback, and reflection. Reflection can be a very personal, individual process. An apprenticeship is a way for the master and apprentice to share the growth spiral, by making tacit knowledge explicit and then translating it back into tacit knowledge again.

When the journalist comes to the editor with a story, she has represented her "reporting knowledge" explicitly, in the form of a document. When the editor and reporter sit down together to review and rewrite the story, the editor is making his tacit knowledge explicit in the form of the rewrite and the questions he asks. When the journalist goes out in the field again to write her next story, she will try to internalize that knowledge and write a better story, and the cycle begins again.

Here's another way to think of it: let's say you are a cook and you like to experiment in the kitchen. One day, you are fooling around in the kitchen, and you come up with a fabulous new dish. Assuming you remember what you did, at this point your learning has become personal, tacit knowledge. Now suppose you want to share that knowledge with a friend. To do that, you will need to find some way to make that knowledge explicit. If it's a difficult or tricky process, you might invite your friend over to show him. If it's relatively simple, you might write down the recipe. Either way, you are making your tacit knowledge explicit so that it can be shared.

Now imagine it was a difficult dish and you had to demonstrate it by showing your friend in person. If your friend wants to be able to replicate that process himself, he will need to try it. He might need to try it several times before getting it right. In this way, your friend is translating the explicit knowledge that you shared back into tacit knowledge.

The problem in most hierarchical organizations is that the majority of the focus is on measuring explicit knowledge—things that are easily counted and quantified. This means that most of the real knowledge and learning in the organization is stripped out as information is abstracted into numbers and moved up the org chart. By the time information reaches the top, senior leaders can only see results and cannot get a deep understanding of what is happening at the edge. Yet the leaders often feel that, based on these abstracted numbers, they are more qualified to make decisions than the people at the front line who are dealing with customer situations on a daily basis.

Hierarchical organizations have a hard time learning because their focus on explicit information, which is easily counted and processed, makes it easy to ignore the real organizational knowledge that exists on the ground.

This is why the best military leaders spend time at the front line mingling with the rank and file. In order to make good decisions, they can't just look at reports; they need to know what's going on.

LEARNING FIELDS

In most organizations, the people who best understand the environment are front-line workers and customers. But their knowledge is tacit, based on experience, and not always easy to share with others. In most organizations, this valuable tacit knowledge is trapped at the edge of the company and never makes the leap to the rest of the organization.

Since organizations are focused on efficiency, they want to optimize the time people spend in operational activities. When people don't have time to socialize and reflect, their knowledge ends up trapped in pockets and silos.

To translate individual learning into organizational learning, companies must create learning fields: times and/or spaces that are designated for learning.

An apprenticeship is one kind of learning field. A team is another kind of learning field, because the action is shared among the members of the team.

This kind of growth system has been a standard practice in knowledge-intensive professions for hundreds of years. When a job requires a lot of experience and creativity, people learn by apprenticing themselves to others who are more experienced, and they learn by doing. Think of a medical intern in a hospital, a lawyer in a firm, or the patrol cops in your favorite police drama. They always team up the rookie cop with the experienced veteran so the new cop can learn the ropes.

If you want the learning that happens in a team to be shared among teams, you will need to create learning fields outside the team so the organization as a whole learns. One example is the GE Work-Out, in which front-line workers come off the line to share ideas and suggest improvements.

IN GE WORK-OUTS, WORKERS COME OFF THE LINE TO SHARE IMPROVEMENT IDEAS.

The idea behind Work-Outs is to gather together the people who have the tacit knowledge and give them some time outside the system to reflect on it, share ideas, and think about improvement. As the name implies, the idea is to take unnecessary work out of the system. Managers are not allowed in the room, because it changes the dynamic and makes it more difficult to get ideas out in the open. In *Jack Welch, in Jack: Straight from the Gut,* former GE CEO Jack Welch writes:

> Work-Out was patterned after the traditional New England town meeting. Groups of 40 to 100 employees were invited to share their views on the business and the bureaucracy that got in their way, particularly approvals, reports, meetings, and measurements... A typical Work-Out lasted two to three days. It started with a presentation by the manager who might issue a challenge or outline a broad agenda and then leave. Without the boss present and with a facilitator to grease the discussions, employees were asked to list problems, debate solutions, and be prepared to sell their ideas when the boss returned.

Managers can't duck the ideas that come from a Work-Out. They are expected to give an on-the-spot, yes or no decision on at least 75% of the ideas. If they can't make a decision on the spot, they must commit to making one by an agreed deadline. Welch says:

It was absolutely mind-blowing to see two union guys arguing over a manufacturing process improvement. Imagine kids just out of college with shiny new degrees trying to fix this manufacturing process. They wouldn't have a chance. Here were the guys with experience, helping us fix things. Small wonder that people began to forget their roles. They started speaking up everywhere.

GE Work-Outs are learning fields, explicitly created by the company to create the space and time for front-line workers to share their tacit knowledge so the company can learn and improve.

Communities of practice are learning fields that share a concern within or across organizations. By interacting on an ongoing basis, they deepen their knowledge and experience over time.

In a community of practice, individuals socialize and externalize their experiences through conversations that may be tenuous at first. Knowledge is born out of ambiguity and redundant information, seeing things from multiple perspectives and finding common themes. But the conversations also define and strengthen the community.

TAIICHI OHNO

Tacit knowledge gained in the field is made explicit through dialogue and rich information sharing, where it is examined and articulated in multiple ways and from multiple perspectives. Once information is explicit, it can be shared with the rest of the organization at a higher level. It can be captured in a shared memory system, allowing it to be shared across the community. As other units try to apply this new knowledge in different contexts, they once again internalize it by doing, trying, copying others, and mimicking behavior. Eventually, new practices become internalized and habitual.

The resulting explicit knowledge is combined and integrated with existing knowledge, and a shared memory and set of mental models is the result.

Organizations are made up of people, and that's how they learn: through the interactions of their people. Toyota's Taiichi Ohno and quality guru W. Edwards Deming encouraged workers to study the system in which they were working. The more that workers can participate directly in the design and improvement of a system, the more the organization can learn and adapt to change. A learning system is always under examination and is always open to improvement.

LEVEL THREE: HOW PLATFORMS LEARN

When things are changing fast, learning must keep up. But not all things change at the same speed. Some things change far more slowly than others.

A company's fast-learning elements and slow-learning elements work best as two complementary forms of organization—pods and platforms—that learn and grow differently. As platforms learn and grow over time, they provide the scaffolding for pods to reach higher and higher.

To get an idea of how platforms learn and coevolve with their constituents, think about how a small settlement becomes a town and how a town becomes a city. The pioneers come first. They carve out a space. Later, as the community grows, people work together to weave the platforms—like schools, police, roads, and plumbing—that support their common purpose.

PACE LAYERS

Pace layering comes from the world of architecture. It was first articulated by Stuart Brand in *How Buildings Learn: What Happens After They're Built* (Penguin Books). The idea is that not everything changes at the same pace. For example, a city's basic infrastructure grid—like sewers, electric grid, roads, and so on—may need maintenance, but it remains relatively constant and doesn't change so much over time. The location or site of a building is constant, too: the address of a building in Manhattan may remain unchanged, even if the building itself is torn down and rebuilt from scratch.

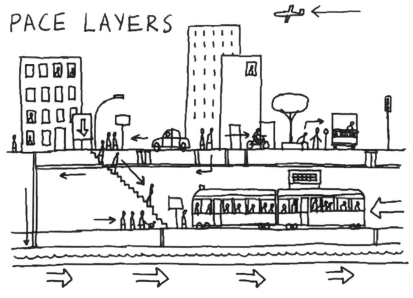

PACE LAYERS

THINGS DON'T CHANGE AT THE SAME PACE

The next layer up in the pace-layer hierarchy is the basic structure of a building—foundation and load-bearing walls—which is expensive and time-consuming to change. So a building's structure tends to remain constant over time. But inside a building are some basic support services, like plumbing, electrical wiring, heating, air conditioning, and elevators, that wear out faster than buildings and occasionally need to be repaired, upgraded, or replaced.

As we move up the pace-layer hierarchy, we find that the rate of change increases gradually, from the things at the bottom—like the land, the building itself, and its address—that change very slowly, to the things at the top—like the building's tenants and uses—which change more frequently. A company might start as a bank or brewery and later evolve into a shopping mall or an office building.

Your company has pace layers, too, like an onion, with many layers between the core and the surface. At the base are the things that are the most constant, like the purpose of the company, and the job you do for customers. At the edge of the company is the front line, the line of interaction, where things may be changing very fast and you are dealing with a high degree of variability. In between are the things that connect the core purpose with the daily interactions and activities at the edge: things like support systems, management practices, technologies, information storage, processing and retrieval, methods, approaches, and so on.

The trick to designing a connected company is to think in pace layers, arranging the layers for maximum flexibility and adaptability. Where change and variability are high, you want to be flexible and adaptive to change. Where change and variability are low, you want to find ways to create stable, reliable platforms to support the layers higher up in the pace-layer hierarchy.

FRONT STAGE AND BACK STAGE

There's a concept in service design called the front stage and back stage. The front stage is where you interact directly with customers, like the dining room in a restaurant, or an ATM, or a web page at Amazon. The back stage includes the services and systems that support the front stage, like the restaurant's kitchen, the bank's transaction systems, and Amazon's warehouses and distribution system.

The front stage and the back stage depend on each other to be successful, but they may operate very differently. An engineer developing web services for Amazon has a very different job than someone who works in an Amazon warehouse.

On the front stage, where change and variety are high, you generally want to be able to absorb a lot of variety, and you want those elements of the business to be able to evolve as rapidly as their external environment requires. On the back stage, things like consistency and reliability are often more important than flexibility. Like the foundations and walls of a building, they provide the stability that supports the faster-changing layers that depend on them.

When it comes to the back stage, you want stability. You want support. Think about the foundational, public systems that support your business, like roads, telephone and internet services, the financial system, and so on. You don't want these things to be changing constantly. For example, when the value of a currency fluctuates wildly, the economic systems it supports fly into a tailspin.

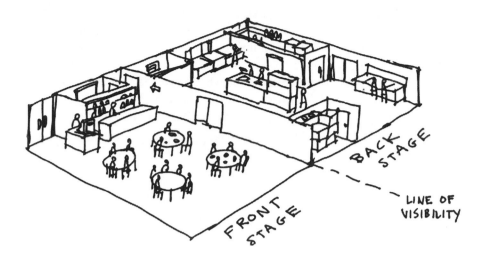

The decision to contain or absorb variety is not simply an either/or choice. Most strategies will require companies to do both: to reduce variety in some areas while absorbing it in others.

BALANCING THE FRONT STAGE AND THE BACK STAGE

In a 2009 paper, Robert Glushko and Lindsay Tabas use the hotel check-in as an example of how the front and back stages need each other.

Imagine you arrive at a hotel and the person at the hotel desk is not able to find your reservation. That is, your reservation was made, but somehow lost by the hotel. This is a back-stage failure that affects front-stage performance. If your reservation is lost and no rooms are available, the customer experience is likely to fail. There is not much the desk person can do other than try to find you a room at another hotel.

Consider the way that Amazon balances front-stage and back-stage operations. Amazon's front stage is its customer-facing website. Amazon can expect that the level of change on the web is likely to remain volatile for some time. Constant innovation in online services will cause customer expectations to evolve accordingly. So it makes sense for Amazon's web-development approach to be highly adaptive and flexible, with lots of room for creative experiments and innovation.

But radical, disruptive innovations on the fulfillment side of Amazon's business are less likely. It's reasonable to predict that customers will continue to want fast, efficient delivery, and that warehousing, shipping, and logistics, because they involve large investments and existing physical infrastructure (ships, trucks, planes, railroads, and so on), won't change anywhere near as rapidly as online services. So it makes sense for Amazon to focus on reducing variety through standards and controls in its back-stage operations, while maintaining maximum adaptability on its front stage with customers. And indeed, Amazon web developers have a very different work experience than workers in an Amazon distribution center, although the company's cost-focused, thrifty culture is in evidence throughout.

When Amazon bought Zappos, it seemed like a strange marriage. At first glance, the companies couldn't be more different when it comes to their approach to customer service. Amazon's approach is, "If the customer is contacting us, there's something wrong." Zappos is delighted when customers call. Amazon Founder and CEO Jeff Bezos explains the difference:

> Every time a customer contacts us, we see it as a defect. I've been saying for many, many years, people should talk to their friends, not their merchants. And so we use all of our customer service information to find the root cause of any customer contact. What went wrong? Why did that person have to call? Why aren't they spending that time talking to their family instead of talking to us? How do we fix it? Zappos takes a completely different approach. You call them and ask them for a pizza, and they'll get out the *Yellow Pages* for you.

So if Amazon doesn't want to absorb Zappos' culture, why buy them? If you look at this through a front-stage/back-stage lens, it becomes clear. Zappos' back stage is the same as Amazon's—customers care about fast and efficient delivery and returns. So it makes sense for Amazon and Zappos to consolidate their back-stage operations to achieve economies of scale and operational efficiency.

On the front stage, Zappos gives Amazon greater variety and optionality. Who's to say if there's a better business in high-touch or high-tech approaches to serving customers? Well, if you don't know, why not try both? In this way, Amazon has a chance to be both the low-cost Walmart and the high-touch Nordstrom of the Web, with the added advantage of a combined, world-class back-stage logistics and delivery system that improves the cost effectiveness and global reach of both companies. Service delivery depends on the ability of the front stage to react creatively and proactively to situations as they come up. But it also depends on the ability of the back stage to support the front stage.

MAKING PLATFORM DECISIONS

When determining how to make these strategic tradeoffs, look at your company's business ecosystem and ask, "Where in the system do we expect a lot of variety, and where do we expect things to remain relatively stable?" In areas where you expect a lot of variety, say, due to changing customer preferences or rapid technological change, efforts to reduce variety are likely to be wasted; by the time you have perfected an approach, the environment around you will have changed. It's like trying to build a perfect sandcastle when the tide's coming in. You're going to have to rebuild it anyway.

Organizational learning starts with individuals and teams, interacting directly with customers and the market. Individual learning becomes organizational learning when the company makes space for reflection, in which individuals and groups throughout the organization can share their ideas and experiences and make them explicit. Some of that knowledge will be so helpful or valuable that it will make sense to build it into the platforms that support the entire community.

Platform decisions must balance individual freedom with the common good in the way that makes the most sense for what the community is trying to achieve. It helps to have decision criteria that are based on your overall purpose. Bezos explains:

> The way we think about it is, on those big things, we want to be stubborn on the vision and flexible about the details.
>
> That's what happened in our third-party selling thing. We launched Auctions and that didn't work. Then we launched zShops and that didn't work. Finally, we launched Marketplace, which is very successful.
>
> We were stubborn on the vision: we wanted a place where we could have universal selection, and we didn't believe that we could have universal selection without a whole bunch of third parties helping us. We knew we had to figure out a way to get third parties to help us. What we finally figured out, the reason Marketplace worked when Auctions did not, was that Marketplace was convenient. It was still one-click shopping, and our customers didn't want to do auctions. They were busy. They wanted to come in find what they want, buy it, and go away.

HOW PLATFORMS LEARN

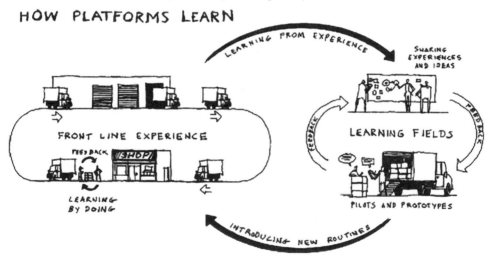

Think of pace layers as a way to separate faster learning from slower learning. Fast and flexible learning becomes knowledge, and with time, slower-changing knowledge can become routine, habitual behavior.

Over time, as routines become embedded in a platform, they operate unthinkingly, unconsciously, like the autonomic functions in your body. You don't consciously focus on your breathing or your heartbeat, but they are there to support you all the same.

This is where our old friend, the hierarchical, bureaucratic organization, can actually be quite valuable and useful. A bureaucracy is an autonomic system, unthinking and unaware.

Bureaucratic hierarchies are good for routine work, while podular networks function well in volatile or changing conditions. Balancing the two is the province and challenge of government.

GROWTH SPIRALS IN THE CONNECTED COMPANY

If you think of the connected company as a living organism, then learning happens as ongoing activity gradually transforms into knowledge and experience.

The individuals who make up the company are its senses, and their learning experiences are based on the company's actions in the world. Learning fields like teams and communities of practice are the company's short-term memory, where it reflects on its experiences and makes sense of the world, formulating thoughts and hypotheses. Platforms are the company's long-term memory, where knowledge and experience is stored and hard-coded into habits, routines, and autonomic functions.

NOTES FOR CHAPTER SIXTEEN

HOTEL CHECK-INS
"Designing Service Systems by Bridging the 'Front stage' and 'Back stage,'" by Robert J. Glushko and Lindsay Tabas, *Information Systems and E-Business Management*, 7, no. 4 (September 2009): 407–427.

CUSTOMER SERVICE AT AMAZON VS ZAPPOS
Steven Levy, "Jeff Bezos Owns the Web in More Ways Than You Think," *Wired*, November 13, 2011.

AMAZON AUCTIONS, ZSHOPS, AND MARKETPLACE
Consumer Reports Talks with Amazon.com, recorded live on May 11, 2011, *http://www.ustream.tv/recorded/14630179*.

An organization's data is found in its computer systems, but a company's intelligence is found in its biological and social systems.

—*Valdis Krebs, researcher & management consultant*

CHAPTER SEVENTEEN

Power and control in networks

Connected companies are networks that live within other networks. To be effective in a networked world requires different ways of thinking and acting. It's less about predictability and control, and more about awareness, influence, and compatibility.

LINKING THINGS CHANGES THEM

Networks change things. When things are linked together, they behave differently. Networks exhibit complex, unpredictable, and sometimes volatile behavior.

The first step in adapting to a networked environment is to understand the characteristics of networks. What is a network? Who holds the power in a network and how do they wield it? What must companies do in order to succeed in a networked environment?

WHEN THINGS ARE LINKED THEY BEHAVE DIFFERENTLY

WHAT IS A SOCIAL NETWORK?

At the most basic level, a network is simply a set of nodes and links (the connections between the nodes). Networks abound in daily life. The electrical grid that supplies power to your house is a network, as are the city streets that you use to go to work.

In this case, we are particularly interested in social networks, in which people and organizations are the nodes, and the connections between them—formal, informal, logical, and emotional—are the links. Social networks include schools, workplaces, churches, clubs, and industry associations, as well as animal networks like flocks, colonies, hives, herds, packs, prides, pods, troops, and so on.

Social networks are patterns of behavior and interaction. As behaviors are repeated, they form stronger associations over time. You form strong bonds with the people in your life with whom you spend the most time. Networks also connect and overlap. You have your network of school friends, your team at work, your neighbors, peers in your industry, and so on. A teammate at work who is also a personal friend and a neighbor forms a particularly strong connection.

Social networks are *interdependent*: members of a network depend on each other for success. Networks can be survival strategies for their members. Both animals and people band together to do things they could not do by themselves. Crows, for example, will band together to harass a predator that none of them could defy alone. Lions will cooperate in hunting parties, to encircle and drive their prey toward companions. And people band together in organizations to achieve a wide variety of shared objectives.

Most real-life networks like this fall into a very specific category called *small-world networks*.

SMALL WORLDS

A small-world network is a combination of densely-connected clusters that are loosely connected with each other.

For example, consider a basketball league. Each team is a densely connected cluster, because team members interact frequently, during every practice and every game. The connections formed by all this activity are called *strong ties*. The connections between the teams are not so strong, because teams interact with each other less frequently. These kinds of connections are called *weak ties*.

Another example of a small-world network is a shopping district, where each store is densely connected internally, because employees see each other every day, but loosely-connected with other stores—for example, because the owners meet once a month to discuss their shared interests in the maintenance and development of the district.

Within a small-world network, the number of connections between any two nodes tends to be quite small. If you don't know someone in your small-world network, the chances are good that you have a connection that can introduce you. Groups of experts, industry associations, schools, and churches all fall into this category. People often go to industry conventions, for example, to make more connections within their small-world network.

A SMALL-WORLD NETWORK

Network researcher Ron Burt has identified two types of activities that create value in small-world networks: *brokerage* and *closure*.

Brokerage is about developing the weak ties: building bridges and relationships between clusters. Brokers are in a position to see the differences between groups, to cross-pollinate ideas, and to develop the differences into new ideas and opportunities.

Closure is about developing the strong ties: building alignment, trust, reputation, and community within the clusters. Trust builders are in a position to understand the deep connections that bond people together and give them common identity and purpose.

These two kinds of activity, bridging and trust building, demonstrate two very different ways in which people and organizations can bring value to a network. Bridging leads to innovation, and trust building leads to group performance.

There is a delicate balance between brokerage and closure. Too much closure and a group becomes subject to groupthink, reinforcing group opinions in an of echo chamber of agreement, tending to perpetuate the status quo. Not enough closure and the group will lose the trust and cohesion that makes it function as a group.

This combination of dense clusters with strong ties with brokers who maintain loose connections between them leads to many performance benefits, including collaboration, creativity, and shared patterns of work. High clustering in business alliances leads to innovation, which is one of the reasons you will find industries clustering together in geographic regions, like technology in Silicon Valley, publishing in New York, and clothing in Milan.

The value that comes from these activities is known as *social capital*. Like every other form of capital, social capital represents stored value—in this case, relationship value—that can be translated into meaningful and tangible benefits.

SCALE-FREE NETWORKS

Networks constantly change and evolve. Existing nodes develop new links and shed old ones, while new nodes continually join the network. As small-world networks grow and connect to other small-world networks, a higher-order pattern emerges. A few nodes become hubs, super-connected relative to the other nodes. This kind of network is called a *scale-free network*, because no matter how large the network grows, the relative distribution of ordinary nodes and hubs doesn't change over time.

Network theorist Albert-László Barabás discovered the mechanism that governs the growth of scale-free networks, called *preferential attachment*. New nodes don't enter a network and connect randomly to other nodes. When a new node enters a network, it will prefer to connect with nodes that are already well-connected. Over time, highly-connected nodes continue to acquire more links than those that are less connected. The result of this growth pattern is that nodes that are rich in links continually get richer relative to their peers.

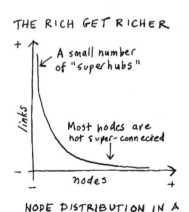

THE RICH GET RICHER

A small number of "superhubs"

links

Most nodes are not super-connected

nodes

NODE DISTRIBUTION IN A SCALE-FREE NETWORK

Examples abound. If you want to start a software firm, it makes sense to start it in Silicon Valley because that area is a locus of talent and knowledge. Financial firms locate on Wall Street. Farmers wanting to sell produce are better off going to a farmers' market. Even though they are clustered with competitors, the increase in customer traffic makes up for the difference.

Developers of malls and business parks use the law of preferential attachment to their advantage. Early in the development process, they secure long-term agreements with anchor tenants, who form the initial center of gravity for the network to grow around. Developers subsidize early "seed tenants," often losing money on the first few tenants. As more firms move in and the cluster grows, they raise the rents.

The mechanism of preferential attachment explains the growth and structure of many real-world networks, including transportation networks, trade networks, social networks, and the Internet, where sites like Google, Amazon, and Facebook dominate web traffic like international ports of call.

Social networks, like small-world and scale-free networks, form the deep social structure that underlies the behavior of people and organizations. They are the fundamental organizing principles and mechanisms by which we coordinate our activities and act collectively to do things.

When people organize themselves collectively to get things done, this deep social structure is always a part of the picture. The way people organize—the design of their organization—will determine what that organization can accomplish.

POWER AND CONTROL IN NETWORKS

Networks are interdependent and control is distributed. Power in networks accrues to those who have connections, can easily access them, and can make or deny connections to others.

POWER IN NETWORKS

The power of an individual node in any network can be considered along three dimensions: degree, closeness, and betweenness.

Degree is the number of connections a node has to other nodes—for example, the number of people in your family or on your team at work, or the number of "friends" attached to your Facebook account. For an organization, it could be the number of sales affiliates or business partners.

The value of a high degree is potential: the potential to connect and interact with a great number of other nodes in the network.

Closeness is a measure of how easily a node can connect with other nodes. For example, you are probably very close to your team at work because it's easy to connect to them—you can contact any person at any time. But you might be farther away from other people in your company. Some you might be able to catch by walking down the hall or popping into their office, while to see others, you might need an appointment, or you might need to be introduced by a mutual acquaintance. Anyone who has tried to make a connection on LinkedIn knows that the greater the distance, the harder it is to make a connection.

The value of closeness is ease of connection: the shorter the distance between you and other nodes, the fewer network "hops" you need to make, and the easier it is for you to make connections when you need to.

Betweenness indicates the degree to which a node forms a bridge or critical link between other nodes. For example, many executives are protected from distractions by executive assistants or secretaries who act as gatekeepers, controlling access to the executive's time and attention.

The value of betweenness is the power you have to block or grant access to others. The more nodes that depend on you to make connections for them, the greater your potential value to them, and thus the greater your power.

Thus, the most powerful person or organization in any network is one that has a high number of potential connections, all of which are relatively close and thus easily accessible, while at the same time enjoying a position within the network such that it can choose to block or grant access to other nodes.

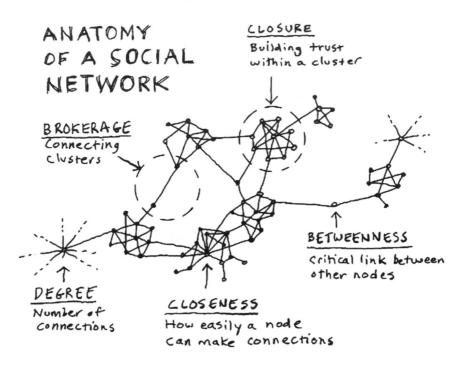

ANATOMY OF A SOCIAL NETWORK

CLOSURE
Building trust within a cluster

BROKERAGE
Connecting clusters

BETWEENNESS
Critical link between other nodes

DEGREE
Number of connections

CLOSENESS
How easily a node can make connections

CONTROL

In hierarchical business systems, control nodes—managers and executives—gain power from their betweenness: they are the critical bridges that connect the top of the hierarchy with the bottom. This is the power of the gatekeeper.

Managers with high betweenness are clearly in powerful positions. Most managers are conduits for information within their companies. Goals, objectives, strategies, and decisions flow downward, while information and feedback from front-line activities flows up. Since managers occupy the nodes through which that information flows, they exert a powerful influence on how events are understood. The way that a manager conveys a company strategy or goal can greatly influence how it is perceived by workers, and the way that a manager conveys information from the field can greatly influence how frontline workers are perceived at the executive level.

But as the number of connections in a network increases, the "betweenness" power of managers decreases. There's a reason for this. More connections create more opportunities to bypass these control nodes, reducing the degree to which the control nodes can limit the flow of information and connection, thus limiting their power.

Starbucks CEO Howard Schultz could do nothing to stop executives from leaking his confidential memo. A restaurant can't change a Yelp review. If you release a movie and it gets bad reviews, that's life. And even the President of the United States can't stop Wikileaks from distributing confidential documents. That's the power of the network.

At the same time that networks tend to reduce the inherent power of betweenness, they also offer more opportunities for nodes to increase their degree and closeness—the number of connections they can easily make with other nodes. As a result, power in networks is more evenly distributed and control more limited than in traditional hierarchical organizations.

The exercise of power in such distributed systems requires an entirely different approach than traditional management, planning, and control.

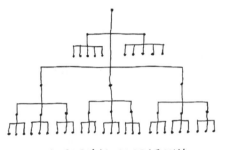

IN A FORMAL HIERARCHY,
BETWEENNESS IS POWER

AS CONNECTIONS INCREASE,
THE POWER OF
BETWEENNESS DIMINISHES

EXERCISING POWER IN NETWORKS

Exercise of power in networks requires high awareness of the network's state, risks, and potential; an ability to influence other nodes; and a high degree of compatibility with existing standards. The greatest power in a network is the degree to which a node can influence or control the platforms and standards that set the rules for connection.

Consider Microsoft's Windows operating system, Apple's iOS mobile operating system, and Amazon's Kindle format. Control of the platform gives these companies powerful influence over software and content providers. When you own the platform, you set the terms.

SITUATION AWARENESS

Situation awareness, like degree, is about optionality. Networks are highly fluid environments—complex, information-rich, and packed with nodes that can detect and respond to events. Opportunities come and go all the time. Like the weather, things can shift and change rapidly with little warning. The more deeply connected you are within the network, the better you will understand its dynamics. The better you understand its dynamics, the better you will be able to spot potential risks and opportunities, increasing the options available to you.

Situation awareness makes it easier to respond in real time to events as they occur. It is even more valuable when it is shared among members of a network, because when nodes have a shared understanding, they can more easily self-organize, collaborate, and coordinate action.

Walmart collects real-time data every time a customer buys something. They can correlate this data with data from other sources, like weather reports and holidays. This is why you will always find an umbrella at a Walmart on a rainy day, and why Walmart doesn't run out of flags on the Fourth of July (in the US, that is).

INFLUENCE

Influence, like closeness, is about capability. Since networks are highly interdependent, success depends on your ability to build strong, trusting, mutually advantageous relationships with other parties in the network. As your reputation improves over time, your influence will increase.

Competitive advantage is important in business, but in networks, you will also find cooperative advantage—significant gains based on cooperative relationships with other nodes in the network.

To build momentum for a network, it is often very advantageous to give a lot away to early adopters. The lower the uncertainty and the easier it is for people to join, the faster the network will grow. Apple gave 70 cents of every 99-cent song sale to recording companies and made iTunes software free to every Mac user in order to jump-start the iTunes network.

Procter & Gamble and Walmart cooperate to combine P&G's deep expertise in market research and product development with Walmart's on-the-ground awareness of in-store purchase activity. This relationship delivers insights for both companies that could never occur within an adversarial relationship.

COMPATIBILITY

Compatibility, like betweenness, is about access. People and organizations join networks because they want to exchange information. They want to share things. Without the ability to connect, there is no network.

More potential connections, along with more ways to connect, means more options for members of the network. High compatibility with other nodes will enable you to do more things: quickly pull in information and resources, connect with complementary services, perform rapid transformations, quickly enter into partnerships, and so on.

Compatibility also lowers risk and uncertainty for new members, making it easier for the network to grow.

For example, if you create a text file in Google Docs, you can save it as a Microsoft Word file. This makes it less risky to upload or create new content in Google Docs. If you create a page on the Web, you can be confident that anyone else on the Web will be able to link to it. When you buy a car, you can be confident that it will be compatible with every gas station because the standards for compatibility have been well established.

THE PLATFORM

The ultimate power position in any network is the power to influence or control the standards for connection. Standards determine what is and is not possible on any network. Standards create the boundaries for the network as a whole, by creating possibilities in some areas while limiting others.

The set of standards and agreements that govern connection in a network are often called the network's platform. Platforms have opinions embedded within their standards—opinions about what is and isn't important. For example, an ATM network places a high importance on security, so it focuses on doing a few simple things in a highly trusted, reliable way. A social network like Twitter places a high value on activity and attention, so it is built to encourage that by making it easier to publish and easier to read.

Developing a strong platform requires a high degree of network fluency—situation awareness, influence, compatibility—and a fair amount of luck.

Without situation awareness, it is unlikely that an organization will recognize and seize the opportunity to create a platform in the first place. And certainly, situation awareness is a requirement for any company to survive the turbulent and frequent shifts in sentiment that constantly ripple through any network.

Strong influence is necessary to convince others to adopt the platform standards, and compatibility is important, too, because new members must be assured that they will increase their overall connectivity by joining the platform.

Exercising platform power is a delicate and political balancing act, because platform providers and network members are interdependent. A platform's power comes from the collective power of its members. The more people and organizations that depend on a platform, the greater its power; but any platform is only as powerful as the people and companies that depend on it. If members decide to abandon a platform, it can become a ghost town. Consider AOL and MySpace.

Facebook developers are dependent on Facebook for the platform they use to build, sell, distribute and manage their services. Thus, Facebook has a great degree of power over the network.

But even Facebook, as powerful as it is, depends on developers as much as the developers depend on it. If developers abandon Facebook's platform, Facebook will be in trouble.

The best platform approach is to extract enough value from the network members to cover your costs, and then share the benefits with members.

THREE PRINCIPLES OF NETWORK POWER

All of this leads us to three guiding principles. Network power is about detection and response, as well as the ability to influence the overall network itself.

1. *The detection principle:* The greater your situation awareness, the more you will be able to detect changes in the environment.

2. *The response principle:* The greater your influence and compatibility, the more effectively you will be able to respond to change.

3. *The platform principle:* The more you can influence the platform, the greater your influence over the network as a whole will be.

NOTES FOR CHAPTER SEVENTEEN

For the thoughts in this chapter, I am indebted to the works of Valdis Krebs, especially "Power in Networks," *http://orgnet.com/PowerInNetworks.pdf,* 2004, and the works of Ronald S. Burt (*Structural Holes,* Cambridge, Massachusetts: Harvard University Press, 1995), and *Brokerage and Closure* (New York: Oxford University Press, 2005).

PART FOUR

How do you lead a connected company?

Connected companies are living, learning networks that live within larger networks. Power in networks comes from awareness and influence, not control. Leaders must create an environment of clarity, trust, and shared purpose, while management focuses on designing and tuning the system that supports learning and performance.

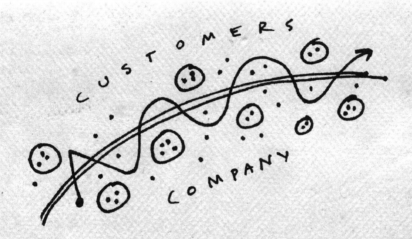

EDGE LEADERSHIP

The best executive is the one who has sense enough to pick good men to do what he wants done, and self-restraint to keep from meddling with them while they do it.

—*Theodore Roosevelt, 26th US President*

CHAPTER EIGHTEEN

Strategy as a pool of experiments

Strategy is usually considered the province of senior executives. But senior executives are in some ways the least qualified to envision the future, because they are the most invested in the past and the least likely to be around in the long term. In a connected company, strategy happens at all levels, across diverse groups and different time scales, generating a rich pool of experiments for senior leaders to draw from.

STRATEGIES DON'T LAST FOREVER

Some things, like the job you do for customers, remain relatively constant over time. Other things, like technology, can be counted on to evolve rapidly and continually create opportunities for companies to disrupt competitors.

GARY HAMEL

Successful strategies can become obsolete. Any successful strategy will attract copycats. Management expert Gary Hamel calls this phenomenon *strategy decay*.

Therefore, strategies must evolve to some degree over time as circumstances change. Sometimes, slow, incremental change is enough keep you ahead of competitors, so long as the environmental conditions don't change too drastically. But technology is a bitch. It affects every industry, often in ways that are difficult (if not impossible) to anticipate. There's always the possibility that a Napster or a Netflix or a Wikipedia, will arrive to completely disrupt your business or industry.

So it makes sense to have some kind of system that allows you to continually develop options and explore possibilities, so that when the day of disruption does arrive, it finds you ready with a few alternatives in hand. The time to seek those alternatives is now—not later, after a crisis has already arrived.

LET A THOUSAND FLOWERS BLOOM

In *The Origin of Wealth* (Harvard Business Review Press), McKinsey Fellow Eric D. Beinhocker writes:

> Typical strategic planning processes focus on chopping down the branches of the strategy decision tree, eliminating options, and making choices and commitments. In contrast, an evolutionary approach to strategy emphasizes creating choices, keeping options open, and making the tree of possibilities as bushy as possible at any point in time. Options have value. An evolving portfolio of strategic experiments gives the management team more choices, which means better odds that some of the choices will be right.

Management theorist Henry Mintzberg makes a distinction between *deliberate* and *emergent strategy*. Deliberate strategy relies on senior leaders to set goals and develop plans and strategies to achieve them. Emergent strategy is a strategy that emerges from all over the company, over time, as the environment changes and the organization shifts and adapts to apply its strengths to a changing reality. Emergent strategy is an organic approach to growth that lets companies learn and continually develop new strategies over time based on an ongoing culture of hypothesis and experimentation.

Instead of focusing on a single goal, allocating resources, and creating a step-by-step plan to achieve the goal, emergent strategies focus on the company's core capabilities, developing a wide array of options and possibilities so they can pounce on opportunities when they come up. Strategy expert Karl Moore, a colleague of Mintzberg, describes emergent strategy this way: "Let a thousand flowers bloom... lop off the heads of most of the thousand flowers, and scale up those experiments and pilots that work."

Deliberate strategy is goal-oriented. It asks, "What do we want to achieve?" Emergent strategy is means-oriented. It asks, "What is possible, with the means we have at our disposal?"

You can see emergent strategy at work at Amazon, where small-scale experiments proliferate and the company "scales up" a few large-scale experiments, like Amazon Web Services, Kindle, and Amazon Marketplace. You can see it at work at Google, where every employee is encouraged to spend one day a week pursuing experiments of their own making, and a few of the most successful ones, like Google News and Gmail, attract resources and scale to become significant new sources of revenue.

A PORTFOLIO OF EXPERIMENTS

Diversity breeds creativity—ecosystems are richest where habitats and species overlap. With more connections and diversity comes more creativity: diverse communities are more interesting, more provocative, and more stimulating.

An emergent approach to strategy requires a large and diverse pool of ideas. Beinhocker writes, "Evolution needs a superfecundity of business plans to do its work." One problem with setting strategy at the top is that senior executives are the most likely to be invested in past success, and hence the least likely to come up with truly innovative ideas.

In *What Matters Now: How to Win in a World of Relentless Change, Ferocious Competition, and Unstoppable Innovation* (Jossey-Bass), Gary Hamel writes:

> Without a lot of exciting new options, managers will inevitably opt for more of the same. That's why renewal depends on a company's ability to generate and test hundreds of new strategic options. There's a power law here: Out of 1,000 crazy ideas, only 100 will merit a small-scale experiment. Of those, only 10 will be worth serious investment, and out of that bundle, only 1 or 2 will have the power to transform a business or spawn a new one. Google gets this. Within its core search business, the company tests more than 5,000 software changes a year and implements around 500.

Emergent strategy requires that the company continually generate a broad range of hypotheses, testing them in small-scale experiments, and feeding the more successful experiments while pruning the failed ones. In order to innovate in a sustainable way, a company should have ongoing bets of all sizes, at all points in the power-law curve—a thousand small, a hundred medium, and one or two large—at any given point in time.

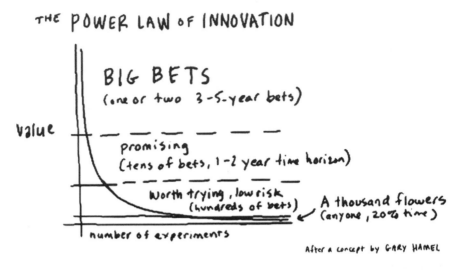

THE POWER LAW OF INNOVATION

BIG BETS
(one or two 3-5-year bets)

Value

promising
(tens of bets, 1-2 year time horizon)

worth trying, low risk
(hundreds of bets)   A thousand flowers
                        (anyone, 20% time)

number of experiments

After a concept by GARY HAMEL

In 2005, Google set a formula for distributing its engineering efforts: 70-20-10. Seventy percent of Google's resources are devoted to improving search and advertising, Google's primary source of revenue and profits. Twenty percent is allotted as free time for people to pursue projects of their own choosing. And ten percent is invested in scaling up the most promising ideas that emerge from the 20% time, the wild cards that could develop into whole new lines of business.

SMALL BETS: SET A LOW BAR FOR INITIAL EXPERIMENTATION

Many companies solicit innovation ideas from employees and customers, but few are successful in generating a large and diverse enough set of ideas to generate valuable insights. This is partly because in many companies, new ideas must run through a harrowing gauntlet of filters before anyone is allowed to make a move.

Companies can increase the number of experiments by lowering the bar. In order to "let a thousand flowers bloom," you need to make it as easy as possible for people to try things.

Diversity requires tolerance for some degree of redundancy and slack in the system. People who are 100% utilized don't have time to generate new ideas. Google and 3M allow employees to spend 20% of their time—that's equivalent to one day a week—exploring ideas for new projects, products, and initiatives. W.L. Gore does the same thing. They call it "dabble time."

Amazon employees are encouraged to continuously experiment, try new things and, test their ideas. CEO Jeff Bezos has said, "Innovation is part and parcel with going down blind alleys. You can't have one without the other. But every once in a while, you go down an alley and it opens up into this huge, broad avenue. And that's so satisfying and, from a shareholder's point of view, so successful, that it makes going down blind alleys worthwhile."

MEDIUM BETS: MANY SOURCES OF FUNDING

Hamel also makes the case that most strategic initiatives rely on a small group of senior decision makers to allocate funding for innovation initiatives. He suggests finding ways to distribute the ability to fund innovation as broadly within the company as possible. As an example, he points to Silicon Valley's rich pool of venture capital investors:

> Imagine what would happen to innovation in Silicon Valley if there were only one venture capital firm. It's not unusual for a would-be entrepreneur to get turned down half a dozen times before finding a willing investor— yet in most companies, it takes only one nyet to kill a project stone dead.

For medium bets, you want to think like a venture capitalist, spreading risk around by making a number of medium-sized bets, with the expectation that only one or two of them will really take off. The idea is to create a market for good ideas, so that a person or team with an innovative idea can shop it around. For example, give managers throughout the company discretionary budgets that can only be used for innovation projects. Let them fund ideas across the organization, not just in their own team.

BIG BETS: THE RESPONSIBILITY OF SENIOR LEADERS

Big bets are the major initiatives that can make or break the future of the company. And big bets are the prerogative—as well as the responsibility—of senior management. Most companies can afford to make only one or two big bets at any point in time.

Investors are skeptical of big bets and will hardly ever endorse them in the early stages. Big bets are even likely to hurt a company's stock price in the short term.

When Jack Welch announced to investors in 1981 that GE would be number one or two in any industry they were in and that this transformation would be driven by a top-to-bottom cultural shift, one investor said, "We don't know what the hell he's talking about."

Apple's decision to go into the retail business in 2001 was another big bet. Investors were skeptical then, too.

In May 2001, as Apple opened their first retail store, *Business Week* analyst Cliff Edwards wrote: "Jobs thinks he can do a better job than experienced retailers... rather than taking on the retailers who ought to be its partners, Apple would do better improving how it works with them."

The same article quoted David A. Goldstein, president of researcher Channel Marketing Corp: "I give them two years before they're turning out the lights on a very painful and expensive mistake."

Arne Alsin of *The Street* wrote:

> It's desperation time in Cupertino, Calif., as Apple is going into the retail store business...This move is fraught with problems...the move into retail takes Apple into an area where it has demonstrated no competence. Now it's going to take on Best Buy and Circuit City? Have the executives at Apple considered the sobering retail experience of Gateway? ...Apple's story now is fodder for business historians—don't make it fodder for your portfolio.

As I write this, Amazon is being punished by shareholders because one of their big bets—the Kindle Fire, a direct competitor to Apple's iPad—is eating into the company's profit margin. Amazon is selling Kindle Fires at cost, or possibly at a loss, to gain market share and put a portable Amazon store in as many hands as possible. The Kindle line is a big bet for Amazon, a company that has never made devices before.

The thing is, Amazon's Kindle bet isn't much different than Apple's retail bet: it's a way to ensure that more people have more opportunities to see and buy things.

MORE EXPERIMENTS MEANS MORE AT-BATS

Larger companies have an advantage because they have the resources to fund more experiments. The more things you try, the better your chances of discovering something valuable. Not surprisingly, GE's Jack Welch, Google's Eric Schmidt, and Amazon's Jeff Bezos have all made very similar statements regarding ongoing experimentation.

- Jack Welch, GE: "Size either liberates or paralyzes. We tried every day to remember that the benefit of size was that it allowed us to take more swings."

- Eric Schmidt, Google: "Our goal is to have more at-bats per unit of time and effort than anyone else in the world."

- Jeff Bezos, Amazon: "You need to set up and organize so that you can do as many experiments per unit of time as possible."

BE CONNECTABLE TO EVERYTHING

We live in a networked world. The more quickly and easily you can link in to other companies, networks, and platforms, the more options you will have.

The US military is standardizing on Internet protocols for its 21st-century network-centric strategy precisely because it's impossible to know in advance what kinds of things they will need to connect to and interoperate with.

In 1995, Wells Fargo was able to launch the first online bank in 60 days because they had already created a standard service interface for use by internal employees.

In the early 1990s, Wells Fargo computer systems were organized by accounts. If a customer wanted an integrated view—that is, if they wanted to see how much money they had in all their accounts combined—employees would have to consult several different systems to find the accounts and then tally them up. A customer view simply did not exist. There was no way for an employee or a customer to see all the accounts they had at the bank. To look at a customer's accounts, one would need to know the account numbers. Wells Fargo VP Eric Castain told developers, "Forget about account numbers...when a customer who owns several accounts calls the bank, they should not be required to know their account numbers."

Developers at the Cushing Group, working with Wells Fargo, developed software that allowed an employee to enter a customer's social security number. The system would then check all existing systems and display a list of the customer's accounts, balances, current status, and so on. Through the same interface, employees could click through to access the accounts in the original systems. The interface was co-designed by developers, Wells Fargo customer service agents, and other participants from the business side.

A few years later, when Wells Fargo wanted to go into Internet banking, the interface was already done, and the only thing left to do was to expose the service layer to the Internet, which the company was able to do in only 60 days. This is the first known instance of a service-oriented architecture in a public-facing business, although today, they are commonplace.

Erik Townsend, who worked on the project, later wrote:

> The idea is that you have systems that are working today and you don't always have time to rebuild them. In the meantime you can "encapsulate them" to shield customers from your internal complexity. Later you can swap in new things behind the service layer without bothering customers.

What Townsend calls a service layer is something that Nicholas Vitari and Haydn Shaughnessy, authors of *The Elastic Enterprise: The New Manifesto for Business Revolution* (Telemachus Press), call *universal connectors*. A universal connector is an interface based on common, shared standards that allows you to connect and share data and capability in a secure, coordinated way. Since the standards for connection are published, everyone knows the rules for interoperating with everyone else who shares that standard.

Vitari and Shaughnessy write, "Universal connectors, particularly APIs and Apps, mean that many new markets, in fact thousands of market niches, can be served with rapidly created, low friction, lightweight content and services, quickly building mass market adoption."

Every team at Amazon is responsible for maintaining a universal connector in the form of a standard service interface. Many of those services are private, available only to other Amazon teams. But they are designed so that, with the flick of a switch, they could be exposed to outside developers and interoperate with any other universal connector on the public Web. In essence, this means that every Amazon team is designed so that it could operate as a stand-alone company if necessary.

STRATEGY BY DISCOVERY

Emergence is self-organization, order that bubbles up from the bottom instead of being pushed down from the top. Emergence is common in complex systems where agents have the autonomy to move around and interact to discover possibilities. For emergent strategy to be successful, there must be enough autonomy, freedom, and slack in the system for people and resources to connect in a peer-to-peer way, like they do in Silicon Valley.

When certain ants need to find a new nest, a few scouts will head out in various directions to search for a new home. When a scout finds a suitable nest, it will spend some time evaluating it. The better the nest, the shorter the time the ant will take. Once the ant has accepted the site, it returns to the main group, where it tries to recruit another ant, whom it then leads to the site. The recruited ant forms its own evaluation, and if the site is acceptable, it will then recruit others in turn. More and more ants are recruited, in an escalating commitment to the site, until the number of ants at the new site reaches a tipping point, which triggers a new behavior. The scouts stop recruiting and begin transporting other ants until the entire colony has moved.

In this manner, an ant colony, working only with local information and without any centralized decision authority, can find the best new site and move the entire colony there in a few hours.

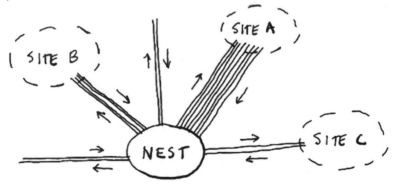

EMERGENT ORGANIZATION: ANTS CAN RAPIDLY
FIND THE BEST NEST SITE IN A PEER-TO-PEER
WAY, WITHOUT ANY CENTRALIZED CONTROL

Employees at Mailchimp, an email marketing company with about 100 employees, decide on new features and services in a similar way. If someone has an idea, they attempt to recruit another person to help them work on a prototype or to help convince others. At Mailchimp, people get excited by good ideas, and they are trusted, so they have the autonomy to follow their instincts. To be recruited, a person must consider it more interesting or useful than the things they are already working on. Like the ants, recruitment turns to escalating commitment over time as more people are recruited to the project. When enough people are recruited, a team is formed and commits to seeing the project through to completion. In this way, ideas compete for resources and the best ideas end up bearing fruit.

Computer game maker Valve allows workers to self-organize based on individuals' interests, passions, and feelings about what's right for the company. Employees are encouraged to manage themselves, to find the work that most interests them, and to contribute wherever and whenever they see a need. There is no management, and nobody reports to anyone else. Employees choose their own projects and are 100% self-directed.

People commit to projects, and project leaders emerge based on informal consensus. Temporary organizational structures arise based on the needs of a particular project or team, but they are disbanded when the work is done.

Valve has no formal management or hierarchy. It is a company designed to tap into—and to feed—the creative energy, passion, and imagination of its workers. In fact, working at Valve is so fun, you might call the employees *players*.

Valve is a privately-held company and doesn't publicly release its revenue figures. But sales are estimated at a billion US dollars per year. And according to Valve Cofounder and Managing Director Gabe Newell, profit per employee at Valve is higher than Google, Amazon, and Microsoft.

These are examples of emergence at work. Nobody is directing people where to go and what to do. Nobody is allocating resources from the top. People and resources self-organize based on horizontal, peer-to-peer activity.

Emergent strategy is not strategy by prediction, it's strategy by discovery.

NOTES FOR CHAPTER EIGHTEEN

"LET A THOUSAND FLOWERS BLOOM"
"The Emergent Way: How to Achieve Meaningful Growth in an Era of Flat Growth," by Karl Moore, *Ivey Business Journal*, November/December 2011.

BLIND ALLEYS
"Jeff Bezos: 'Blind-Alley' Explorer," *Bloomberg Businessweek*, August 19, 2004.

"ONE NYET TO KILL A PROJECT STONE DEAD"
Gary Hamel, "Outrunning Change—the CliffsNotes version," *Management 2.0* blog, *The Wall Street Journal*, October 21, 2009.

APPLE STORES
Cliff Edwards, "Commentary: Sorry, Steve: Here's Why Apple Stores Won't Work," *Bloomberg Businessweek*, May 21, 2001.

"DESPERATION TIME IN CUPERTINO, CALIF."
Arne Alsin, "Apple's Scraping the Bottom of the Barrel," *The Street*, October 25, 2001.

SERVICE-ORIENTED ARCHITECTURE
Erik Townsend, "The 25 Year History of Service Oriented Architecture," white paper, July 17, 2008, *http://www.eriktownsend.com/white-papers-technology/doc_view/4-1-the-25-year-anniversary-of-service-oriented-architecture.raw?tmpl=component*.

MAILCHIMP
Interview with Aarron Walter, MailChimp, conducted by the author, 2011.

VALVE MANAGEMENT
"Steam generated $1 billion in 2010," by Matthew DeCarlo, *Techspot*, February 4, 2011, *http://www.techspot.com/news/42289-steam-generated-1-billion-in-2010.html*.

VALVE SALES
Oliver Chiang, "The Master of Online Mayhem," *Forbes*, February 9, 2011.

The primary task of leadership is to communicate the vision and the values of an organization. Second, leaders must win support for the vision and the values they articulate. And third, leaders have to reinforce the vision and the values.

—*Frederick Smith, Founder, Chairman, & CEO, FedEx*

CHAPTER NINETEEN

Leading the connected company

A connected company is a network of loosely coupled, semi-autonomous units. So what is the role of a leader? Leaders should focus on creating an environment of clarity, trust, and common purpose so members know what the company stands for and how it intends to fulfill its promise to customers. And then leaders should get out of the way.

LEADING FROM THE EDGE

So, if a connected company is a network of autonomous, loosely coupled pods, how do you lead it? What is the role of managers in a connected company?

First, let's make a distinction between *leadership* and *management*. Leadership is about engaging and motivating people. Management is about designing and running the systems that organize the work. Both are important, and certainly one can be both a leader and a manager.

LEADERSHIP IS
WORKING WITH PEOPLE

MANAGEMENT IS
WORKING WITH SYSTEMS

Peter Drucker once said, "Management is doing things right. Leadership is doing the right things." If Drucker is right, and I believe he is, then leadership must come first. For if the leader isn't setting the right direction in the first place, then it doesn't matter how well the company is managed, because it will be managing the wrong things.

THREE TYPES OF STRATEGY

Business has changed, and so has business strategy. Reknowned fighter pilot and military strategist John Boyd described three types of military conflict, each characterized by a different core strategy: attrition warfare, maneuver warfare, and moral warfare.

Attrition: Much of business strategy in the industrial age was much like military strategy in the American Civil War or World War One: clashes of force against force—wars of attrition—where victories are won an inch at a time. Exxon versus Shell. Pepsi versus Coke. This kind of war is capital intensive. Companies invest huge sums in pitched battles for customer attention and market share.

Maneuver: New technologies shift strategy. In World War II, the German army introduced *blitzkrieg*, or "lightning war": the strategy of maneuver. Maneuver warfare wasn't new; it was practiced by the Genghis Khan in the 11th century. But maneuver strategies defeated attrition strategies because they operated at faster cycles, with multiple centers of gravity. When you can operate at a faster pace than your adversaries, they can't keep up with your moves, and they become disoriented and confused. Boyd described this as "getting inside their decision loops."

Many companies today find themselves in a state of disarray, because they are fighting pitched battles of attrition against more agile, maneuverable adversaries who make decisions faster than they can keep up. Maneuver warfare requires that central commanders trust their forces to make tactical decisions in the field, within the context of a larger strategy. Thus, a central tenet of a maneuver strategy is distributed control.

You can see maneuver strategies employed today by companies such as Amazon, which operates at a faster strategic pace than traditional booksellers and publishers, and software-as-a-service companies like Salesforce, which can run circles around traditional enterprise software vendors by making their software so easy to buy and start using that their sales cycles move much faster than competitors.

Moral: Boyd said "People, not weapons, win wars." Moral warfare concentrates on the people factor, focusing on winning the hearts and minds of the people while undermining the adversary's efforts. This is the primary strategy in guerilla operations such as Washington's troops in the American Revolutionary War, or the Viet Cong in Southeast Asia. Guerillas focus on moral, not material, superiority. Guerilla forces are even more broadly distributed than those in maneuver warfare, and they maintain cohesion based on trust and strong bonds to a higher cause. Guerillas are given wide latitude to exercise creativity and initiative to achieve their aims.

Moral conflict is a battle for moral authority, which undermines the moral authority of your adversaries and wins the uncommitted to your point of view. Google and Apple are in such a struggle today to be the world's dominant mobile operating system. Will it be Android or iOS? Both companies have engaged "guerilla" advocates outside their company walls, such as developers and users. You can see the battle for moral authority unfolding all over the Web as both sides try to win over the uncommitted.

This brings us to a fundamental tenet of connected companies: in uncertain times, the faster you can learn and maneuver to seize opportunities, the greater your advantage.

The more you can distribute control, the faster you can learn and maneuver. The greater your moral authority, the greater your leverage and the greater the cohesion of your forces. Therefore, the more you can distribute control and the greater your moral authority, the greater your advantage.

EDGE LEADERSHIP

When examining anything, one of the first things you need to determine is the unit of analysis. For a chemist, the unit of analysis is molecules; for a physicist, it's atoms. For a leader, the unit of analysis is people. Companies are made up of people, and people are the fundamental building blocks of leadership.

PEOPLE FIRST

From this, we derive leadership rule number one: attract good people. Good people have more choices about where they go to work. Good people don't tolerate bad bosses. Good people commit themselves to the work because they enjoy the work, they enjoy the challenge, and they enjoy making things happen. And good people manage themselves, for the most part. The better your people, the better your performance will be.

As a leader, if you attract and hire good people in the first place, half of your leadership problems are solved right out of the gate. Your job is to set an example, articulate the strategy, appreciate people, and for the most part, get out of the way.

The role of leader is not given or appointed, it is earned. There are leaders in every organization, and they are not always at the top. You are a leader not because you say you are, but because people listen to you and because people follow you. Do people like their bosses and get along with them? Do people feel appreciated?

Former IBM executive Irving Wladawsky-Berger describes distributed leadership this way:

> Distributed leadership is all about empowering individual leaders throughout the organization, so they will step up to help address problems as they arise, as well as work together, self-organize into communities of interest, and collaborate in tackling the toughest, most complex problems. Such an entrepreneurial culture based on individual and community empowerment represents a fairly radical departure from the industrial age corporate culture that was common in the twentieth century.

A system of distributed control is a fertile ground within which leaders will naturally develop. As a leader, you are leading and developing leaders by creating the conditions that are ripe for leaders to emerge.

AWARENESS

Connected companies are loosely-joined networks of semi-autonomous pods. Since pods aren't coordinated from above, you want to create the conditions that allow them to self-organize and coordinate their own activity. That means they need as much information about each other's actions and the conditions of their environment

SITUATION AWARENESS

as possible. This is known as *situation awareness*—the ability to perceive and understand the context (see Chapter 17). To have situation awareness means you understand what is going on around you well enough to understand the impact of your actions. The better you understand your situation, the more quickly and intelligently you can respond and adapt.

ADAPTIVE TENSIONS

Tension is the difference between where you are and where you want to be. For example, imagine you are on your way to meet a close friend and you run into a traffic jam. You worry that you might be late. The things that make it more difficult to achieve your goal create tension, and you take action to relieve that tension. The greater your desire to see your friend, the greater the tension will be and the more you will be motivated to do something about it.

Companies are constantly faced with tension created by customers and the environment. Complexity researcher Bill McKelvey calls them *adaptive tensions*, because they represent external pressures on the company, forcing it to adapt or die.

The problem in many companies is that the workers in the company are insulated from these adaptive tensions. Many people just don't feel them, and they don't have any sense of urgency about them. The job of the leader is to bring these adaptive tensions front and center in the company to make them the topic of ongoing conversations, and to ensure that they are deeply and tangibly felt by the people who make up the company.

Jack Welch was a master at making the adaptive tensions of the marketplace real to GE employees. He said, "We're a performance culture. We've decided that our strategy is going to be, you're going to be number one or number two in your industry, or we're going to sell you." The adaptive tension is made real in that statement in two ways. First, there's an aspirational goal: you're going to be number one or number two in your industry. And there's also a threat: if you can't make it, we will sell you.

As a leader, your job is to make adaptive tensions real to people so they feel them and are motivated to act. You create the tension, then you provide the resources, coaching, encouragement, and support that help them get there. At GE, Welch invested heavily in leadership training, creating a leadership university in Crotonville, New York.

Leaders at Vanguard bring adaptive tension inside the company in their Voice of the Client Program, where employees get an email every day with verbatim statements from customers collected via focus groups, comments on the website, and support calls with company representatives. And every executive fields customer support calls. What they are doing is bringing external market forces inside, and putting them to work inside the organization. They are distributing that outside economic pressure internally, putting pressure on internal units to respond and adapt.

But you can't bring the adaptive tensions inside if you don't feel them yourself. That's why you need to spend time on the front line, talking to customers and employees at the points of interaction. As a leader in a connected company, you are going to be out there on the edge a lot more than traditional leaders are. You're going to be out there learning, finding the things that are working, and helping to share that learning inside the company.

Your job is to move from someone in an ivory tower, planning stuff, to being a person who is helping to exemplify the culture, the principles, and the behaviors that will help the company win. You're looking for stories to tell that demonstrate what you are trying to achieve as a group.

Connected companies require a different kind of leadership that we call *edge leadership*. Edge leaders are good listeners and synthesizers. They gather a deep sense of what is going on at the front line by interacting with front-line employees and customers.

DIVERSITY MATTERS

One danger of a strong culture is that it can lead to blind spots and groupthink over time. You can see this in biology as well: when a population loses its genetic diversity, it becomes more vulnerable to invaders. Without diversity, there can be no mutation, no variation, no real learning. If everyone is the same, a network offers no real advantage. In a healthy system, both genes and ideas need to crosspollinate, and that requires a diverse population. Creative ideas emerge when different ideas and concepts interact. Evolution requires two things: variation and selection. As long as you have both, new and improved versions will continue to emerge.

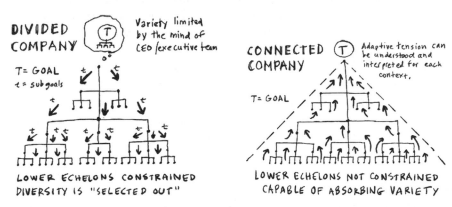

As a senior leader, it's all too easy to be blinded by past successes. In *The Future of Management* (Harvard Business Review Press), Gary Hamel says, "You can't let the top team dominate the strategy discussion. The conversation about what's next should be dominated by those who have their emotional equity invested in the future, not the past."

The more diversity you have in your ecosystem, the more perspectives you will have to draw from when you want to make sense in an uncertain environment.

YOU ARE A LEARNING FIELD

A leader in a connected company is a connector and system builder, not a controller. Connect the people and do your best to make sure that the systems support them.

We talked a bit about learning fields in Chapter 16, and how they are an important link in the chain that connects individual and organizational learning. As a connected leader, you are a learning field; as you move around the organization, you are pollinating the company with ideas, energy, and emotion. You bring your learning field with you wherever you go, and the more you move around, the more the organization can learn. So if your company needs to learn a lot, you need to move a lot.

The higher you are in the organization, the more broadly you need to connect. "It's lonely at the top" is a platitude for a different age. In a connected company, senior leaders should be the most connected people in the company. They should spend their

EDGE LEADERSHIP

FRONT LINE, THE EDGE OF THE ORGANIZATION

THE EDGE LEADER
Leader as pollinator

time listening, connecting, and empathizing. If you are a leader, then you are a synthesizer and an amplifier. To truly understand the front-line jobs, you may need to do them yourself.

Prefer richer communication whenever possible. You can reach out via email, but you can only hug someone or put a hand on the shoulder in real life. As a leader, you embody the purpose, and the purpose needs to be not only seen and heard, but also felt.

Look for emergence. Listen, find, tell, and amplify the stories; synthesize, look for the patterns, and help others see them, too. Leaders are not good because they are right, they are good because people follow them, and people follow those who are willing to listen and learn.

INFLUENCE—GIVE MEANING AND MORAL AUTHORITY TO THE PURPOSE

Without awareness, people have no way to make sense of a situation. But awareness by itself is not sufficient. You also need to be able to act in order to improve the situation.

People act to resolve tensions, and they act based on emotion and beliefs. People act when they care. One thing that motivates people to care is a sense of common purpose.

PURPOSE

When the situation is too complex or uncertain for detailed orders, the US military manages by something they call *command intent*. Command intent is a set of goals and a vision for possible methods of achieving those goals. It's sufficiently high-level that it can be broadcast widely to everyone in the system, while leaving front-line troops the freedom to translate those plans and interpret how to put them into action, depending on the immediate situation.

A connected company's promise to customers is the core of its business strategy, and so command intent is oriented around the keeping of that promise. Especially today, when customers have easy access to social network services that exponentially amplify word-of-mouth messages, your company cannot afford a mismatch between promise and provisioning, between expectations and experience.

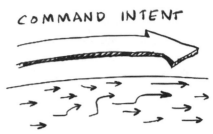

COMMAND INTENT IS A BROAD VISION THAT LEAVES SMALL UNITS THE FREEDOM TO INTERPRET HOW TO PUT PLANS INTO ACTION

A company is a network of promises and commitments, and a company's performance is a function of how well people inside and outside the company trust each other's promises and keep their commitments.

WHAT YOU STAND FOR

It's important to give people a sense of who you are and where you are going so that your people understand what membership means and why they should devote time and energy to the enterprise.

Take Amazon, for example. You can look at everything that Amazon does, and you can see that they're focused not only on helping customers make good buying decisions, but also on making sure that the process is transparent to customers, that the gap between what they expect and what they get is as slim as possible. You can clearly see that they are focusing on a long-term relationship. Amazon obsesses about customers.

A friend told me a story about how she ordered something on Amazon and didn't receive it. The delivery guy signed it off as delivered, but it never came. She told Amazon about it, and the customer service representative said, "No problem, we're wiping it off your record. If you do get it, please send it back." She was very impressed by that.

I'm sure that if a customer tried something like that five times, Amazon might start to be a little less understanding, and they might start to write that person off as a customer. But the point is that customers like Amazon because Amazon starts with trust, and when a company trusts you first, you are more likely to trust that company later. You're more likely to give them the benefit of the doubt.

The basis of a company's relationship with the customer is not transactional; it's a relationship that unfolds over a long period of time, and Amazon invests in that relationship. People tend to appreciate that.

And from the perspective of an employee at Amazon, knowing what Amazon stands for makes it much easier to make decisions. They don't need to check with anybody, because they know what Amazon stands for. So they can simply act.

MORAL AUTHORITY

You are a leader when people follow you, trust you, are inspired and motivated by you. Leaders set an example for others to live by. They embody the purpose and principles of the company. They simplify, enlarge, and enrich the people that follow them.

Leaders stand for something and live the principles they stand for. If your company is about service, serve. Every executive at Vanguard fields customer support calls. So does Jeff Bezos at Amazon. If your company is about low prices, drive a beat-up pickup truck, even if you're a billionaire. Sam Walton did.

Leaders have moral authority that attracts people to their cause.

Moral authority isn't easy to obtain. It's not a sprint, it's a marathon. Reputations take a long time to build, but they can be destroyed overnight. You gain moral authority by living your principles, in public and in private. By allowing conflicts to exist, you put your reputation at risk. The financial industry has taken severe hits in recent years because of a general failure to put customers before profits.

Here's what John Boyd said about moral authority and moral leverage:

> Identify our flaws, blemishes and contradictions. Find ways to overcome them. They destroy internal harmony, paralyze us and alienate us from each other. Emphasize the traditions, experiences and unfolding events that build harmony and trust. Identify the flaws and weaknesses of adversaries. Point them out. Regarding the uncommitted: respect their culture and achievements. Demonstrate that we bear them no ill will. Provide benefits and favorable treatment for those who support our cause. Demonstrate that we will not support or tolerate ideas and interactions that undermine our cause and philosophy.

Easy to say, but difficult to do, especially if, like many companies, you are addicted to short-term returns and bad profits that result from trapped or abused customers.

The simplest strategy for acquiring moral authority has been articulated by just about every moral leader and authority in history. It's called the Golden Rule. Treat people as you would have them treat you.

The Golden Rule strategy is a long-term strategy. It often involves things that seem like sacrifices in the short term, like trusting a customer and accepting a returned product without questions or skepticism, or promptly paying an insurance claim. This means valuing long-term relationships over transactions and short-term profits. In the long run, the Golden Rule strategy is the most winning strategy of all.

Make people feel good. Happiness is contagious. Happy employees create happy customers. Happy customers create happy shareholders. As Tony Hsieh of Zappos has said clearly and often: happiness is a business model.

PRINCIPLES TRUMP PROCESSES

Every connected company stands for something. It has opinions. Its people are bound together by shared purpose and principles.

One way to help people make good decisions in uncertain environments is to have a strong, constant purpose so everyone understands the job to be done, and a few clear principles that they can use to guide their decisions about "how" to do that job.

Principles are liberating, whereas policies are constraining. Principles are rules of thumb that can help people make decisions in all kinds of situations. Principles make use of human judgment. Policies, on the other hand, restrict and constrain and reduce the human element.

You know you have a good principle when you can write a simple yes-or-no question that will enable anyone in your company to make strategy decisions at both macro and micro scales. For example, "Will this decision put the customer first?" Nordstrom employees know that they will never be punished or reprimanded for making a decision that puts a customer first.

The principles will be different depending on the strategy of the company. What a good principle does is embody the strategy. For example, Walmart's "every day low prices" can be articulated as a principle with the question, "Will this decision reduce prices?" At Amazon, you might find principles like, "Will this help customers make better buying decisions?"

Technology hosting company Rackspace has grown to be a leader in its industry by focusing on a single core principle: fanatical customer support.

Hosting is a very competitive business, and most companies focus on providing a basic service at the lowest possible cost. To most companies, that means spending as little as possible on customer service and support.

In 1999, then-CEO (now Chairman) Graham Weston launched the "fanatical support" initiative by eliminating the automated phone queue. He felt that the phone queue effectively said to customers, "Our time is more valuable than your time." When the phone rings at Rackspace, someone has to answer.

The focus on fanatical customer support is a strategic principle that serves as a foundation for the company's decisions and actions, from the boardroom to the front line.

Fanatical support drove the company to adopt the Net Promoter Score (NPS) as a key measure. In board meetings, the focus is first on customer NPS, second on employee NPS, and third on financials. A sustained focus on NPS led to insights that changed the business.

Fanatical support drove the company to reorganize front-line operations around cross-functional, customer-focused teams. In the early days, Rackspace was organized by function, like most companies. Based on customer feedback, the company has reorganized into small, cross-functional pods made up of 10–12 people. Each pod owns a customer or customer category. NPS for the cross-functional teams was higher than peer groups, and first-call resolution of customer problems rose from 55% to more than 90%.

Says Mary Walker, VP of Sales Operations:

> A lot of stuff at Rack makes sense when you understand the fundamental principle: fanatical support. It's about pushing the power and the authority and as much of the information down to the front lines as humanly possible. If you've been in mainstream corporate America, you have picked up some unconscious approaches that are the exact opposite of the behaviors that you need at Rackspace.
>
> A lot of managers have been trained in corporate America to believe that, if you don't know how to defend yourself and your team, you are screwed. Frankly, reaching out to collaborate and help people gets you screwed. You're looked upon as the naive sucker at the poker table.
>
> At Rackspace, you can reach out to anyone to help solve a problem. You can ask your co-worker. You can call up your buddy who you were in orientation with, or the person you met at the barbeque last week. You don't need anybody's approval to do that. You don't have to ask your manager. You don't have to ask their manager. You just reach out, because we are all bound together by the principle that says 'take care of the customer.' That kind of deeply collaborative behavior is punished in most companies.

When principles are at the core of your competitive strategy, you must hire for attitude first. You can train people on skills, but you can't train them on attitude. Employees must be a good fit. Hire for attitude, orient for values, and train for skills.

Rackspace CEO Lanham Napier says, "It really comes down to core values, and we don't train our employees in core values. Their parents did that a long time ago."

IT TAKES TRUST TO BUILD RELATIONSHIPS

A system that distributes authority out to the edge also needs a lot of trust. You have to trust people to make good decisions, and they have to trust that they won't be punished when they make mistakes. Because there will be mistakes. Any learning system must tolerate some degree of trial and error. Mistakes are a part of learning.

Services are based on trust and reputation and long-term relationships. If customers don't come back, you've squandered a really precious asset. A Southwest Airlines employee once said, "We know, if we can get someone to try us three times, that we've got them." Their focus on any new passenger is going to be to try to get them to come back three times. If they do that with new customers, they've really got to do it with every customer, because they don't always know who the new ones are. So Southwest's focus is always on getting people to come back for the next time.

If you're focused on selling a product, it's easier to avoid thinking in terms of a long-term relationship with customers. It's easier to focus on the transactions.

When you make and sell a car, it's easy not to think about things like, "What about when I sell them the next car and the next car and the next car?" When you're dealing with services, there's no way to avoid that.

The best profits come from these kinds of Golden Rule behaviors that build long-term customer relationships and loyalty.

A focus on long-term, relationship-driven profits will increase your moral authority. A focus on short-term, transaction-driven profits will destroy it.

In the end, it all comes down to trust. Do people trust that you will keep your promises? Do they trust you to treat them well? Do they trust the information you provide? Do they trust your intentions? Whole Foods' CEO John Mackey says it well:

> We tend to see human beings as human resources, which is a metaphor that reflects back to an industrial age, where people were a resource to be used on the assembly line. It's a very stultifying view of human nature. In fact people bring their whole selves to the workplace. They want to be full human beings. If we want to create organizations of trust...we need to view them as whole people, that are striving to fulfill their own individual purposes, to learn and grow, to self-actualize, to find friendship and love and community in the workplace.

> We need to create workplaces that allow human beings to flourish, unified around the purpose of the organization. It's not a touchy feely kind of thing. You have important work to do. You're trying to fulfill the mission and purpose of the organization. But while you're doing that, you're part of a community of people that are there as full human beings.

The strategies of a connected company are strategies of learning, maneuvering, and moral authority. When you lead a connected company, you are leading a network: a distributed control system that allows people and teams varying degrees of freedom to do their work as they see fit. A connected leader focuses not only on those who are inside the company, but also on the entire ecosystem of partners, suppliers, customers, and investors. We are all interconnected today, and our fates are in many ways bound together.

You are leading a company, but you are also leading a social network.

NOTES FOR CHAPTER NINETEEN

DISTRIBUTED LEADERSHIP
Irving Wladawsky-Berger, "The MIT Distributed Leadership Forum," blog post, November 23, 2009, *http://blog.irvingwb.com/blog/2009/11/the-mit-distributed-leadership-forum.html.*

ADAPTIVE TENSIONS
Bill McKelvey, "Improving Corporate IQ," published in the *Workshop on Managerial Implications of Complexity Theory in the Network Economy,* July 14, 2001.

JOHN BOYD & MORAL AUTHORITY
A Vision So Noble: John Boyd, the OODA Loop, and America's War on Terror, by Daniel Ford (CreateSpace, 2010).

JOHN MACKEY & TRUST
"John Mackey: Want trust? Let people be their whole selves," MIX TV, *http://www.managementexchange.com/video/john-mackey-want-trust-let-people-be-their-whole-selves.*

Life is like riding a bicycle—in order to keep your balance, you must keep moving.

—*Albert Einstein*

CHAPTER TWENTY

Managing the connected company

The job of management is to design and run the systems that support the company in achieving its purpose. Managers must carefully balance individual freedoms with the common good, involve people in platform decisions, and tune the system to keep the company's metabolism at the right temperature—too cold and the company sinks into rigid bureaucracy; too hot and the company breaks apart into anarchy and chaos.

MANAGEMENT IS A SUPPORT SYSTEM

The purpose of management is to design and run the systems that enable the organization to effectively pursue its goals. Assuming that leaders have effectively focused the company on doing the right things, it is then the focus of management to ensure that the company is designed and organized to do those things as well as possible. Management is the design and operation of the system that supports the work.

Note the word *support*. In an earlier, industrial era, the keywords were "organize and supervise," but in a connected company, the focus is on support. The management system needs to function less like a traditional command-and-control system and more like a city, in which you create invitations and opportunities by the way you design the architecture and environment.

The purpose of management is to design, operate, and improve the system by which work gets done. W. Edwards Deming said often that more than 90 percent of the problems with work are due to the system, not the workers. He suggested that managers should encourage workers to study the system at all times and look for ways to improve it.

Watch the leaders, see what they do, and try to build systems that support and encourage the right kinds of behaviors. A light touch and a willingness to listen are always a good idea.

In a connected company, the first job of management is to design and build the structure and system that supports the work. The second job of management is to operate that system.

DESIGNING THE SYSTEM

A management system for a connected company is not so much designed for control as it is for flexibility and emergence. What you want from the system is enough structure that people are not endlessly repeating routine work, with enough flexibility that you are not overly constraining work.

Too often in today's companies, people feel overly constrained by the structure and processes that are put in place to manage the work. They feel like a rat in a maze when they should feel like a driver in a car. The difference is that, in a car on a road, you can see where you are going and have control over where you go.

BALANCE THE INDIVIDUAL FREEDOM WITH THE COMMON GOOD

The most delicate and important balancing act is to balance individual freedom with the common good. Individual freedom is important if you want to encourage risk taking and experimentation—if you want people to be free to use their good judgment rather than being tightly bound by rigid rules, procedures, and bureaucracy.

Some things make a lot more sense if they are common. In a large city, it just doesn't make sense for everyone to generate their own electricity or maintain their own roads, when everyone's needs are far better served by centralized resources. Common infrastructure and standards make it easier for people to connect and share information. But everything that is standardized for the common good also constrains individual freedom. For example, it's easier to connect if everyone uses the same instant-messaging system. But that also means everyone can't choose their own.

Cities create zones and boundaries to minimize conflict and cluster similar activities together. For example, a commercial shopping district creates clusters of shopping activity that are beneficial to customers and retailers alike. In a connected company, boundaries and parameters create zones where the limits and shared resources benefit everyone.

THE MOST IMPORTANT BALANCING ACT

For example, Amazon Marketplace does not allow the sale of certain items, like alcohol and firearms, and retailers are held to strict ethical standards. But those restrictions create a trusted system in which customers can feel safe to buy. At the same time, Amazon Marketplace clusters retailers together under the same roof, making it easier for customers to find the right retailer and item quickly.

Boundaries might be tight or loose, depending on what you are trying to achieve. Tighter parameters ensure greater consistency. For example, McDonald's has strict rules and frequent, unannounced inspections to ensure a consistent customer experience. Looser parameters, like Nordstrom's "Use your best judgment in all situations," give workers the flexibility to surprise and delight customers.

Boundary-setting is a balancing act that depends on the kind of company you're running and identifying where customers and employees value consistency as opposed to flexibility.

PARTICIPATION
Since boundaries are all about supporting the workers and helping them manage their work, the best way to set the boundaries is to include the population in your boundary designs. Let the community be your guide. If you pay attention to the community, they will probably guide you in the right direction. When people don't get the support they need from a platform, you will often find them building it themselves.

For example, when Apple first launched the iPhone, they did not plan to support outside developers right away. But within weeks of the iPhone's launch, outside developers had hacked the iPhone and were developing apps. Apple responded by accelerating the release of the iOS software development kit (SDK) and released it in early 2008. Apple was listening to its community and accelerated the launch of a platform because the community was doing it anyway.

BUILD SLACK INTO CENTRAL RESOURCES TO ENSURE AVAILABILITY

The natural tendency when developing support systems is to make good use of your centralized resources by making them as efficient as possible. And that's a good idea to a point. But the demand on central resources will not be consistent. If you focus only on efficiency, you will pay a price in availability because in peak periods, people will have to wait too long.

The reason for this lies in a branch of mathematics called *queueing theory*, which deals with how providers manage capacity in order to deal with multiple customers. As a provider attempts to serve more and more customers, the wait time per customer increases. For example, the more people who want to use an ATM, the longer the line (hence the name *queueing theory*). What it comes down to is that the more efficiently you utilize resources, the longer the wait times will become. This is mathematically inevitable.

And as wait times increase, the effectiveness of that central resource declines. For some people, it won't be worth the wait. For others, by the time the system could respond, it would be too late.

So how efficient should you be? There's no hard-and-fast rule, but there is one very useful rule of thumb. Waiting time increases gradually until utilization reaches a critical tipping point (around 70%), after which response times

THE EFFICIENCY PROBLEM

ELAPSED TIME (MINUTES)

UTILIZATION

As utilization increases, wait time goes up dramatically

start to shoot up exponentially. So incremental increases in efficiency are good up to a point, after which they become a very bad thing indeed. In other words, an ambulance that arrives after the patient has died is of no use at all.

What this comes down to is that if you want your central services to be useful and available, you will need to build in some slack. The amount of slack will depend on how important availability is for that particular service. The more critical it is to have fast response times, the more slack you want in the system.

RELY ON PEER-TO-PEER REINFORCEMENT WHENEVER POSSIBLE

Bureaucracy has a tendency to feed itself. Like weeds in a garden, rules and procedures will proliferate unless you actively guard against them. The most flexible structures are also the most lightweight. Whenever possible, let peer-to-peer reinforcement and cultural norms do the work for you, instead of introducing rules that you will then have to police.

For example, Google examined their expense policy and realized that enforcing the policy would cost more than the few people who abused it. So Google has no formal rules about expenses. Each employee is issued a credit card and is expected to use their good judgment and follow Google's code of corporate conduct, which is clearly and publicly posted on the Web.

At W.L. Gore, performance-based incentives determined by peer review. In his book *What Matters Now: How to Win in a World of Relentless Change, Ferocious Competition, and Unstoppable Innovation* (Jossey-Bass), Gary Hamel quotes Gore CEO Terri Kelly on how Gore manages incentives:

USE PEER-TO-PEER REINFORCEMENT WHENEVER POSSIBLE

> An associate will be evaluated by 20 or 30 peers and will, in turn, evaluate 20–30 colleagues. You rank your peers from top to bottom. It's a forced ranking. You're asked to rank only people you know. What we find is that there's typically a lot of consistency in who people view as the top contributors, and who they put at the bottom of the list...We have a cross-functional committee of individuals with leadership roles who look at all this input, debate it, and then put together an overall ranking, from first to last, of those particular associates. Then, in setting compensation, they ensure there's a nice slope to the pay curve so that the folks who are making the biggest contributions are also making the most money.

Second Life founder Philip Rosedale let employees distribute the company's bonuses to each other. Here's how it worked: each employee got a thousand dollars and had 24 hours to decide how to distribute that money to fellow employees. They could distribute it evenly or give the whole amount to a single worker. But it had to be anonymous, and they couldn't give any money to themselves. He found that the money always was distributed in the most equitable way. Workers are good at recognizing value in their co-workers when given the chance.

REWARD TEAMS, NOT INDIVIDUALS

When designing incentive systems, consider rewarding team performance rather than individuals. Individual incentives encourage people to compete with each other in order to stand out from their peers. If you want people to work effectively, reward their performance on a team basis. When servers at a restaurant pool their tips, you often find that overall service improves. At Whole Foods, for example, it's the performance of the teams that matters, and profit-based incentives are designed to match. There's still competition, but it's between teams, and not individuals.

OPERATING THE SYSTEM

Even the best-performing machines require periodic maintenance. Likewise, no management system runs itself. Management in a connected company must think about the company as a complex adaptive system and manage it accordingly.

CRITICAL VALUES IN COMPLEX ADAPTIVE SYSTEMS

Think of your company as a system, where individuals and groups are organized in order to do work. Work requires energy, and depending on the way the system is organized, it can constrain or release the inherent energy in the people that make up the system.

In any system, motion generates energy. The faster molecules move, the more energy they generate. This is why your hands get warmer when you rub them together. The longer a motor runs, the hotter it gets. This is why cars have coolant systems and many computers have fans inside: to regulate the temperature.

Companies put rules and procedures in place to intentionally reduce workers' freedom of motion. One byproduct of these constraints is that they reduce the amount of energy that people can put into the system. By reducing or eliminating constraints, you increase the freedom of motion available to employees, creating more potential energy in the system.

A motor is a mechanical device. As a motor gets hotter, it expands a bit, but its fundamental shape and structure do not change. But some things—and this is especially true for complex adaptive systems—change their structure as their temperature changes. For example, when water is cooled past a certain point, it freezes, and when it is heated past a certain point, it boils.

These points are called *critical values* or *tipping points*, and the structural changes that occur when critical values are reached are called *phase transitions*.

Since companies are complex adaptive systems, made up of people rather than mechanical parts, they undergo phase transitions when certain critical values are reached.

Think of your company as having a temperature. If the system is too cold, then the company will

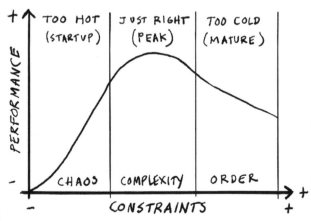

feel like ice: rigid, bureaucratic, unmoving. It will feel stifling, because people will feel like they have no room to breathe. If the system is too hot, then it will feel chaotic, like a gas, with energy scattered all over the place, with no sense of cohesion or direction. If your company is at the right temperature, you will feel that things are moving fluidly. Not too cold or too hot, but like Goldilocks' porridge, when the temperature is just right, your company will enter a state of flow.

SYMPTOMS

As a manager, you can take the temperature of your company. Is it too hot, too cold, or just right? The right temperature for any company is a temperature that matches the pace of change in the business environment, that is the same temperature, or slightly hotter than, customers and competitors. Like a doctor, you can look for symptoms that your company is operating at the wrong temperature.

A company that is running too cold will have rules that are so strict that they get in the way of the work. You will find people working "around" the system to get things done. Processes will be tightly coupled and over-coordinated. Business divisions and groups will be interdependent such that each group cannot make a move without consulting other groups, stifling innovation and slowing down business processes. People are likely to be territorial, hoarding information to consolidate or increase their power. When in doubt, people will fall back on rules and traditions, taking refuge in habits and routines, rather than doing what the business environment demands. Strategies are reactive. Innovation initiatives will narrowly focus on a small group of known competitors and existing paradigms, and breakthrough ideas will be stifled at birth.

A company that is running too hot will find itself reinventing the wheel, solving the same problems over and over again. Every project or initiative will be started from scratch, with no consideration for lessons learned in the past. Communications between groups will be random and sporadic, and in general, people will not feel like they know what's going on or what others are doing. Fiefdoms and cliques may develop as people try to build "safe havens" amid the chaos. It may be difficult or impossible to coordinate activities that involve more than one unit. Ideas flow freely, with intense experimentation in short bursts of energy, but they die quickly due to lack of follow up and an inability to prioritize among the multitude of options. There's plenty of creativity, but uncontained and unfocused, it simply results in endless thrashing about.

Some companies may find themselves in an oscillating pattern, with periods

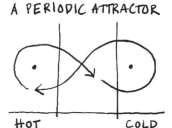

A PERIODIC ATTRACTOR

HOT   COLD

of creative chaos followed by periods of overbearing structure. In such cases, a management team might give workers wide latitude, and then, recognizing chaotic tendencies in the system, overreact with draconian controls. In complex systems, this kind of oscillation cycle is called a *periodic attractor*, because the system is periodically attracted to two or more radically different states. An example from nature is seen in feast-and-famine predator-prey cycles that never seem to settle down. The rabbits breed and quickly proliferate. The foxes, faced with an unprecedented feast, hungrily eat up the rabbits, and their population grows to an unsustainable level. Soon, the rabbit population has dwindled and all but a few of the foxes starve, allowing the rabbits to proliferate again. And the cycle repeats itself. For companies caught in such oscillation cycles, the resulting endless fluctuation is demoralizing and exhausting. Oscillating systems like this can be the most difficult to change.

TUNING THE SYSTEM

One job of management is tuning the system to keep the company's temperature within the critical "Goldilocks" range—the fluid flow state where people are productive and enjoy their work—without feeling stifled or overly stressed.

If you can recognize the symptoms in your company, here are 10 things you can do to tune the system to manage the temperature and stimulate phase transitions.

ADAPTIVE TENSIONS

You can tune the system by changing or adjusting the adaptive tensions to better reflect the outside environment.

GE found that its focus on "being number one or two in your market" had unwittingly encouraged teams to define their markets too narrowly. By broadening the definitions of what market the groups were in, GE was able to increase their adaptive tensions, and consequently, their performance.

Vanguard's Voice of the Client program increases adaptive tension by bringing customer concerns front and center—to every employee's email inbox, every day.

ATTRACTORS

Attractors are the things that motivate and energize people to excel at their work. You can amplify or dampen attractors based on how well they are working. You can strengthen attractors by clarifying the company's purpose, by giving people more freedom, or by tying compensation and other rewards to the things that matter.

Semco employees are motivated because they get a third of the profits from their work, which they share equally. Nordstrom salespeople get a portion of their sales. Whole Foods employees benefit when their team creates profit for the company.

Strengthening or dampening attractors will change behavior. For example, if people are too competitive and it's negatively affecting teamwork, you can change your incentives to focus on team rewards instead of individual rewards.

But it's not always about financial rewards. At Amazon, an old shoe can be just as effective. Greg Linden, who worked at Amazon in the early days, tells of Amazon's "Just do it" awards. Those who won the prize were called up in front of the entire company and given an old, used, Nike shoe. Linden says:

> I got a couple of these—including one for shopping cart recommen-
> dations—but after moving to Stanford and back to Seattle, the old, stinky,
> mismatched shoes have long been lost. What was not lost was the sense

of pride. I was proud to have gotten that crappy old shoe. Of course, it was not the prize itself that mattered. It was the recognition. It was that someone had noticed and said thanks. That was what I wanted...That used shoe was worth far more than it might appear. It was a thank you. It was recognition. These are things valued by many, but offered far too rarely.

The appreciation of leaders can go a long way. Linden recalls another incident when he was working on the "customers who bought this also bought" feature, known within Amazon as "similarities." He recalls:

After much experimentation, I discovered a new version of similarities that worked quite well. The similarities were non-obvious, helpful, and useful. Heck, while I was at it, I threw in some performance improvements as well. Very fun stuff. When this new version of similarities hit the website, Jeff Bezos walked into my office and literally bowed before me. On his knees, he chanted, 'I am not worthy, I am not worthy.' I didn't know what to say then, and I don't know what to say now. But that memory will stick with me forever.

INFORMATION TRANSPARENCY

The more you share information, the more you will build trust and increase the company's overall situation awareness. People who can see their impact and compare their performance with others can more easily learn, improve, and coordinate without guidance from supervisors.

In "cold" bureaucratic companies, people tend to hoard resources and information. This locks up learning, talent, and knowledge, concealing it from the rest of the company. Finding ways to release and unlock this hidden value will increase the energy flow in the system. Putting people in cross-functional teams for a project, for example, puts people from different divisions on the same side for the duration of the project, helping them build relationships, share knowledge, and learn to trust each other.

Another example: a lot of valuable knowledge is locked away in email when it could just as easily be shared across the organization via social channels. To release this hidden value, one company decided to slowly reduce the space people had to save information in their inbox. The rate of social adoption increased as people started putting their information and documents online.

7-Eleven and Walmart share performance data widely, throughout the company and with suppliers, so each member of the community can self-adjust based on awareness of what's going on in the system. For example, 7-Eleven store managers can see how every item in their store is performing relative to similar items in other 7-Eleven stores. Walmart suppliers can compare their sales across regions and stores. Every Friday, Google holds a "TGIF" meeting in which one of the company's founders answers questions frankly and honestly. Any and every question may be asked, and employees use an online voting system that bubbles the most popular questions to the top.

Sharing information also tends to increase adaptive tension by exposing people to the complexities and conflicts of the environment—internal and external—broadly within the company. When people know what's going on, you set the stage for emergence.

DENSITY

Separating people from each other cools the system. Putting them closer together heats it up. Every time a city doubles in density, its productivity rises by about 20%.

There are many ways to create opportunities for connection. The smoking area, the break area, the lunch room, the coffee machine, and the water cooler are areas where people from different parts of the company come when it's time to take a break. These are natural areas for people to mingle and make connections with people in other departments, groups, or divisions.

Those interactions aren't planned or organized. But such areas create conditions that are conducive to connection. Those very casual, simple conversations, when repeated over a long period of time, give people a greater awareness of the information patterns in the company as a whole.

INCREASE DENSITY
TO HEAT THE SYSTEM

Google's Director of Facilities, George Salah, intentionally increased density to increase the energy in the company. Steven Levy tells the story in his book *In the Plex: How Google Thinks, Works, and Shapes Our Lives* (Simon & Schuster):

> Salah was surprised that when Silicon Graphics occupied the building, all the cubicles had relatively high walls. And the desks were all oriented inward, with almost no one facing out. So as you walk through the building, you couldn't find a soul," he says. "They were all there, you just didn't know it. It was dead space." His job, he felt, was to make it as alive as the company he worked for. The key to vibrancy, he believed, was human density. Though the campus was built to accommodate around two thousand people, Silicon Graphics had had only 950 workers. Not long after Google took it over, it had more than nine hundred people in one building alone. Eventually there would be about 2,500 in those four large buildings. "We want to pack those buildings, not just because it minimizes our footprint but because of the interactions you get, just accidental stuff you overhear," says Salah. "Walking around, you feel good about being here. And that's what's Googley.

An SGI employee from the 1990s would not recognize those offices today. The GooglePlex, as they call it, is designed like a mixed-use urban space. Googlers eat for free from a selection of cafeterias, managed by top chefs, which offer more options than most city streets. A snack or drink is always just around the corner, and comfy chairs, tables, and common meeting spaces abound. Bicycles and scooters are handy for travel between buildings. Googlers enjoy access to volleyball courts, gyms, and even a concierge service.

DIVERSITY

As we said in the previous chapter, diversity matters. Constancy of purpose is one thing, but single-mindedness can all too easily lead to groupthink, narrowly focusing the company on a single way of seeing the world.

One way to increase diversity is by rotating people from team to team or throughout the company, so they are able to see the company from different perspectives.

Another way is to bring in people from different industries. When Apple decided to go into the retail business, they started by asking people to talk about their most memorable service experiences. Realizing that most of the memorable experiences came from the hospitality business, they went straight to the experts: Ritz-Carlton. Bringing people from the high end of the hotel business inside Apple helped the company build a new competency of service excellence on top of their existing knowledge and skills in building "insanely great" products.

ROTATE PEOPLE BETWEEN TEAMS TO INCREASE DIVERSITY

Another way is to give workers access to education and professional development programs, sabbaticals, leaves of absence, and exchange programs. Give people opportunities to learn from the outside world and bring those valuable experiences back into the company.

PERMEABILITY

A more open, permeable system is more connected to its environment. Making your systems more permeable is another way to invite more energy and ideas into the company. For example, Zappos is moving into the old Las Vegas City Hall and investing in developing the surrounding neighborhood, recruiting startups and small companies like restaurants and coffee shops to move to the area, developing residential properties, and investing in schools in a deliberate attempt to increase the permeability between their organization and the surrounding business ecosystem.

In a 2012 *Fortune* article, Leigh Gallagher reported:

> When it came time to think about a new home for the company, Hsieh decided the best way to create those interactions is to drop his employees in the middle of a vibrant downtown and let the surroundings facilitate the interaction. "When you're in a city, the bar or the restaurant becomes an extended conference room," he says. Since downtown Vegas didn't really have that yet, Hsieh says, "The idea went from 'let's build a campus' to 'let's build a city.'"

Zappos is also planning a 21,000-square-foot coworking space and a shared technology platform that anyone in the community will be able to use for finance and accounting.

Another form of permeability pertains to levels of management. In a permeable organization, people have regular informal contact with people at all levels of the hierarchy. Senior executives spend time on the front line, observing customer interactions and talking to front-line workers about their issues and concerns. Skip-level conversations, between superiors and people two levels down in the hierarchy, are a common occurrence. Conversations and connections are not limited to cliques within pockets and silos but spread are throughout the company.

Customer communities can also increase permeability. For example, Starbucks invited customers to participate more deeply with the company by launching *MyStarbucksIdea.com*, a community where customers can make suggestions and vote up the best ideas. One result of this open community was the splash stick, a customer innovation that keeps coffee from spilling by plugging the sip hole in their cups.

PERMEABILITY INCREASES SITUATION AWARENESS

RATE OF FLOW

Making information transparent helps increase a company's metabolism and capacity for self-organizing behavior. But equally important is the rate at which information flows. The faster the flow, the greater the situation awareness.

For example, every time a customer buys a product at 7-Eleven Japan, the in-store system captures the age and gender of the buyer (estimated by the cashier), the combination of products sold, and the time of day. Each store in the system captures about a thousand transactions per day. By 9 a.m. the following morning, all of the data from all 7-Eleven stores across Japan are available to every store. This allows store managers to compare their sales with every other store in Japan in near real time. The system also correlates that data with weather patterns and historical sales trends.

These data are presented graphically so that they are easy for store managers to understand and analyze, which allows them to make better decisions about what to stock in their stores. Store managers can order three times a day and get nine deliveries by van each day.

The pace of information flow at 7-Eleven Japan allows it to run circles around competitors. The approach has been so successful that sales at 7-Eleven Japan exceeded sales of the parent 7-Eleven company, and in 1991, 7-Eleven Japan bought the debt-burdened American parent. In 2007 7-Eleven became the largest chain store in the world, bigger even than McDonald's, with over 40,000 locations.

PARAMETERS

If your company is running too cold, another thing to look at is the degrees of freedom given to individuals and teams to pursue their business objectives. One powerful way to stimulate your company's metabolism is to focus on removing the obstacles and barriers that keep people from focusing on their work.

One major such obstacle is bureaucracy, rules, and procedures. GE Work-Outs are designed to break the bureaucratic chains that constrain workers from doing their best work. GE managers look for "rattlers"—bureaucratic constraints that can be shot on sight—and "pythons"—which are trickier and must be unraveled first. But the shared goal of a GE Work-Out is to give workers a voice, as well as a chance to propose improvements and eliminate the obstructions that keep them from being successful.

When setting parameters, the simplicity or complexity of the rules can expand or reduce the latitude people feel that they have to do their jobs. Rules that people can keep in their heads are easier to follow and easier to share. Here is the Nordstrom employee handbook in its entirety, written on an index card:

> WELCOME TO NORDSTROM. We're glad to have you with our Company. Our number one goal is to provide outstanding customer service. Set both your personal and professional goals high. We have the great confidence in your ability to achieve them. Nordstrom rules: Rule #1: Use your good judgment in all situations. There will be no additional rules. Please feel free to ask your department manager, store manager, or division general manager any question at any time.

STRUCTURAL CHANGE

Sometimes tuning isn't enough. The design of the management structure itself must be open to continual evaluation and review. While structural changes may be more costly and time consuming, an ongoing dialogue between the platform and pods will help keep you honest. Remember, the system is about support, not control, and the best platform managers have a system for listening to constituents and encouraging their participation, as well as prioritizing and implementing their ideas. Not every idea should be implemented, but every idea should be heard and recognized.

EMERGENT LEADERSHIP

People need something to aspire to, to believe in. Every company has a story, and the best stories are stories that inspire and motivate. There are times in the life of a business that the story has gone stale, when the business is at risk, when the bureaucratic barriers are weak and breakthroughs near. Think about the Berlin Wall in 1989, a time when stifling Soviet controls had been weakened and the energy on both sides of the wall was eager for connection. At such moments, the story wants to change, and these are the times when new leaders can emerge by telling a powerful new story.

As a manager, these are the times to listen for emerging leaders and find ways to amplify their stories.

THE JOB OF MANAGERS

The manager's job in a connected company is not an easy one. It's a support role, one that requires listening, diplomacy, an eye for detail, and a sense of the big picture. The design of the system should be as simple and lightweight as possible. Involve constituents in platform decisions. Look for symptoms that the company is running too hot or too cold, and tune the system over time to keep the company's metabolism in that "just right" Goldilocks range.

NOTES FOR CHAPTER TWENTY

I'm indebted to the writings of business complexity researcher Bill McKelvey for many of the thoughts expressed in this chapter.

GOOGLES' CODE OF CONDUCT...
The Google Code of Conduct can be read online at *http://investor.google.com/corporate/code-of-conduct.html.*

"SECOND LIFE FOUNDER PHILIP ROSEDALE"
"Decentralized Organizations: Do They Work?" SXSW panel discussion, 2012.

AMAZON'S JUST DO IT AWARDS
Greg Linden, "Early Amazon: Just do it," *Geeking with Greg,* blog, April 26, 2006, *http://glinden.blogspot.com/2006/04/early-amazon-just-do-it.html.*

"I AM NOT WORTHY"
Greg Linden, "Early Amazon: Similarities," *Geeking with Greg,* blog, March 22, 2006, *http://glinden.blogspot.com/2006/03/early-amazon-similarities.html.*

"IN A 2012 FORTUNE ARTICLE..."
"Tony Hsieh's new $350 million startup," by Leigh Gallagher, *Fortune,* January 23, 2012.

PART FIVE

How do you get there from here?

Any enterprise involves risk, and connected companies are no exception—they can fail, too. But in times of change and uncertainty, their ability to learn and adapt faster than their competitors gives them an edge. If you want to become a connected company, there's no reason you can't start today.

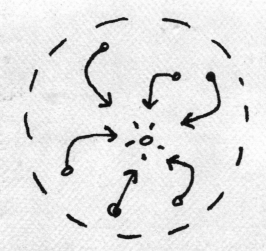

THE CORPORATE
IMMUNE SYSTEM

History is a race between
education and catastrophe.

—*H. G. Wells*

CHAPTER TWENTY ONE

The risks of connectedness

The speed and flexibility of connected companies gives them clear advantages over slow-moving adversaries. But no advantage comes without associated risk. How can connected companies go wrong? There are three ways: failure at the pod level, failure at the platform level, and failure of purpose.

NETWORKS ARE NEUTRAL

Networks in themselves are morally neutral. They are a method of organization. Like any other method, they have strengths and weaknesses, and they can be used for good or ill. Highly connected systems spread ideas faster, but they also spread viruses faster. Risky behavior in networks can have cascading effects that can't always be anticipated in advance, as we have seen in the financial crisis of the late 2000s.

Connected companies learn faster—they can coevolve with partners and competitors, and they more easily adapt and respond to change. They do this by distributing control to semi-autonomous pods, supported by platforms and connected by common purpose. Pods, platforms, and purpose. All have strengths and weaknesses, and all are subject to failure. We will examine each in turn.

POD FAILURE

Success in a connected company hinges on the concept of distributed control. By breaking the company into the smallest pieces possible, you can create a network of small, agile teams that can operate much faster than a large company or business unit ever could.

The question when distributing control is how much control to distribute. What freedoms should pods enjoy, and what are the limits of those freedoms? The answer will be different for every company. But the dangers are real. Too much freedom, and the network will lose cohesion and may overexpose the company to risk. Too little freedom, and you will defeat the purpose of distributing control, and pods will be unable to learn or innovate.

TOO MUCH AUTONOMY

Freedom in a network, like freedom in any community, is not absolute. The boundaries set by a company or community designate what is and isn't acceptable. Your rights do not include the freedom to impinge on your neighbor's rights. A pod should not have so much freedom that it can incur serious liabilities or put the entire company at risk.

In *The Service Profit Chain* (Free Press), James Heskett and W. Earl Sasser report that Ritz-Carlton employees can spend up to $2,000 to resolve a customer's problem. Since the Ritz-Carlton is a luxury hotel, this limits the hotel's liability in any one case to about the price of a five- to six-night stay.

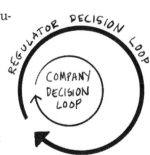

CONNECTED COMPANIES CAN OPERATE FASTER THAN REGULATORS CAN KEEP UP.

But at American International Group (AIG), one small unit had so much autonomy that they were able to put the entire company at risk. AIG's financial products unit entered into contracts without putting up sufficient collateral, exposing the company to billions of dollars in liabilities.

Note that AIG was in compliance with federal regulations. Compliance with regulations is not enough. Because they operate faster than other companies, connected companies can also innovate faster than regulators can keep up. A company that is ahead of the regulatory curve must be especially vigilant. If not for an $85 billion federal bailout, AIG would have ceased to exist. Despite the federal bailout, AIG's market value was destroyed and has yet to recover.

NOT ENOUGH AUTONOMY

Too many constraints can be equally dangerous. The purpose of giving autonomy to pods is so they can learn and improve over time. There is no way to know in advance what kinds of new knowledge will emerge. Too many constraints can cripple a pod such that it is unable to learn and successfully compete in its business environment.

When major airlines decided to compete with low-cost competitors like Southwest and JetBlue, they failed to give the baby airlines the flexibility they needed to compete effectively.

For example, Southwest offers short, frequent flights at low cost. They have optimized for this activity by focusing on small airplanes that can be more easily filled. Small airplanes can also be turned around more quickly at the gate, so they spend more time in the air and generate more profits. Standardizing on one type of short-haul plane also allows Southwest to maintain and repair planes more rapidly, because mechanics only need to understand one type of plane, and it's easier to manage a spare parts inventory. Southwest reduced costs by flying point-to-point to secondary airports instead of main hubs. Southwest focuses on long-term, win/win relationships with workers and their unions.

But when United, Delta, and Continental launched low-cost airlines, they saddled the new ventures with existing systems. They had to use the same workers and deal with the same unions. They had to use existing planes and reservation systems. They had to operate out of the same centralized hubs.

These attempts to gain cost advantages by using existing systems hampered the ability of the low-cost airlines to compete.

LA Times writer Jane Engle said of United spin-off TED:

> I was disappoint-TED...At the gate, there was a forest of orange signs, offering cheery greetings such as "It's a great day to be flying," and "Ted is happy to see you." But onboard, it was much like flying United, with its pleasant but business-like crew and cramped legroom. Plus one unsettling oversight: a used tissue in my seatback pocket.

If you want to start from scratch, you need to create enough space for startups to operate free from the constraints of your existing system.

It's tempting for a large company to force new ventures to use existing systems and infrastructure, but this puts the startup at an immediate disadvantage relative to competitors.

PLATFORM FAILURE

Platforms are systems that support a community. A platform is an investment, often a long-term investment that will only pay for itself over a long period of time. A platform supports a network—a shared resource—and in order to thrive, it must attract and retain members. Before they will join, people and companies want to know they can trust the platform provider to support them and adjust over time to meet their needs. That's a big leap.

FAILURE TO INVEST IN THE PLATFORM

Building networks and the platforms to support them takes time and money. If you run out of cash before you reach critical mass, the platform will fail.

People Express, another low-cost airline, launched in 1981 and initially grew very rapidly. Early success led the company to go on a buying spree, acquiring three airlines in its fourth year of operations. But People Express bit off more than it could chew. Three acquisitions in a row created a massive debt load. Labor struggles emerged with unions at the newly acquired companies. People Express's no-frills service was a turn-off to customers of the acquired airlines. Attempting to pay down the debt, People Express tried to attract more business travellers by introducing first-class cabins, a frequent flier plan, and complex fare structures, and in the process became nearly indistinguishable from the airlines it was trying to disrupt.

The rapid expansion proved too much for the company, and it was merged into Continental Airlines in 1987.

In 2007, Yahoo launched an innovation studio called Brickhouse, in order to better compete with nimble startups. Yahoo opened a 14,000-square-foot office far away from corporate headquarters, in the South of Market Area (SOMA) of San Francisco, a hotbed of startups and innovation, and seeded the effort with entrepreneurs such as Flickr cofounder Caterina Fake. Basically, Brickhouse was an innovation pod, set up to rekindle the startup flame and encourage experimentation and the exploration of new ideas. The Brickhouse team moved quickly, developing products in a third of the time it took at Yahoo proper. Brickhouse launched several innovative services for managing streams and feeds (Yahoo Pipes), streaming video (Yahoo Live), and location sharing (Yahoo Fire Eagle).

But for all its successes, Brickhouse failed. Employees at the main office were jealous of the freedom given to their peers at Brickhouse. And since Brickhouse was isolated from the corporate parent, that left no one at headquarters to protect it. So, just like People Express, Brickhouse ran out of runway, and in 2008, only two years after its launch, Yahoo shut it down.

Salim Ismail, the Yahoo VP who took charge of Yahoo Brickhouse in 2007 , explains the failure this way: "When you do innovation in a large company, the immune system will come and attack you. A large company is basically an organism, and it has antibodies and an immune system, and those things will come and attack."

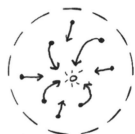

OVER-CONTROLLING THE PLATFORM

Before people will join a platform, they must trust the provider to look after their interests and be there for the long term. In addition, good platforms have broad value and are easy to adopt. The more people join a platform, the greater its value.

WHEN YOU INNOVATE
IN A LARGE COMPANY,
THE IMMUNE SYSTEM
WILL ATTACK YOU

But the temptation for a platform provider is to ask for too much in return. Sony has repeated this mistake several times in its history. In 1975, Sony released Betamax, a recording format for videocassettes. A year later, JVC came out with a rival format, VHS. Although the technology of the two formats was similar, neither was compatible with the other. At first, Sony tried to go it alone, maintaining Betamax as a proprietary technology. Meanwhile, JVC licensed the VHS standard to competitors, making VHS an open standard. With more manufacturers making devices and tapes, the VHS platform grew more rapidly, and in networks, a small advantage in rate of growth leads to a very large advantage over time. Eventually, Sony capitulated, shutting down its Betamax group and adopting VHS as a standard.

Later, Sony made the same mistake in the portable music business. In 2001, Napster had already disrupted the music business, and there was no safe, easy, legitimate way to buy music online. While Apple's Steve Jobs set out to recruit music companies and artists to offer their songs for sale on iTunes, Sony announced it would go forward with a proprietary format called Pressplay. Apple announced a rival technology called FairPlay.

Both Pressplay and FairPlay protected the digital rights of any song bought online. But there was a critical difference. Sony's Pressplay would only play authorized, protected files, but Apple's FairPlay would protect files bought in their store, and also play any file in a user's existing library. This made Apple's platform more valuable, because users did not have to start from scratch to build a music library.

In addition, Apple aggressively courted musicians and record labels, giving away all of the money from music sales to partners: record companies made 70 cents on every 99-cent purchase, with the rest split between artists and merchandising costs.

The temptations to use a platform for your own company's advantage are great. And if you succeed, the rewards can also be great. But over-controlling the platform comes with significant risk: if people don't trust you, or if your platform doesn't have broad value, or if it's not easy to adopt, the chances are that it will fail.

The purpose of any platform is to serve its members and constituents. Fail to remember that at your peril.

FAILURE OF PURPOSE

Profits are not a purpose. They are a result. Profits accrue when a company consistently does a good job for customers, building relationships and loyalty. When customers trust a company to do a good job for them, they will come back over and over again. Therefore, a company is healthy and sustainable when its primary purpose is creating value for customers. There is no other way. When a company's purpose shifts so that it is serving itself first at the expense of customers, then it has lost its way, and its demise is only a matter of time.

Enron was a connected company. *Fortune* named Enron "America's most innovative company" six years in a row. The company distributed control to workers—every trader had her own profit-and-loss statement.

In annual performance reviews, employees at Enron were rated from 1-to-5 on how well they lived the company's values: communication, respect, integrity, and excellence. But the company didn't walk the walk. Employees who rated high on values were often fired, while lower-ranked workers were promoted based on the profits they brought in to the company. It was clear to everyone that profit was what mattered.

For Enron, the problem was a failure of purpose. Enron stopped being about creating value for customers. The numbers became the goal. Keep the stock price up. Keep income and cash flow up. Inflate asset values. Keep liabilities off the books.

In March of 2012, Greg Smith, an executive director at Goldman Sachs, resigned after 12 years at the company. In a resignation letter published in The New York Times, he claimed that Goldman had lost touch with its customers and its purpose. He wrote:

> What are three quick ways to become a leader? a) Execute on the firm's "axes," which is Goldman-speak for persuading your clients to invest in the stocks or other products that we are trying to get rid of because they are not seen as having a lot of potential profit. b) "Hunt Elephants." In English: get your clients—some of whom are sophisticated, and some of whom aren't—to trade whatever will bring the biggest profit to Goldman. Call me old-fashioned, but I don't like selling my clients a

product that is wrong for them. c) Find yourself sitting in a seat where your job is to trade any illiquid, opaque product with a three-letter acronym...Over the last 12 months I have seen five different managing directors refer to their own clients as "muppets," sometimes over internal email...It astounds me how little senior management gets a basic truth: If clients don't trust you, they will eventually stop doing business with you. It doesn't matter how smart you are.

A company can't exist without customers. So if a company is to survive and thrive in the long term, it must build trusted relationships with customers. You have to treat them right. Any company can abuse or rip off customers in the short term, but customers learn fast, and they will not be abused for long, especially when there are alternatives available.

CUSTOMERS FIRST

Connected companies operate at a faster pace than other companies in their ecosystem. To use John Boyd's phrase, they get inside their adversaries' decision loops, leaving adversaries in confusion and disarray. Speed is an advantage. This makes leadership and moral authority more important than ever.

Creating value for customers must come first. It is the only sustainable strategy. Leadership has failed when a company starts to see the stock price as the goal instead of a result. Profits are a reward that comes from creating value for customers. They are not an end in themselves.

If a connected company uses its speed advantage to outrace the law, to hoodwink customers and investors, and to avoid regulators, then it is sowing the seeds of its own destruction. When a company begins to see investors and government regulators as people to be fooled, as adversaries to be outrun and outgunned, when customers become an afterthought, secondary to profits—the company is doomed.

Eventually, customers and regulators will catch on. The laws will catch up. The lesson for regulators is that what you don't see or understand can hurt you. A government that can't keep up with criminals is an accident waiting to happen. The lesson for companies is that customers must always come first.

NOTES FOR CHAPTER TWENTY ONE

TED

Jane Engle, "Flying the frugal skies can be fun," *The Los Angeles Times*, March 21, 2004.

IMMUNE SYSTEM ATTACKS

"Keen On...How Yahoo Screwed Up and Lessons for Other Silicon Valley Giants," Techcrunch TV, October 11, 2011, *http://techcrunch.com/2011/10/11/ keen-on-how-yahoo-screwed-up-and-lessons-for-other-silicon-valley-giants-tctv/*.

GOLDMAN SACHS

"Why I Am Leaving Goldman Sachs," by Greg Smith, *The New York Times*, March 14, 2012.

You can't connect the dots looking forward; you can only connect them looking backwards. So you have to trust that the dots will somehow connect in your future. You have to trust in something—your gut, destiny, life, karma, whatever. This approach has never let me down, and it has made all the difference in my life.

—*Steve Jobs, Cofounder & former CEO, Apple*

CHAPTER TWENTY TWO

Starting the journey

Connected companies today are the exception, not the rule. But as long as the environment is characterized by change and uncertainty, connected companies will have the advantage. There are four ways your company can start that journey today: organic growth; top-down, leader-driven change; pilot pods; and network weaving. You can take the first steps on Monday morning.

HOW TO GET THERE FROM HERE

Connected customers are adopting disruptive technologies faster than companies can keep up, and the resulting complexity is overwhelming current business structures, causing confusion and disarray.

To survive, companies must develop the means to absorb complexity and variety. They must be able to respond, learn, and adapt more rapidly, and the only way to do this is to distribute control to front-line units and help them build the capabilities that they need to win.

All this is well and good. But what can you do on Monday morning to begin your company's transformation? How can you get from here to there?

IT WON'T BE EASY

The problem for many companies is that when customers and the market change gradually, it's easy to live in denial, especially when a company is large and has been successful in the past. Some people call this the boiled frog effect, based on a metaphorical story about a frog in a pot of water. If the water is heated up slowly enough, the story goes, the frog will not notice the gradual, incremental increase in heat, and it will stay in the pot, slowly boiling to death.

It's very difficult for a company to reinvent its core architecture. In *The Future of Management* (Harvard Business Review Press), Gary Hamel reports a conversation he had with senior executives at a big American auto manufacturer. He asked them why, after 20 years of benchmarking studies, the company had been unable to catch up to Toyota's productivity. Here's the answer he got:

> Twenty years ago we started sending our young people to Japan to study Toyota. They'd come back and tell us how good Toyota was and we simply didn't believe them. We figured they'd dropped a zero somewhere—no one could produce cars with so few defects per vehicle, or with so few labor hours. It was five years before we acknowledged that Toyota really was beating us in a bunch of critical areas. Over the next five years, we told ourselves that Toyota's advantages were all cultural. It was all about wa and nemawashi—the uniquely Japanese spirit of cooperation and consultation that Toyota had cultivated with its employees. We were sure that American workers would never put up with these paternalistic practices. Then, of course, Toyota started building plants in the United States, and they got the same results here they got in Japan—so our cultural excuse went out the window. For the next five years, we focused on Toyota's manufacturing processes. We studied their use of factory automation, their supplier relationships, just-in-time systems, everything. But despite all our benchmarking, we could never seem to get the same results in our own factories. It's only in the last five years that we've finally admitted to ourselves that Toyota's success is based on a wholly different set of principles—about the capabilities of its employees and the responsibilities of its leaders.

DO YOU WORK AT A PLACE THAT IGNITES YOUR PASSION?

The first step on the journey is to ask yourself what you want. Do you identify with the purpose of your company? Is it a place you want to be? Companies run on passion, and if you can't find the passion in the work you're doing today, then you're in the wrong place.

The core of a connected company is a shared purpose that everyone in the company can get excited about. That's the starting point. Companies are in many ways just like people. They all have their lovable qualities and they all have flaws. If you can't find something to love about your company, then you are not doing yourself or the company a favor by staying. Even if it is deeply flawed in many ways, you need to be able to believe in a future that's worth pursuing, or there's no point. I'm not suggesting you need to quit today, but the world is too exciting and there are too many opportunities out there to stay in a job you don't enjoy. Start looking for something you can get excited about.

DESIGN AROUND CUSTOMERS

Companies of the future will be designed around customers. How easy is it for customers to find your company? How easy is it for them to talk to you, engage with you, and start buying from you? How easy is it for customers to build a long-term relationship with you? Do you answer when they call? Are you responsive to their requests? If you are an airline, don't compare yourself to other airlines. Compare yourself to Nordstrom or the Ritz-Carlton or Amazon.

A connected company starts with customers. The people and systems must be organized to support the activity of serving customers.

It's possible that you don't come into direct contact with customers in your day-to-day job. Managers and senior executives spend their time in meetings, managing information that is abstracted from the work, like profit and revenue numbers, cash flow, product sales, and so on. The people who are directly connected with customers, like sales and support staff, are often those with the lowest status in the organization.

Front-line people are often excluded from conversations about strategies, processes, and policies that directly affect their ability to perform. When those decisions are made based on abstracted numbers, without a real understanding of the situation on the ground, chaos and confusion can result. But front-line workers have deep domain knowledge and are in continuous contact with customers. The front line is where the action is, where the information is richest and most concrete. If you want to understand the company from the customer's perspective, you will have to visit the front line.

It may not be pretty. The front line can be messy and disorderly. It's where the battles get fought, where they are won and lost. But there's a reason that the best military commanders spend time on the front lines: it's the only way to get an honest and deep understanding of what's really going on. Anything else is just hearsay.

TAKING STEPS VERSUS CROSSING CHASMS

As you improve your understanding of customers and the experiences they have with your company, you will begin to identify gaps. Some things you can address one step at a time, but others will seem like uncrossable chasms. In these cases, you need to build a bridge.

In our research, we have identified four paths to connectedness: the organic path; top-down, leader-driven change; pilot pods; and network weaving.

THE ORGANIC PATH

Every company starts small—so all companies are born connected. If you're a start-up or a small company, the challenge is to grow intelligently and avoid dividing in a way that disconnects your people from the purpose of the work.

Often, this will mean ignoring the advice of well-meaning professionals who belong to the "old school" command-and-control philosophy, including seasoned executives, lawyers, and financial advisors. They usually mean well, but are so embedded in industrial-age paradigms that they have trouble understanding more organic structures.

Small companies and startups organize and distribute work informally among a small team of people who all feel connected to the work and to customers. If you are lucky enough to work at a company in this category, your path to connectedness is easier than most. Focus on growing in a podular way:

- *Shared purpose.* The primary force that keeps people in a connected company aligned and working together is a shared commitment to a common purpose, combined with a set of core principles that guide decisions. Everyone at Nordstrom understands that the company is committed to outstanding service. This allows them to make deci- sions without consulting policies and procedures and without needing permission from supervisors.

- *Autonomous pods.* When people are committed to a common pur- pose, the best way to get them to do the work is to give them the freedom and autonomy to organize it for themselves. Freedom is not absolute: it exists within a framework of boundaries set by the organization and consistent with the purpose. But a pod has the greatest potential when it has the most degrees of freedom within the system.

- *Growth through reproduction.* Divided companies scale up, organiz- ing work into divisions and functions, and putting like work with like (for example, all the programmers together). Connected com- panies scale out, organizing work into fully functional units (for ex- ample, sales and operations in one unit) that operate as businesses within the business, like franchises. Form new pods by seeding them with individuals from existing pods. In this way, tacit knowledge, as well as the passion and energy for the work, are maintained and spread as you grow. You need to do this to keep the flame alive. When Nordstrom opens a new store, they pay employees to move to the new location for exactly this reason.

· *Platforms that support rather than control.* Growth does offer opportunities to gain efficiency and economies of scale. Historically, these economies have been gained by hierarchical management and control systems. But in a connected company, those economies come from consolidating routine or repeating operations into well-oiled structures that are focused on support more than control. Grow your platforms slowly and conservatively, and make sure the pods have a voice in their design and management.

TOP-DOWN, LEADER-DRIVEN CHANGE

If you happen to be the boss or a senior leader in your company, you can follow the path laid down by Jack Welch at GE and Lou Gerstner at IBM. Welch and Gerstner wrote two of the best manuals for top-down, leader-driven change in their books *Jack: Straight from the Gut* (Business Plus) and *Who Says Elephants Can't Dance?* (HarperCollins).

To take this path, you need to be a committed leader, willing to declare war on the existing organization and its culture, which is often zealously guarded. Jack Welch described his approach as, "throwing hand grenades, trying to blow up traditions and rituals that held us back."

There is no getting around it: top-down, leader-driven change is hard work, the kind of hard work most executives would avoid if they could. Lou Gerstner only tacked IBM's culture because there was no other way:

Frankly, if I could have chosen not to tackle the IBM culture head-on, I probably wouldn't have...changing the attitude and behavior of hundreds of thousands of people is very, very hard to accomplish. Business schools don't teach you how to do it. You can't lead the revolution from the splendid isolation of corporate headquarters. You can't simply give a couple of speeches or write a new credo for the company and declare that the new culture has taken hold. You can't mandate it, can't engineer it. What you can do is create the conditions for transformation. You can provide incentives. You can define the marketplace realities and goals. But then you have to trust. In fact, in the end, management doesn't change culture. Management invites the workforce itself to change the culture. Perhaps the toughest nut of all to crack was getting IBM employees to accept that invitation.

Both Welch and Gerstner agree on the following.

· *Focus on customers.* Welch and Gerstner did everything they could to get their companies re-focused on customers and the market. Welch famously declared that every GE division would be number one or two in its market, or else. One of Gerstner's first moves was to send senior executives out to meet directly with customers and give him a one-page report on their issues and concerns.

LOU GERSTNER

· *Fight bureaucracy.* In both companies, what had once been a customer-oriented culture had become stultified and bureaucratic. Both executives declared war on bureaucracy and fought hard to remove the barriers that kept people from doing the right things for the company and its customers. GE Work-Outs are designed to give frontline workers a chance to rethink and improve the systems they work in, and GE expects management to accept the majority of worker proposals.

· *Move decisions close to the customer.* Both CEOs distributed control wherever possible so decisions could be made close to the work and close to customers. Gerstner said, "Big companies are inevitably slow and cumbersome; small companies are quick and responsive." Therefore, break big companies into the smallest pieces possible.

· *Foster teamwork.* One problem with hierarchies is that the goals of sub-groups become isolated from each other, and often find themselves in conflict with the goals of the organization as a whole. As each division works to achieve their goals and targets, it's easy to forget or ignore the idea that everyone is working for the same company. When Gerstner inherited IBM, it had become a collection of fiefdoms in which one geographical group had no incentive to work with the others. He reorganized the company into customer-focused units and changed the compensation and bonus structure to pin executive compensation to the performance of the whole company.

JACK WELCH

· *Put people first.* Changing the company means changing the people. They need to commit with their hearts as well as their minds. Welch said, "People first, strategy second." Gerstner agrees: "In the end, an organization is nothing more than the collective capacity of its people to create value." Top-down change doesn't have to originate with the CEO. As change expert John Kotter says, "You need something you can draw a box around." If you manage a division or group in a larger company, you may be able to get more connected by simply taking charge of the pod you're in.

CONNECTING AN INTERNAL GROUP AT MARRIOTT

Livia Labate is Senior Director of User Experience Design for Marriott International. She is responsible for the user experience across all of the company's websites and mobile applications. When she came on board, Labate's group was made up of about 40 people who were divided into groups based on their function. They were pulled together to collaborate on a project-by-project basis, and when projects were done, the individuals involved dispersed back to their separate groups.

She says, "When I started with the team, I found that they were feeling really disempowered and morale was really low...The user experience design practice was supposed to be composed of these chefs who had real deep knowledge and expertise and could create these amazing cuisines, but we were really line cooks. We were flipping burgers."

Project managers would come in to her department and say things like, "I need an information architect for 10 hours to do a thing." Labate felt that the focus on projects and tasks was too hierarchical and process-oriented, and that a new approach was needed.

"I started thinking, okay, what would a pod look like? How can I mix these sub-specialties up into one group so they can be more empowered and make more decisions?"

One of her first actions was to change the physical space. The office was the kind you see in corporations all over the world, segregated by cubicle walls. So Labate started by taking down the walls. "That was the lowest-cost option at the time," she says. And immediately she started

LIVIA LABATE

to see changes in the way people interacted. They were starting to engage more with each other and their work.

Labate did other things to encourage cross-functional interaction. She found opportunities to pull together cross-functional groups to work together on small problems. She took the entire team offsite for a day to socialize and get to know each other better. They visited museums and went bowling.

Almost immediately, she noticed a small but important shift. Before the change, people would refer to each other by job title: "The information architect said this. The designer said this or did that." After the change, people started to refer to each other by name. They were starting to connect on a social level.

Next she looked at leadership. Labate had four direct reports, who managed four functional teams. She knew that leadership would have to change. She needed leaders who saw their roles as support, rather than control, and who could help individuals grow:

> I still had to frame things in the old way, so that was really difficult. That was probably the hardest part of the process, was trying to do something new using old words and old structures. But ultimately, I was able to establish what I wanted out of these roles, and then opened them up as new positions, and interviewed the people who had played director roles on the old teams, and also interviewed new candidates...When I interviewed them, I was just trying to assess, can they really embrace that level of leadership and management culture?

She decided that two of her four direct reports were ready and willing to embrace the change. Of the other two, one was simply unhappy as a manager and was happy to go back to front-line work. He was a great person who was simply in the wrong place. The other manager was not a good fit, and Labate let her go. The two empty spots were filled by promotions from the front line.

She reorganized the teams into cross-functional pods that would work together on larger initiatives. Each pod was responsible for a big chunk of the customer experience. For example, one pod took charge of the reservation experience. She met with each member of her team individually, explaining the concept of pods and where she thought that person would be the best fit.

The day after the change, Labate announced the change to the larger organization. She went on a "road show," explaining to other groups how and why her team had reorganized, and answering questions about workflow.

The response to the change has been overwhelmingly positive on all fronts.

Labate's internal customers have started working more collaboratively with her group. They ask less for functional expertise and started treating her group more like a strategic partner, asking for advice rather than demanding tasks. More conversations are happening between her group and other groups.

The actual changes Labate made to people's jobs were relatively small. It was really the system around them that changed. "At the end of the day, I didn't really change people's goals or their levels of responsibility very much," she says. "But the mindset has changed...The real change here is that instead of saying 'No,' by default, the system says 'Yes,' by default. That just allows people to flow. It takes the gates away."

Employees are more engaged now than they have ever been. As one worker put it, "Something strange happened when we shifted to the new pod format. I suddenly feel free to be awesome."

CONNECTING WITH CUSTOMERS AT U.S. CELLULAR

When Sharif Renno took a job as store manager for U.S. Cellular in Milwaukee, Wisconsin, sales were flat. So he started looking for new ways to connect with customers. He quickly gravitated to Twitter, where he could engage in ongoing conversations with customers and also build relationships in the community:

> I started to establish a rather lengthy list of customers and prospects that enjoyed speaking with me, had an understanding of where I worked and where I was located. Eventually I had the opportunity to work with many of these people... What happened is they started to select the location where I worked to do their wireless shopping.

When customers had a problem, they would tweet or call Renno rather than call customer support, and he would take care of their problems. The time and effort he spent solving customer problems paid off. People became so satisfied that they started recommending him, his store, and U.S. Cellular to friends. When people complained about phone service on Twitter, Renno's growing army of advocates would say things like, "Hey, I've worked with this store, they're on Twitter, let's connect the dots, they can help."

"I started to have sales people that weren't paid sales people," says Renno, "essentially just throwing softballs our way. It was really exciting when customers began to generate buzz for our store online, and it took me about six to eight months to establish enough credibility in the space where people wanted to refer their friends and family into the store by way of Twitter."

To strengthen the bond he was building with customers, Renno created opportunities for customers to connect with him—and each other—face to face. He partnered with local restaurants and bars to sponsor "Tweetups" where people could meet each other and get discounts on food and drinks. Renno recruited company associates to attend the event, but instructed them that they were not there to sell. Rather, they were to focus on building relationships:

SHARIF RENNO

> We weren't there to sell a product. We were just there to make sure people knew we were a part of the community and they could count on us. If they happened to have a question while we were present we would answer it. Really it was about getting to know the community and networking and just being top of mind so when they reached that moment in their customer journey where they're like, hey, I'm thinking about a change in wireless or I need to upgrade my phone, they were thinking about U.S. Cellular instead of competitors.

Soon, more than 20% of Renno's sales were coming from social activities. The entire energy of the workplace changed, as employees started building relationships with customers:

> By doing something different and creating that atmosphere of energy and excitement, it drove the morale in the store to the point where everyone was excited to come to work, because they knew we had this atmosphere of fun, that the community was in love with the store, that we probably had some traffic that talked to us online in the morning that would now be stopping by to either buy something, get a phone, get an accessory, or just swing by to say hi, which happened quite a bit.

Renno was concerned that his initiative might get shut down. At the time, U.S. Cellular did not have a strong social media policy. What they did have was vague, and most associates chose not to participate in work-related social media activity. So he let senior executives know what he was doing and kept them in the loop as his experiment progressed. But his approach was to try things first, and explain later.

"I would rather ask for forgiveness than ask for permission," he says. "Organizations can be stodgy, and in general, most don't want to say yes to new ideas, because their first and foremost responsibility is to protect the organization and protect the business. I'm really grateful for the flexibility of the leadership team here."

Renno's advice to managers in other companies is to focus on happiness. Yes, happiness:

> Try and find what does make you happy or why you come to work, and try and build upon it, try and build your team around it, try and get them excited about it. The more people that get excited about your ideas, the more fun you're going to have together at work. The more fun that you have at work, the more excited your customers are when they're in your store. When your customers are excited, they're more willing to buy from you, so it's kind of a cycle. You just have to find that nugget that you're jazzed about, and dedicate yourself to blowing it out. Once you do that, and your senior leaders see that the store environment is contagious, that your sales are on the rise or are increasing, opportunities will start to present themselves to you.

The company's leaders know a good thing when they see it. Renno has been pulled out of the field so he can work on trying to replicate his results nationwide, to help U.S. Cellular become a more connected company.

COMMON THREADS

Leader-driven change is difficult. Because it runs against the grain of an organization, it requires a fresh mindset, a vision for change, and the willingness to stick to your guns in the face of strong resistance. It's like running into a strong wind or rowing against the current. Since it is so difficult, successful examples are hard to find. Far more common are the organizations that fail to change and die a long, lingering death. The evidence is anecdotal, but Jack Welch of GE, Lou Gerster of

IBM, Livia Labate of Marriott, and Sharif Renno have one thing in common: all of them were, to one degree or another, outsiders.

Jack Welch came out of the very young and entrepreneurial plastics division, far outside the politics of GE headquarters. He was a dark-horse candidate for CEO, and most senior executives were against his appointment.

Lou Gerstner was brought in to IBM at a time of crisis, when the company was on the brink of financial disaster. He was formerly the CEO of American Express, an IBM customer.

Livia Labate was a newcomer to Marriott. Before she took the job, she asked her interviewers, "What is the appetite for change in this organization?" She came on with a clear understanding that she would be changing things.

Sharif Renno was not new to U.S. Cellular, but he was new to the Milwaukee store when he took it over.

Conclusion: a crisis may not be necessary. But a fresh perspective, and the willingness to act on it, is critical.

PILOT PODS

Most real, significant change does not happen from the inside. IBM may have transformed, but it did not give birth to Microsoft. Xerox did not give birth to Apple. If top-down change is out of the question, then another option is to launch a pilot pod. A pilot pod is an experiment that happens outside the regular structure of the company. Pilot pods are like special forces in the military: they operate outside the norm and are not subject to the same rules and restrictions as the regular forces, because they operate in areas where they must be completely self-sufficient, sometimes for months at a time. They work in areas that are hard to reach, like behind enemy lines.

A pilot pod is similar, because it works directly with customers and independently of the parent company. Like military special forces, pilot pods function as probes or reconnaissance units, gathering valuable intelligence that the parent company couldn't get on its own. They are trusted to operate independently, with a great degree of freedom to experiment and learn.

LAUNCH A PILOT POD TO SHIFT TO A NEW BUSINESS MODEL

When a company finds that its business model is in trouble, one approach is to pivot—to shift the company's purpose to one that has more value to customers. It's a risky move, but one well suited to podular innovation.

Microblogging platform Twitter started as a pilot pod. The parent company, Odeo, was a podcasting platform, but the company was feeling heavy pressure from Apple. Team members gathered together for a day-long brainstorming session, during which they broke out into small groups to discuss ideas for new initiatives. In one of the groups, team member Jack Dorsey described his idea for an

SMS service that allowed you to text message a group of friends at the same time. Each group presented their ideas and a few were chosen for prototyping. After a brief prototyping round, the teams presented demos, and Jack's idea, which had morphed into a status-update tool, rose to the top.

A small team was assigned to build out the service, while the rest of the team continued to maintain and grow Odeo. Twitter was launched on the Web in 2006. The parent company, Odeo, no longer exists, but Twitter is thriving.

LAUNCH A PILOT POD TO SERVE UNMET CUSTOMER NEEDS

In 1988, P&G had 12 Global Product divisions with salespeople all calling on Walmart separately, with different strategies and approaches. The salespeople were accountable for the sales results in their respective divisions (like Fabric Care, which sells Tide), and Walmart could never deal with P&G as a whole: a classic example of a divided company, with units measured separately that had no incentive to come together. Even though the company was doing $375 million a year with Walmart, from Walmart's perspective, they were inflexible, difficult, and complicated to do business with. When Sam Walton tried to call P&G's CEO to give him Walmart's "Vendor of the Year" award in 1985, he was transferred six times and never got through. He decided to give the award to another vendor.

Today, Procter and Gamble has created a podular team that focuses on only one customer: Walmart (which is responsible for about a third of the company's revenue). The team—a global team of 250 people, reporting directly to the COO of the company, that is basically a customer for all the other divisions—gives Walmart a single, easy interface for all their buying. A salesperson from each business unit reports to the head of the Walmart team.

Walmart now does $10 billion a year in business with P&G. They have a joint scorecard to measure success, which includes profits for both companies as well as other financial and logistics measures. They work together to reduce costs on distribution and logistics and share data to gain insights.

Walmart had loads of data that came from scanners in all of their stores. P&G had data that it used to develop products. By putting the information together, they could answer questions like, "What products do customers buy in combination, and why?" By analyzing Walmart's in-store data, the companies, working together, were able to eliminate losing products from store shelves and replace them with winners, increasing sales by 32.5%.

DISRUPT YOURSELF BEFORE SOMEONE ELSE DOES

Intel's Andy Grove said, "Only the paranoid survive." If you are successful, then fast, tough, nimble competitors will find you, and they will do their best to mop up the floor with you. But most disruptive competitors start small. So instead of waiting for an outside company to disrupt your business, do it yourself. Here are a couple of examples.

DISRUPTING DESKTOP SOFTWARE AT AUTODESK

Autodesk is probably the largest software company you've never heard of. Founded in 1982, Autodesk makes the CAD (Computer-aided design) software that architects and industrial designers use to create blueprints, 3D models, and plans for the things we use every day, from blenders to cars to office towers.

In the late 1990s, all of Autodesk's software was desktop software, and the rise of the Internet did not escape their attention. Autodesk realized that since software was digital, there would be many opportunities to deliver software and improve it using the Internet and its rich set of potential connections.

The company was also sitting on about $700 million in cash. In 1999, Autodesk created Autodesk Ventures, a separate division to invest in promising web startups and ideas that complemented their existing business.

One of the first ideas, dubbed Buzzsaw, came from within the company. The idea behind Buzzsaw was to create a marketplace for the digital 3D "building blocks" that architects use to develop their designs. Parts manufacturers could submit 3D models of the parts in their catalog, so when an architect created a 3D model, the parts of the model would be automatically linked to the suppliers catalog, including the exact price, part number, and purchase information. Buzzsaw was iTunes for CAD components.

After incubating the startup for six months, Autodesk spun it out as a separate company, retaining some equity in the company and raising additional capital from outside investors.

Another internally incubated idea named RedSpark was an Internet hub for manufacturing services. It was launched in April 2000. But of the two pilot pods, only one was successful. RedSpark was shuttered in October of 2001, although Autodesk absorbed some of the people and technology back into the parent company.

Buzzsaw raised about $90 million. Autodesk invested about $40 million altogether, including $22 million in Buzzsaw, which it bought back for $15 million, a fire-sale price, in 2001. Buzzsaw is now called Building Collaboration Services, and Buzzsaw CEO Carl Bass is now the CEO of Autodesk.

DISRUPTING FULL-SERVICE TELECOM AT O2

In 2008, Gav Thompson, Head of Brand innovation at UK telecom provider O2, came up with an idea for a pilot pod while sitting in a Web2.0 conference in San Francisco, doodling in his notebook. He envisioned a company that was designed and run mostly by customers, and a new service called giffgaff—an ancient Scottish word for "mutual giving"—was born. O2 started the pod by launching a community first, so prospective customers

GAV THOMPSON

could talk about what they wanted in a service. Early members of the community, now known as founders, helped to shape and craft the offering.

Giffgaff is a mobile phone service that uses O2's cellular network, but in every other respect operates as an independent company. Giffgaff is a low-cost service with no physical sales or service locations. All operations are online. Customers order a SIM card online that is delivered to their home. They pay bills online and receive statements online. The service is cheap—about half the price of most competing services.

But that's just the beginning. Giffgaff rewards its customers for helping them run the business. In exchange for providing value to the business, customers get "payback points" that they can redeem for services or cash. Thus, giffgaff pays its customers for providing support, bringing in new customers, creating advertisements, and so on. Some customers subsidize their service with their contributions, and others even make a profit. The community responds to questions and support requests 24 hours a day, and most questions are answered within 60 seconds.

When difficult decisions come up, giffgaff management gets customers involved. For example, giffgaff provides unlimited data, and in January of 2012, management revealed that 1% of users were generating more than a third of the data traffic. This was economically unsustainable for the company, so management brought the situation to the community, asking, "What should we do about this?" Customers responded with a range of suggestions, from a "wall of shame" that exposed the offenders, to cutting them off or throttling data services once a daily limit had been reached. (As this book went to press, the problem had not yet been solved, but the conversation was ongoing.)

This method of organizing work allows giffgaff to run a mobile telecom company for the entire UK with a staff of less than 20 people, with a ratio of subscribers to staff of about 5,000 to one.

By launching a pilot pod, O2 has successfully disrupted its own business before an agile startup could do so. Not only that, it seems they are disrupting the entire mobile industry. Mobile telecom in general has one of the worst customer satisfaction rates of any industry—a sign that an industry is ripe for disruption. The average Net Promoter Score (NPS) for mobile providers is an abysmal 19 percent. But giffgaff's NPS is 73%. This blows away all other mobile providers, and is on a par with customer-focused companies like Google and Apple. Customer satisfaction at giffgaff is 91%.

THE DIFFERENCE BETWEEN A PROOF-OF-CONCEPT AND A PILOT

A pilot is an experiment. A proof of concept is an experiment in which the conclusion is determined in advance. And as any scientist will tell you, if you already know the conclusion you want to reach, you will probably introduce bias into the experiment.

The thing is, when you embark on a pilot, you don't know in advance what you might learn. If a pilot is positioned as a proof of concept, then the team will be focused more on achieving a predetermined result than on learning from the environment. Rather than start with a "concept" to be proved, start your pilot with a "hypothesis," which can be proved or disproved. Either way, you are learning something new.

A pilot pod doesn't have to be a whole new company. It can be a small experiment, like a new service or a cross-disciplinary initiative. But in order to learn and deliver real innovation, a pod must be independent and connected to the environment. That means that, unlike skunkworks or black box–type innovation efforts, pilot pods need to operate in the field, with real customers.

NETWORK WEAVING

If you're not the CEO and you can't find a way to launch a pilot pod, then your last resort is network weaving. Network weaving is the most common approach being taken by most large companies today that have decided that they want to become more connected.

The concept is that better networks and more connections can make companies more effective and adaptive. To that end, companies are introducing social and collaboration technologies and developing guidelines and policies for the use of social media.

There are two approaches to network weaving. The first is to create a central, core group, sanctioned by the organization, that is charged with developing a set of social media policies and guidelines, and then rolling out social technologies and practices to the company as a whole, much like you would introduce a new technology, procedure, or policy.

The second approach is what social business expert Chris Brogan calls the "pirate approach." Pirates are people and groups who simply start forging connections and operating based on the way they think work ought to be done. Pirates take initiative; they don't ask permission, although they may apologize if scolded. Pirate activities are not officially sanctioned, but in many cases, managers turn a blind eye because they help work get done faster and more effectively. Most social networking technologies are free or so cheap you can put them on a credit card, and they can be found everywhere.

The only real problem with network weaving is that it's an incremental, step-by-step approach. Like a lot of things in the corporate world, it's a workaround rather than a solution. Network weaving by itself can't change organizational control structures. It can't change compensation systems. It can't reorganize the hierarchy.

What customers want is not just connectedness. They want people who can serve their needs and solve their problems. If employees have access to social technologies but are still bound by scripts and procedures, if workers can connect with customers but don't have the power to act, then you haven't got a connected company. You've got a connected prison, and your employees will be worse than demoralized when they find they are connected to customers but unable to do anything for them.

But if network weaving is your only option, it's a good first step. Weaving networks creates social ties that connect pockets and silos inside and outside your organization. As you forge those connections and increase the flow of information horizontally and across channels, you begin to create the conditions for people to find each other, connect, self-organize into teams, and develop communities where they can share ideas and formulate projects and plans. Like vines on a brick wall, those connections slowly but surely weaken the bureaucratic structures of control that suppress creativity and initiative. With persistence, cracks will appear.

Network weaving may not solve the problems of the divided company, but it will expose them, because networks allow people to see and share what's happening across the organization.

IT'S TIME TO CHANGE

In the future, every company will be a connected company. Although they may be able to survive for some time, eventually every company must give customers what they want—or they will die. And connected customers are already demanding more than divided, industrial-age companies can deliver. This future is inevitable and it's only a matter of time.

Some leaders are rising to the challenge. They are organizing for adaptiveness by distributing control and building platforms to support autonomous teams. They are creating open environments of trust and connection with employees, partners, and customers. They are managing their companies as complex adaptive systems where continual learning and experimentation are part of the game.

The challenges are substantial, but there is no choice. As connected company pioneer Jack Welch said, "Change before you have to."

NOTES FOR CHAPTER TWENTY TWO

MARRIOTT AND U.S. CELLULAR
Based on interviews conducted by the author, 2011.

WALMART AND P&G
Michael Grean and Michael J. Shaw, "Supply-Chain Integration through Information-Sharing: Channel Partnership between Wal-Mart and Procter & Gamble," *http://citebm.business.illinois.edu/it_cases/graen-shaw-pg.pdf.*

BIBLIOGRAPHY

Brokerage and Closure: An Introduction to Social Capital
By Ronald S. Burt, Oxford University Press, 2007.

Catalyst: How You Can become an Extraordinary Growth Leader
By Jeanne Liedtka, Crown Business, 2009.

The Cluetrain Manifesto
By Rick Levine, Christopher Locke, Doc Searls, David Weinberger, and McKee Jake, 1999.

Creative Destruction: Why Companies That are Built to Last Underperform the Market – and How to Successfully Transform Them
By Richard Foster and Sarah Kaplan, Broadway Business, 2001.

Delivering Happiness: A Path to Profits, Passion and Purpose
By Tony Hsieh, Business Plus, 2010.

Drive: The Surprising Truth about What Motivates Us
By Daniel H. Pink, Riverhead Trade, 2011.

Effectuation: Elements of Entrepreneurial Expertise
By Saras D. Sarasvathy, Edward Elgar Pub, 2008.

Evolving to a New Dominant Logic for Marketing
By Stephen L. Vargo and Robert F. Lusch, Journal of Marketing, January 2004.

The Elastic Enterprise: The New Manifesto for Business Revolution
By Nicholas Vitari and Haydn Shaughnessy, Olivet Publishing, 2012.

Emergence: The Connected Lives of Ants, Brains, Cities, and Software
By Stephen B. Johnson, Scribner, 2001.

Freedom from Command and Control: Rethinking Management for Lean Service
By John Seddon, Productivity Press, 2005.

The Future of Management
By Bill Breen and Gary Hamel, Harvard Business School Press, 2007.

The Ghost in the Machine
By Arthur Koestler, Macmillan, 1968.

The Great Reset: How New Ways of Living and Working Drive Post-Crash Prosperity
By Richard Florida, Harper, 2010.

How Buildings Learn: What Happens After They're Built
By Stewart Brand, Viking Adult, 1994.

Human Sigma: Managing the Employee-Customer Encounter
By John Fleming and Jim Asplund, Gallup Press, 2007.

In the Plex: How Google Thinks, Works, and Shapes Our Lives
By Steven Levy, Simon and Schuster, 2011.

Information Rules: A Strategic Guide to the Network Economy
By Carl Shapiro and Hal R. Varian, Harvard Business Review Press, 1998.

The Innovator's Dilemma: When New Technologies Cause Great Firms to Fail
By Clayton Christensen, Harvard Business Review Press, 1997.

An Inquiry into the Nature and Causes of the Wealth of Nations
By Adam Smith, 1776.

Jack: Straight from the Gut
By Jack Welch and John A. Byrne, Business Plus, 2001.

Just in Time for Today and Tomorrow
By Taiichi Ohno and Setsuo Mito, Productivity Press, 1988.

*The Knowledge-Creating Company: How Japanese Companies
Create the Dynamics of Innovation*
By Ikujiro Nonaka and Hirotaka Takeuchi, Oxford University Press, 1995.

Linked: How Everything is Connected to Everything Else and What it Means
By Albert-Laszlo Barabasi, Perseus Book Group, 2002.

The Living Company
By Arie de Geus and Peter M. Senge, Harvard Business School Press, 1997.

The Management of Innovation
By Tom Burns and G.M. Stalker, Routledge Kegan & Paul, 1961.

Maverick: The Success Story Behind the World's Most Unusual Workplace
By Ricardo Semler, Warner Books, 1993.

Moments of Truth
By Jan Carlzon, Harper Business, 1989.

The New Economics for Industry, Government, Education
By W. Edwards Deming, Quality Enhancement Seminars, 1992.

The Nordstrom Way: The Inside Story of America's #1 Customer Service Company
By Robert Spector and Patrick McCarthy, Wiley, 1995.

Onward: How Starbucks Fought for its Life without Losing its Soul
By Howard Schultz, Rodale Books, 2011

The Origin of Wealth: Evolution, Complexity, and the Radical Remaking of Economics
By Eric D. Beinhocker, Harvard Business School Press, 2006.

Out of the Crisis
By W. Edwards Deming, MIT Press, 1982.

The Power of Pull: How Small Moves, Smartly Made, Can Set Big Things in Motion
By John Hagel, John Seely Brown, and Lang Davison, Basic Books, 2010.

The Rise of Hypercompetition From 1950 to 2002: Evidence of Increasing Structural Destabilization and Temporary Competitive Advantage
By L.G Thomas and Richard D'Aveni, 2004.

The Sciences of the Artificial
By Herbert A. Simon, The MIT Press, 1981.

Service Orient or Be Doomed!: How Service Orientation Will Change Your Business
By Jason Bloomberg and Ronald Schmelzer, Wiley, 2006.

The Service profit Chain: How Leading Companies Link Profit and Growth to Loyalty, Satisfaction, and Value
By James L. Heskett, W. Earl Sasser, and Leonard A. Schlesinger, Free Press, 1997.

The Seven-Day Weekend: Changing the Way Work Works
By Ricardo Semler, Portfolio Hardcover, 2004.

Simply Complexity: A Clear Guide to Complexity Theory
By Neil Johnson, Oneworld, 2009.

Steve Jobs
By Walter Isaacson, Simon and Schuster, 2011.

Structural Holes: The Social Structure of Competition
By Ronald S. Burt, Harvard University Press, 1995.

Toyota Production System: Beyond Large-Scale Production
By Taiichi Ohno and Norman Bodek, Productivity Press, 1988.

The Ultimate Question: How Net-Promoter Companies Thrive in a Customer-Driven World
By Fred Reichheld, Harvard Business School Press, 2006.

A Vision So Noble: John Boyd, the OODA Loop, and America's War on Terror
By Daniel Ford, CreateSpace, 2010.

What Matters Now: How to Win in a World of Relentless Change, Ferocious Competition, and Unstoppable Innovation
By Gary Hamel, Jossey-Bass, 2012.

Who Says Elephants Can't Dance: Inside IBM's Historic Turnaround
By Louis V. Gerstner Jr., Collins, 2002.

INDEX

A

A/B testing, 151
Accenture survey, 25
Ackoff, Russell, 57
adaptive moves, impact of, 66–69
adaptive tensions, 213–214, 230
adaptive walk, 70
agile development
  about, 124–125
  organizing for, 128–131
  tightly coupled systems and, 132
Agile Manifesto, 124
AIG (American International
    Group), 243–244
aircraft carriers, 117–118
Alamo car rentals, 106
Alice in Wonderland (Carroll), 66
Alsin, Arne, 202
Amazon (company)
  adaptive moves by, 69
  allowing negative reviews, 10
  attractors for, 230
  boundary-setting by, 225
  building long-term customer
    relationships, 103
  connectability of, 203
  customer service
    example, 216–217
  experiments at, 200, 202
  maneuver strategies, 211
  platforms and, 156, 158, 160,
    162–164
  podular nature of, 150–152
  principles for, 218
  products as service avatars, 27

purpose for, 90
  Zappos and, 178
American Express, 25, 34, 49, 93
American International Group
    (AIG), 243–244
ant colony, 204
AOL (company), 191
Apple (company)
  community support
    and, 225–226
  diversity and, 233
  expansion into retail, 201
  iTunes, 245
  moral warfare, 211
  Net Promoter Scores at, 106–107
  platforms and, 163–165
  Xerox and, 45
apprenticeships, 171–173
Ashby's Law, 114
Asplund, Jim, 102
ATM revolt (Bank of America), 8
AT&T (company), 150
attractors, 160, 230
attrition warfare, 210
authoritarian power structure, 80
Autodesk software
    company, 263–265
automobiles
  loose coupling in, 132
  self-driving cars, 19, 21
  services for, 19
  urban populations and, 18–20
autonomy
  balanced with common
    good, 224–225

cultures, risk-avoidant, 47–51
Cushing Group, 203
customer relationships
    absorbing variety in, 115–116
    Amazon example, 216–217
    bad profits and, 93
    building, 103, 219–220
    company purpose and, 91
    cost and quality
        considerations, 36–37
    declining satisfaction
        levels, 25, 34–36
    fanatical customer
        support, 218–219
    feedback from, 99–109
    focusing on, 51–52
    freedom to experiment
        in, 116–118
    Golden Rule strategy and, 217
    hated companies, 34
    issue ownership with, 37–39
    moments of truth in, 112
    promotors and
        detractors, 102–103

D
Dalton, Richard, 37, 38
Darwin, Charles, 71
de Geus, Arie, 84
degree measure in networks, 187
deliberate strategy, 198–199
Dell (company), 6, 102
Dell, Michael, 6
DeLong, J. Bradford, 14
Delta Airlines, 243
Deming, W. Edwards
    on cost and quality, 36
    on management, 224
    quoted, 93, 154

on studying systems, 174
detection principle, 192
detractors, 102–103, 104
distributed control, 211–212, 242
diversity
    creativity and, 199–200, 214
    importance of, 214
    tuning the system regarding, 233
division of labor, 56, 58, 137
Domino's videotape, 7
Dorsey, Jack, 261
Dow Jones Industrial Average, 48
Dropbox service, 70
Drucker, Peter, 210

E
eBay site, 156
edge leadership. *See* leading con-
        nected companies
Edison, Thomas, 48
Edwards, Cliff, 201
Einstein, Albert, 222
The Elastic Enterprise (Vitari and
        Shaughnessy), 203
Emergence (Johnson), 82
emergent
    strategy, 198–199, 204–205
Engle, Jane, 244
Enron (company), 246
Enterprise Rent-A-Car, 104–106
entrepreneurial method, 168–170
Evolving to a New Dominant Logic
        for Marketing (Vargo and
        Lusch), 24
experimentation by companies
    absorbing variety, 115–116
    freedom to experiment, 116–118
    front line versus production
        line, 113
    Law of Requisite Variety, 114

M

machines
  as closed systems, 81
  companies as, 78–81
  design by division, 85
  purpose of, 78, 90
Mackey, John, 220
Mailchimp (company), 204
management
  designing system for, 224–227
  leadership versus, 210
  operating the system, 227–230
  purpose of, 223
  role of, 236
  as support system, 224
  tuning the system, 230–236
maneuver warfare, 210
Marriott International, 257–258
mass marketing, product saturation
  and, 14–15
mass production
  product saturation and, 14
  standardization and, 57–58
Maverick (Semler), 142
McCarthy, Patrick D., 118, 140
McDonald's (company)
  adaptive moves by, 68–69
  boundary-setting by, 225
  reducing variety, 114–115
  size of, 235
  support structure, 161–162
McIntyre, Tim, 7
McKelvey, Bill, 66, 213
Microsoft Corporation, 156
minimum viable product (MVP, 124
Mintzberg, Henry, 198–199
mobile phones. *See* cellphones
Moments of Truth (Carlzon), 112

Moore, Karl, 199
Moore's Law, 32, 46
moral authority, 211, 215–220
moral leverage, 217
moral warfare, 211
Morita, Akio, 95
Morning Star (company), 138–139
Mosser, Fred, 68
Mullikin, Harry, 140
multidivisional
  organizations, 136–137
MVP (minimum viable
  product), 124
MySpace service, 191
MyStarbucksIdea.com site, 234

N

Napier, Lanham, 219
National car rentals, 106
Netflix service, 69, 70, 128–130
Net Promotor Score. *See* NPS (Net
  Promotor Score)
networks
  about, 184–187
  compatibility in, 190
  control in, 188–189
  exercising power in, 189–192
  influence in, 190
  platforms in, 191
  power in, 8–10, 187, 192
  scale-free, 186–187
  service, 28
  situation awareness in, 189–190
  small-world, 184
network weaving, 265
Newell, Gabe, 205
New York Times, 246
Nielsen study, 9

profits and, 92–95
risk of failure in, 246–247
setting context for
learning, 95–96

Q

quality
cost-cutting and, 36–37
judging, 100
mass production and, 57
measuring for products, 113
measuring for services, 113
as moving target, 102
Netflix example, 130
queueing theory, 226

R

Rackspace (company), 218–219
rate of information flow, 234
Rational Software, 140–141
Redbox rental kiosks, 69
Red Queen race, 66, 71
RedSpark services hub, 263
Reichheld, Fred, 30, 92, 103–104
relationships, services and, 27
Renno, Sharif, 259–261
Requisite Variety Law, 114
Research in Motion (RIM), 7
response principle, 192
return on assets, 64
revisionist history, 169
RIM (Research in Motion), 7
risk-avoidant cultures, 47–51
risks in connected companies
platform failure, 244–246
pod failure, 242
purpose failure, 246–247
Ritz-Carlton Hotel
Apple recruitment from, 106, 233

customer issue resolution, 116
employee autonomy, 242
purpose for, 96
Roosevelt, Theodore, 196
Rosedale, Philip, 227
Rothschild, Nathan, 14
Ruby language, 163
Ruby on Rails framework, 163–164
Rudisin, Jerry, 140
rules
boundary-setting in companies
and, 224–225
breaking, 117
cultural standards and, 159
problem with, 112–113
Russell, John, 98

S

Salah, George, 232
Sarasvathy, Saras, 169
SAS Airlines, 112
Sasser, W. Earl, 96, 242
Sasson, Steve, 46
scale-free networks, 186–187
Schiller, Ron, 7
Schmidt, Eric, 202
Schultz, Howard, 4–5, 22, 43, 189
Sears (retail stores), 51
Second Life (company), 227
self-manageed teams. *See* podular
organizations
Semco (company), 142–143, 230
Semler, Ricardo, 142–143
service avatars, 25–26
service contracts
about, 126
Whole Foods Market
example, 130

velocity, increasing demands
for, 32–33
venture capital (VC) firms, 161, 201
Vitari, Nicholas, 203
Vogels, Werner, 151–152
von Moltke, Helmuth, 113

W
Walgreens (company), 69
Walker, Mary, 219
Walmart (company)
adaptive moves, 67–68
focusing on customers, 51
information transparency, 231
principles for, 218
Procter and Gamble and, 262
purpose for, 96
Walton, Sam, 217, 262
Watchmakers Parable, 136
weak ties, 185
Wealth of Nations (Smith), 160
Welch, Jack
adaptive tensions and, 213
General Electric
and, 48, 94–95, 201
learning fields and, 173
quoted, 54, 71, 88, 110, 202
on top-down, leader-driven
change, 255–256
Wells Fargo services, 202–203
Wells, H. G., 240
Weston, Graham, 218
What Matters Now (Hamel), 199
Whipcar service, 28
Whitmore, Kay, 46–47

Whole Foods Market
agile management and, 130–131
attractors for, 160, 230
Golden Rule and, 220
peer-to-peer reinforcement, 227
platforms and, 156, 160–161
Who Says Elephants Can't Dance?
(Gerstner), 49, 255
WikiLeaks (organization), 9
Wikipedia site, 156
Wladawsky-Berger, Irving, 212
W.L. Gore (company), 200, 227

X
Xerox (company), 45–46, 150

Y
Yahoo! site, 150, 244–245

Z
Zale Jewelers, 131
Zappos (company)
absorbing variety, 115–116
Amazon and, 178
moral authority and, 217
Mosser and, 68
permeability of systems, 233

DISCUSSION QUESTIONS

Get even more for your money.

Join the O'Reilly Community, and register the O'Reilly books you own. It's free, and you'll get:

- $4.99 ebook upgrade offer
- 40% upgrade offer on O'Reilly print books
- Membership discounts on books and events
- Free lifetime updates to ebooks and videos
- Multiple ebook formats, DRM FREE
- Participation in the O'Reilly community
- Newsletters
- Account management
- 100% Satisfaction Guarantee

Signing up is easy:

1. **Go to: oreilly.com/go/register**
2. **Create an O'Reilly login.**
3. **Provide your address.**
4. **Register your books.**

Note: English-language books only

To order books online:

oreilly.com/store

For questions about products or an order:

orders@oreilly.com

To sign up to get topic-specific email announcements and/or news about upcoming books, conferences, special offers, and new technologies:

elists@oreilly.com

For technical questions about book content:

booktech@oreilly.com

To submit new book proposals to our editors:

proposals@oreilly.com

O'Reilly books are available in multiple DRM-free ebook formats. For more information:

oreilly.com/ebooks

O'REILLY®

Spreading the knowledge of innovators   **oreilly.com**